Aesthetics, Politics, and Educational Inquiry

Studies in the Postmodern Theory of Education

Joe L. Kincheloe and Shirley R. Steinberg
General Editors

Vol. 117

PETER LANG
New York • Washington, D.C./Baltimore • Boston • Bern
Frankfurt am Main • Berlin • Brussels • Vienna • Oxford

Tom Barone

Aesthetics, Politics, and Educational Inquiry

Essays and Examples

Foreword by William F. Pinar

PETER LANG

New York • Washington, D.C./Baltimore • Boston • Bern
Frankfurt am Main • Berlin • Brussels • Vienna • Oxford

Library of Congress Cataloging-in-Publication Data

Barone, Tom.
Aesthetics, politics, and educational inquiry: essays and examples / Tom Barone.
p. cm. — (Counterpoints; vol. 117)
Includes bibliographical references.
1. Education—Research—Methodology. 2. Education—Research Social aspects.
3. Education—Philosophy. 4. Postmodernism and education. 5. Aesthetics.
6. Literature—History and criticism—Theory, etc. I. Title.
II. Series: Counterpoints (New York, N.Y.); vol. 117.
LB1028.B345   370'.7'2—dc21   99-15092
ISBN 0-8204-4520-7
ISSN 1058-1634

Die Deutsche Bibliothek-CIP-Einheitsaufnahme

Barone, Tom:
Aesthetics, politics, and educational inquiry: essays and examples / Tom Barone.
–New York; Washington, D.C./Baltimore; Boston; Bern;
Frankfurt am Main; Berlin; Brussels; Vienna; Canterbury: Lang.
(Counterpoints; Vol. 117)
ISBN 0-8204-4520-7

Cover design by Nona Reuter

The paper in this book meets the guidelines for permanence and durability
of the Committee on Production Guidelines for Book Longevity
of the Council of Library Resources.

Printed in the United States of America

Table of Contents

Foreword by *William F. Pinar*   vii

Acknowledgments   xix

Introduction   1

Section I
Beginnings: Elliot Eisner and Literary Nonfiction   7

1. From the Classrooms of Stanford to the Alleys
   of Amsterdam: Elliot Eisner as Pedagogue   9
2. Effectively Critiquing the Experienced Curriculum:
   Clues from the New Journalism   19
3. Insinuated Theory from Curricula-in-Use   51
4. Ambiguity and the Curriculum: Lessons from the
   Literary Nonfiction of Norman Mailer   61

Section II
Deweyan Influences: The Aesthetics of the Everyday   71

5. Things of Use and Things of Beauty:
   The Swain County High School Arts Program   73
6. Educational Platforms, Teacher Selection, and School
   Reform: Issues Emanating from a Biographical Case Study   101
7. Breaking the Mold: The New American Student
   as Strong Poet   119

Section III
The Neopragmatism of Richard Rorty   **135**

8. Using the Narrative Text as an Occasion for Conspiracy   137
9. On the Demise of Subjectivity in Educational Inquiry   161

Section IV
**Rediscovering Sartre: Social Justice
and Issues of Audience**   **179**

10. Ways of Being at Risk: The Case of Billy Charles Barnett   181
11. Beyond Theory and Method: A Case of Critical Storytelling   191
12. A Narrative of Enhanced Professionalism: Educational
    Researchers and Popular Storybooks about Schoolpeople   201
13. On Kozol and Sartre and Educational Research as
    Socially Committed Literature   229

Section V
Bakhtin and Beyond   **243**

14. Persuasive Writings, Vigilant Readings, and
    Reconstructed Characters: The Paradox of Trust
    in Educational Storysharing   245

Foreword

William F. Pinar

How lucky for us to have Tom Barone's essays between two covers! How easy it is to miss a scholar's intellectual formation when articles appear here and there, when everyone feels (and is) submerged under the tidal wave of scholarly publication. While every serious curriculum scholar has heard of Thomas Barone, not all of us have been able to follow his intellectual career over the last two decades. Now we can. And now we can make available to our students Barone's unique and important contribution.

Thinking about these past twenty years, Tom is quite clear about the autobiographical character of his writings. He says at the outset that these writings can be recoded as a life story. Five writers have influenced him most, he tells us, have "alter[ed] most the course of my quest," producing "invaluable disruptions and advancements in the flow of my professional and personal identity." One of these happens to be one of my five (if I were to make a list), Jean-Paul Sartre, the early (or in Tom's words) the "optimistic Sartre." By that he means the Sartre before his Marxist conversion—the author of *Nausea* and *Being and Nothingness*, almost twenty years before the *Critique of Dialectical Reason* appeared—the Sartre "still infatuated with the possibilities of a socially committed literature as a means for promoting critical awareness." This is a theme that Tom will emphasize throughout his work.

While Sartre may be one of Barone's intellectual heroes, the one who was present concretely, in a pedagogical relation to him, was his doctoral mentor Elliot Eisner, whom Tom terms his "mentor," "friend," "teacher/ critic," a "connoisseur of life." The first and distinguishing feature of Eisner's intellectual leadership, he tells us, was "a courage born out of a deep sense of professional responsibility." Second was his civility. Barone must have been an exemplary student, for these two qualities also mark his achievement. We can discern Eisner's influence in Barone's early concern for "the experienced curriculum," the lived reality of those in classrooms, a reality he wants from the start to honor. How? As a curriculum theorist, he wants to honor it by describing it precisely, by which he means "qualitatively," narratively, and specifically, fictionally. Not only empathetic loyalty to the experience of those in schools prompts him to structure his research so, but a larger sense of professionalism leads him to argue for writing that inspires and persuades a seemingly indifferent public. Early on he suggests that the point of curriculum inquiry is inspiration.

Characterizing the work of scholars such as Dwayne Huebner (and Pinar) as curriculum "philosophy" (in contrast to "theory"), Tom argues that "curriculum theory can also serve a somewhat more traditional purpose: that is, to be more directly helpful to practitioners in planning and using actual curricula." While both Dwayne and I would insist we are trying to be helpful to teachers too, true enough it is not our, especially my, only motive. Faithful to his mentor, Tom writes,"The kind of theory envisioned here is for thoughtful practitioners . . . portraying curriculum-in-use. And so, a research agenda for interested parties: to insinuate such theory in portraits of curricula-in-use, to provide these critiques to practitioners, and to carefully watch what happens." Over time, as you will see, he also wants these portraits to persuade politicians and policymakers to change their perceptions of schools and schoolpeople. But for now, in the early essays, Barone is thinking about a new version of curriculum inquiry, one that, like "great literature . . . lures he or she who experiences it away from the shores of literal truth and out into uncharted waters where meaning is more ambiguous." With writers such as Truman Capote, Norman Mailer, Tom Wolfe, and Joan Didion in mind, Barone writes: "Ultimately, I erased the boundary between the realm of the text which purports to give only the facts and that of a metaphor-laden story which dares to (as Sartre once put it) lie in order to tell the truth."

For those who may have pigeonholed Barone's scholarship as "aesthetic" or "simply" an extension of Eisner's, think again. Barone demonstrates throughout his work an explicit political commitment, one which he situates generationally and historically:

> For I remain deeply appreciative of the opportunity for coming of age in an irreverent, socially committed era like the 1960s, a time which fostered sensitivity to the imperfections of society, which opened our eyes to the plight of the less fortunate around us, to the groups of disenfranchised—including (since my eyes are still open) today's public school teachers whose professional autonomy and

status have steadily eroded within our increasingly bureaucratized and depersonalized system of schooling.

The obsession with equating education to business, the naive faith in
technology (which hardly began with computers; examine the literature
on slides, educational radio, TV—see Pinar et al. 1995, p. 704 ff.), and
the epistemological narrowness of mainstream social science research in
education are all related, Barone suggests. They have to do with the fact
that:

> We Americans are indeed inhabitants of a callow culture, a nation in its adoles-
> cence, one lacking the maturity that could provide a strong sense of who we are
> and where we want to go as a people. This partially explains, I believe, our
> infatuation with the tools which science gives us. With no clearly defined vision of
> our own we find it convenient to partake of the half-hidden values implicated in
> the use of technology.

He adds: "Educators, we too are children of our culture, and have lacked
the vision and the voice, the will to question where we are being led by
our inventions."

Self, Society, and the School

Given these cultural conditions and such macro-political initiatives as
America 2000, Barone asks: "Can schools of education hope to transform schooling from the 'bottom up'?" Discussing that 1991 example of
school reform, Tom finds it "hard to argue with the premise that the rigid,
omnipresent, traditional organizational structure of the American public
schools needs rethinking." But he doubts that the kind of school designs
sought in America 2000 would break that mold. Indeed, the promise of
most macro-reforms has been a "continuation of pedagogical practices
aimed at molding American students into a standardized product." Observing that "it is hardly news to note that the American school is patterned after the industrial workplace," Barone reminds us that "standardized schools with standardized visions of success tend to produce
standardized human beings." Truly "New American Schools," ones that
would break the mold of standardization,

> would offer students and teachers the autonomy of the artist who works toward
> an end that is emergent, and not yet in view. They would be concerned less with
> molding students in accordance with "national consensus standards" than with
> providing the growth of unique, powerful, integrated identities. They would sup-

port a process wherein teachers assist each student in the weaving (and reweaving) of profoundly educational, aesthetic experiences into a narrative, or story, of a unique and responsible *self*.

If only we were in a position to pull this off!

Barone then explicates the main points in this vision of school as profoundly autobiographical. Narrating one's life story, he reminds us, represents nothing less than the construction of self. It is in a fundamental sense an aesthetic and interpretative (i.e., hermeneutical) process. Relying on George Herbert Mead, Barone views personal identity as neither a material substance nor a spiritual soul, but a sense of oneself constructed by a conscious human person. So conceived, he conceives of "schools as communities of strong poets and storytellers" in search of the good life.

But what, you ask, is the good life? To answer he invokes the work of Charles Taylor, Richard Rorty, Harold Bloom, and Friedrich Nietzsche. Like Nietzsche, Barone suggests that "a good life is like a good original story or poem insofar as disparate thoughts and actions are consciously shaped into a narrative unity, an aesthetic form." Such a coherence does not derive from "weakness and imitation, but through will and autonomy"; it is what Nietzsche called "style." And style, Barone suggests, is the primary attribute of the "strong poet," by which he means:

> someone who refuses to accept as useful the descriptions of her life written by others. Instead, the strong poet is a strong storyteller, continuously revising her life story in the light of her own experience and imagination. The strong poet constantly redescribes her past interactions with the world around her, constantly reinvents her self, so that she may act in the future with greater integrity and coherence. The strong poet plots her life story toward her own emergent ends and purposes.

These ends and purposes are not of course formulated "in solitary confinement." A strong poet is no "disengaged esthete," busily weaving an effete self in rarefied existential isolation. Instead, s/he is very much "a social being and a moral agent, a responsible citizen of a shared community." Barone thinks of Dewey here, who reminded us that the renewal of self and community are interwoven and can occur only within a democratic culture. The more democratic and equitable the distribution of power in any given society, the more likely, Barone suggests, that strong poetry will be composed and communicated broadly. "Now," he asks, "what if the New American Schools adopted the notion of a strong poet as the ideal student?"

Now that *would* be revolutionary. But Tom Barone is clear that we'll get no help from "above," that whatever gains we make we will make by ourselves in collaboration with our friends teaching in the schools. So it is "we" who will have to elaborate an agenda based on the notion of "strong poet," and to that end Tom asks: "[w]hat educational moves could we make toward realizing our hopes for students who have style?" He suggests two, "two phases of the educational act, each of which must, to be successful, exhibit certain aesthetic attributes." In the first of these the teacher "reads" those narratives of the life-text of the student that s/he has composed and lived through. In the second the teacher invites the student to explore aesthetic experiences that, the teacher hopes, will provide "wondrous" avenues toward the future.

Of course, autobiographical work is not certain, as Tom is well aware. He points to a sharp sense of "uncertainty that accompanies this process of self-creation," uncertainty that is (after Frank Kermode) the source of considerable human anxiety. There is, then, a certain courage prerequisite to the process of self-fashioning, not only a courage that enables one to dwell in uncertainty over one's self, but a courage that supports one in facing up to others, including those one encounters in the often predatory world of politics. So understood, stories "can be, as Foucault put it, *transgressive*," offering "radical alternatives for thinking about the world and acting within it." Most fundamentally perhaps, "composing stories is an additional mode of sense-making that offers practice for the imposing task of living."

Key to this process is the teacher's presence, and it is a particular modality of being present that Barone pinpoints: "The pedagogue plays an important role in making these engagements more likely to occur. . . . [S/he] must engage in the aesthetic project of empathic understanding." As an "aesthetic project," empathetic understanding is, Barone suggests, "more than mere intuition or feeling because what is striven for is not purely emotional identification but rather an *idea* of a piece of subjective life," one, I would add, that must not collapse one's own critical distance. As I have suggested elsewhere, empathy conceals as it reveals, and I think Tom's distinction between "identification" and an "idea" of another subjective life helps reduce the risk. Risky business even so, empathy can permit one to encounter another's "life expression," a process that "can deepen the teacher's appreciation of the student's *funded biography* (Dewey, 1963), the integral mass of her accumulated life experiences."

"The learning event," understood from this perspective, "may become the kind of aesthetic experience that Dewey called *educational*: a growth-inducing experience that grants the capacity for having even richer experiences in the future." Key to this capacity is storytelling, by means of which "a student may have discovered new options for interpreting the world and new possibilities for living." These possibilities offer, perhaps, greater autonomy, including the possibility of redescribing, refashioning the self. Moreover, "with the guidance of a wise and empathetic teacher, she may have written some mighty strong poetry." That is the point of empathy: educational experience. Tom puts it this way: "[T]he educator comes to understand empathetically the lives of her students in order to arrange the environment intelligently toward the promotion of aesthetic experiences," experiences that lead "toward the continual revision of the poem of who that student, specifically, can be." Yes.

Qualitative Inquiry

None of this is, of course, self-evident or easy. The rigor and discipline of such pedagogical labor requires regular rest, and in one essay Tom thinks of Sunday morning as one occasion for a "sabbatical." Perhaps, as Tom says he does, one listens to music, reserving "Sunday mornings for engaging in a musical kind of celebration, for listening to the contrapuntal harmonies of a fugue." Barone seems to be thinking of educational research as a kind of fugue, for he writes: "When used for educational purposes, a text of qualitative inquiry is, I propose, better viewed as an occasion than as a tool. It is, more precisely, an occasion for the reader to engage in the activities of textual re-creation and dismantling." Tom goes on to point out that such activities—re-creation and dismantling—require a narrative mode of thinking, one that suggests "a reordering of the totem pole of qualitative inquiry genres, a challenging of important premises of the educational research establishment."

He is *not* thinking about "the high priests Campbell and Stanley," who "offered holy communion in strict accordance with paradigmatic canons, and *every day was Sunday*." In this testament, qualitative inquiry is a kind of heresy, a research heresy involving the "steady recovery of the human voice." This trend leaves Barone optimistic about the future of qualitative inquiry, so much so that he imagines a day when "editors of prominent journals of educational inquiry will publish the most accomplished pieces of literary fiction with educational themes," when "the teacher-educator should act as critical-co-investigator . . . serving as leader of a discursive community of professionals in which each member shares responsibility for critical reflection and discussion." This form of qualitative inquiry, Barone suggests, transcends distinctions between objectivity and subjectivity, terms which, he suggests (after Richard Rorty) have become "nuisances." Instead, he continues, "I will recommend that as educational inquirers we no longer talk about research texts as being objective or subjective but about texts that are more or less useful or, in varying degrees and ways, persuasive."

To help us think about what such texts would look like, Tom turns to literature, not education. He summons Charles Dickens, Theodore Dreiser, Harriet Beecher Stowe, and Richard Wright, whom he praises for having "offered readers occasions for reconstructing their tired, safe views of social conditions into more radical and utopian one. My hope is for educational inquirers soon to do the same." Barone's emphasis upon social justice leads him to think of another novelist (and playwright and essayist and philosopher): Jean-Paul Sartre. "I explicitly endorse," he tells us, "a Sartrean brand of storytelling that is both popular and socially conscientious." To illustrate, Tom tells us the story of Billy Charles Barnett. It is, I think, the most poignant piece in the collection.

Billy Charles

Eschewing "professional" labels of expert and client, Tom names himself and the fifteen year-old boy as "representatives of two subcultures, meeting at a McDonald's along an interstate highway in northeastern Tennessee." Across from him is "Billy Charles Barnett, a tall lanky boy with dark hair, green eyes, a pug nose, and an infectious grin. He is a member of the rural 'disadvantaged,' a fifteen-year-old nominated by the vice-principal as the student least likely to remain in Dusty Hollow Middle School. I am a middle-aged urban academic who, secure in a tenured university position, will never leave school." There are echoes of Dickens here. And there is Sartre's commitment to classlessness, as Barone positions himself, not the boy, as the one lacking knowledge: "Even more jolting is a sudden realization of my vast ignorance about the ways of people who live within a two-hour drive of my home and about the fundamentals of a world no longer honored in the dominant culture." Stuck in seventh grade for a second year, "Billy Charles . . . has expressed on numerous occasions his intentions to drop out of school as soon as he can. And I know that, on occasion, he has entertained fantasies of dropping out of life, as well." Part of Billy Charles's story has to do with class and region, and part of it, as Barone tells us, has to do with his father. There had been a period—"a glorious time, according to Billy Charles"—when he and his father were very close, when the older man guided the younger one "into his own Appalachian manhood. Almost daily Billy Charles and his father went out in the wilds, the two of them together, teacher and apprentice. Billy Charles was joyously receiving an education in the *real* basics, eagerly learning the time-honored skills of survival. . . . He was absorbed in the fundamentals of the world around him. Almost daily for more than a year, rain or shine, this wilderness school was in session." But the son is forced from the Garden after the father begins beating him. Barone: "So a father turns viciously on a son, who, in a time of delicate adolescent need, is reluctant to leave—until the final incident of abuse when the new family decides to vacation in Florida." While there Billy Charles writes his mother for help, to which she responds, and "so, on the verge of manhood, Billy Charles went back to Mama, back to a place strewn with so many obstacles to his escape."

Back with mother, Billy Charles finds himself in the wilderness that is the school, a place from which he is rather completely estranged. But here too Barone refuses to blame the boy, writing that "what use, after all, are passivity and punctuality to denizens of the forest?" I leave the remainder of the tale to Tom, but I do want to underline the conclusion he draws, for it is at the center of the essay and of this book:

> His case revives our fading dreams of a broader sort of empowerment that schools once hoped to provide for *all* American children, regardless of their economic or social backgrounds. This included the power to use the disciplines for penetrating more deeply into one's own past and present world, the power to imagine a wide range of alternative worlds in other times and places, and the power to express these understandings by employing many forms of literacy—verbal, visual, musical, kinesthetic, and so on.

That is a dream many of us share, however faded the last thirty years have rendered it. For all his determination and hopefulness, Tom has his somber moment. "Empowering teachers (and students) in this way," he admits toward the end, "may require more resources than our society is willing to provide. We will need to reeducate teachers, to reduce their workload, and to purchase material resources to link the local community with the larger one." As unlikely as that is in the short term, we have no choice but to work to make this dream come true, "because Billy Charles Barnett has reminded us that doing anything less is still a very risky business."

Socially Committed Literature

Risky business indeed, but as Tom Barone realizes, the public sleeps, complicit in the failure of the school to do what it could, must, do. That sleep and complicity call to mind another historical period in which the public denied what was happening around it, Europe in the 1930s, a time during which the young Sartre formulated his concept of a socially committed literature. No doubt that, plus his experience as a resistance fighter in Vichy France (he was captured and served time as a prisoner of war), formed in him a strong commitment to participate in the predatory politics of postwar Europe. Sartre was determined to speak to that world, to influence its formation through his writing, to reach not only other intellectuals but literate readers everywhere through his essays, articles (in *Les Temps Modernes*), plays and, in the 1960s, street politics. In the shadow of this great twentieth-century intellectual, Barone is not asking so very much of us, education professors who might, he hopes, try to influence the public to support the formation of a world that children and teachers might gladly inhabit: the school.

We in the academy, Barone urges, must "strive to reverse the usual pattern of research-follows-funding by going over the heads of government policymakers to the primary source of our political democracy." Yes, he wants us to speak with our neighbors, our friends, with politicians, with anybody who will listen. "We speak to them," he tells us, "not from a distance, not through texts that need translation by intermediaries, but directly and compellingly so that the public ceases to imagine teachers and schoolkids as essentially negligent and malevolent characters in need of externally imposed discipline, and begins to understand the nature of the unfortunate culture and institutional forces that impinge upon their lives."

There have been nonfictional examples of educational writing that, in part, achieve this aim of speaking directly to the larger public on behalf of teachers and children in schools. Barone thinks of Kozol's *Savage Inequalities*, which "exemplifies the kind of writing I call socially committed literature"; it is "a latter-day example of the sort of literary endeavor favored by John Paul Sartre." Barone reminds us that Sartre was committed to the "irreducible historicity of the writer, but that "as an inhabitant of a later era, a participant in a postmodern intellectual culture, I cannot endorse every Sartrean assertion about the nature and purpose of committed writing." What Barone does draw from Sartre is the primacy of the researcher/author's commitment to social justice, a sharp sense of her/his intended audiences, and her/his conscious choice of rhetorical tools for engaging those audiences in the issues in which one is engaged. Sartre was not satisfied with mere description, for description is "pure contemplative enjoyment." Nor was he content to explain, for, again in Sartre's words, "explanation is acceptance, it excuses everything." Why did he write? Tom answers: "Sartre wrote to transform the world." As Sartre put it: "The world and man reveal themselves by *undertakings*. And all the undertakings we might speak of, reduce themselves to a single one, *making history*" (1988, p. 104). In this respect, like Sartre, we must become committed to the elaboration of "particular historical contingencies [i.e., schools] at the expense of academic abstractions."

This capacity and commitment to speak to the public in the name of making history is not limited to exceptional individuals like Sartre. "I believe," Barone asserts, "that many of today's educational researchers (especially qualitative researchers) also possess, to a much greater extent than they can imagine, the 'very special talents' needed for making history." "What has prevented us from trying?" he asks. The answer, he suggests, has to do in part with our conception of what our work is. We must, he urges us, move

> away from a posture of scholarly detachment toward one of passionate commitment to a redistribution of social resources; away from texts aimed exclusively at our academic colleagues toward direct communication with additional constituencies (such as educational practitioners, policymakers, and the public-at-large) who must join in the enactment of such a redistribution; away from the detached, arcane, technical languages of philosophical and scientific theory, toward modes of discourse feared by powermongers throughout history, the vernacular languages of literature. . . . I believe we can transform, not only the field of educational research, but also the landscape of American schooling.

As the title of this collection suggests, Thomas Barone links aesthetics with politics in the context of educational inquiry, an inquiry he reformulates as directed to the larger public, inquiry that is at once fictional and socially committed. In this respect, he has extended and made more complex and provocative the rich legacy he inherited from his mentor, Elliot Eisner. He has honored his own autobiographical and generational commitments as well as demonstrated a perceptive, judicious grasp of contemporary curriculum scholarship. These essays perform what they ask us to consider, namely, a self-reflexive political commitment to social justice, justice for students and for teachers. Barone asks us as scholars and teachers in the university to reposition ourselves, to decline our roles as polite facilitators of policymakers' pronouncements, in fact to bypass policymakers in an effort to persuade the public to see the schools as they are, the places where our children live much of their childhood, engaged in projects of self-fashioning and world transformation, in a word: education. Tom's loyalty to the school is no knee-jerk gendered reaction to lost influence, but a historically situated, socially engaged commitment to concretely existing individuals, young and old alike. For that he merits not only our sustained applause, but our support.

Reference

Pinar, William F., Reynolds, William M., Slattery, Patrick, & Taubman, Peter (1995). *Understanding curriculum.* New York: Peter Lang.

Acknowledgments

The author and publisher wish to thank those who have generously given permission to reprint the following material:

"From the classrooms of Stanford to the alleys of Amsterdam: Elliot Eisner as pedagogue" originally published in *Teachers and Mentors: Profiles of Distinguished Twentieth-Century Professors of Education*, edited by Craig Kridel, Robert Bullough, Jr., and Paul Shaker, pp. 105–116. Copyright 1990. Reprinted by permission of Garland Publishing. All rights reserved.

Barone, T., "Effectively critiquing the experienced curriculum: Clues from the 'new journalism'." *Curriculum Inquiry, 10* (1), pp. 29–53. Malden, MA: Blackwell Publishers, Copyright 1990 by the Ontario Institute for Studies in Education. Reprinted by permission of the publisher. All rights reserved.

Barone, T. (1992). Insinuated theory from curricula-in-use. *Theory into Practice, 21* (1), 38–43. (Theme issue on "Curriculum theory") Copyright 1982 College of Education, The Ohio State University. Reprinted by permission of the publisher. All rights reserved.

"Ambiguity and the curriculum: Lessons from the literary nonfiction of Norman Mailer" reprinted from *Reflections from the Heart of Educational Inquiry*, George Willis and William Schubert, (Eds.), by permission of the State University of New York Press. Copyright 1991, State University of New York. All rights reserved.

"Things of use and things of beauty: The story of the Swain County High School Arts Program" reprinted by permission of *Daedalus, Journal of the American Academy of Arts and Sciences,* from the issue entitled "The Arts and Humanities in America's School," Summer 1983, Vol. 112, No. 3.

Reprinted with permission. Copyright by the American Association of Colleges for Teacher Education. Barone, Thomas, "Educational platforms, teacher selection, and school reform: Issues emanating from a biographical case study." *Journal of Teacher Education, 38* (2), 1987, pp. 13–18.

Barone, T. (1993). Breaking the mold: The new American student as strong poet. *Theory into Practice, 32* (3), 236–243. (Theme issue on "Using the arts to inform teaching") Copyright 1993, College of Education, The Ohio State University. Reprinted by permission of the publisher. All rights reserved.

"Using the narrative text as an occasion for conspiracy" reprinted by permission from Eisner, E. & Peshkin, A. (Eds.), QUALITATIVE INQUIRY IN EDUCATION: THE CONTINUING DEBATE (New York, Teachers College Press. Copyright 1988 by Teachers College, Columbia University. All rights reserved.), pp. 305–326.

Barone, T. (1992). "On the demise of subjectivity in educational inquiry." *Curriculum Inquiry, 22* (1), 25–38 Malden. MA: Blackwell Publishers. Copyright 1992, The Ontario Institute for Studies in Education. Reprinted by permission of the publisher. All rights reserved.

Barone, T. (1989). Ways of being at risk: The case of Billy Charles Barnett. *Phi Delta Kappan, 71* (2), 147–151. Bloomington, IN: Phi Delta Kappa International, Inc. Copyright 1989. Reprinted by permission of the publisher. All rights reserved.

Barone, T. (1992). Beyond theory and method: A case of critical storytelling. *Theory into Practice, 31* (2), 142–146. (Theme issue on "Qualitative issues in educational research") Copyright 1992, College of Education, The Ohio State University. Reprinted by permission of the publisher. All rights reserved.

Barone, T. (1992). A narrative of enhanced professionalism: Educational researchers and popular storybooks about school people. *Educational Researcher, 21* (9), 15–24. Copyright 1992 by the American Educational Research Association. Reprinted by permission of the publisher.

Barone, T. (1994). On Kozol and Sartre and qualitative research as socially committed literature. *The Review of Education/Pedagogy/Cultural Studies, 17* (1), 93–102. Lausanne, Switzerland: Gordon and Breach Publishers, Copyright 1994. Reprinted by permission of the publisher. All rights reserved.

Barone, T. (1995). "Persuasive writings, vigilant readings, reconstructed characters: The paradox of trust in educational storysharing" in *Life History and Narrative,* J. Amos Hatch & Roger Wisniewski, editors, Qualitative Study Series, Volume 1, Ivor Goodson, general editor.), pp. 63–74. London: Falmer Press, copyright 1995. Reprinted by permission of the publisher. All rights reserved.

Introduction

In this era of the narrative, it seems reasonable to suggest that a set of writings composed by a single author over a period of decades be read as a life story. Of course, at least in Western cultures, a story needs a theme, a unifying topic that binds together and bestows meaning upon the story's disparate elements. The theme that gives coherence to this group of essays and research texts—and the theme that has long given meaning to my professional life story—is one of educational inquiry.

Over the years I have wondered about how best to explore and reveal the nature and outcomes of educational encounters, about the aesthetics and politics of educational inquiry as they relate to the institution of the school. Questions have plagued me since my years as a high school teacher negotiating daily with successive platoons of adolescents, and as a Master's student laboring over a statistically supersaturated thesis in which individual students never made an appearance. When, circa 1973, the members of my quantitatively oriented thesis committee seemed to value the technically elaborate, persona-free work much more than I, and when my research aspirations grew too large to be contained within the confines of a school teacher's schedule, I decided to leave the high school classroom in pursuit of a university career.

My hopes then were somehow to make things otherwise for the practitioner colleagues I was leaving behind. So I sought out a doctoral program (and mentor) where I might be encouraged to pursue alternative forms of research and writing, kinds that honored educational meaning and significance. By then the various questions about how to understand and to write about what constitutes educational virtue had merged into a full-fledged quest, the kind of which I would later hear Maxine Greene (1995) eloquently speak.

My quest, like Greene's, has existed in a dialectical relationship with a professional self. I have defined the project as it has defined me. It has served as a theme throughout my professional life, shaped its course, allowed it to be understood as a story. It has offered me, I mean, a narrative self, a version of which you, the reader, may reconstruct in your negotiations with this book.

But if there is a narrative identity to be found within these pages, it is not, I suggest, the kind most associated with modernist thinkers, the kind Paul Ricouer (1992, 119) critiqued as one of "uninterrupted continuity and permanence in time." If the reader does sense an "otherness" lurking between the lines in these pages, s/he should not conclude that it is a seamless and continuous entity. A narrative self can thrive on change, on growth, sometimes on a reconstitution or redefinition so fundamental that it may seem to produce a profound dislocation, a fragmentation, even a dissolution, of identity.

And in one sense, the author of the early essays in this book is not the same person as the later author. While the senior self acknowledges his debt to the person he previously was, he nevertheless believes, perhaps arrogantly, that he is wiser than the callow youngster. Indeed, the elder author finds himself resonating with a remark by the character of Nathan Zuckerman in Philip Roth's (1988) *The Facts*: "The truth you told about all of this long ago, you now want to tell in a different way."

Shifts in outlook (and therefore in identity) do indeed occur within these writings. But they are hardly the results of exertions of the private will of an existential isolate. They are, rather, evidence of a relational self, one who acts only within a world of others who also think and write, one whose very selfhood is reconditioned by those others whom he seeks out in the name of his own personal quest for meaning.

Indeed, I can only admit to constructing my narrative self out of the words of others. Most of these "others" have each contributed only brief passages to the script (although, taken together, these contributions are substantial indeed). And there are perhaps dozens who have made more profound differences in my view of the world and my place in it. But I have identified five prominent authors as altering most the course of my quest, enormously persuasive writers whose words have produced invaluable disruptions and advancements in the flow of my professional and personal identity. They are Elliot Eisner, John Dewey, Richard Rorty, Jean Paul Sartre, and Mikhail Bakhtin. The influences of these thinkers have provided important subthemes in the story of my professional life and have enabled me to organize the enclosed collection of articles accordingly.

The first set of articles highlights the influence of my mentor at Stanford University in the mid-1970s. Indeed, while traces of Elliot Eisner's intellectual impress can be discerned throughout this book, his greatest influence can be found in my initial probes into the formally aesthetic character of educational inquiry. My early fascination with literary nonfiction as a mode of representing research findings (considered avant-garde at the time) was fed by Eisner's groundbreaking work on arts-based approaches to educational research and evaluation. Eisner also reinforced the proclivity of my practitioner self to remain close to the classroom in thinking about research, to regard the dailiness of school life as worthy of scrutiny, to see education as a project that is simultaneously aesthetic and institutional.

My initial attraction to Eisner's work was due in part to its extension of the ideas of someone whose writings I had already discovered. Even before my Stanford days, I had woven John Dewey's progressivist educational theory, his pragmatist epistemology, and his antipathy toward various unwarranted dualisms, into my own professional narrative. But Eisner must be credited with introducing me to the elderly Dewey's perspective on the place of aesthetics in education and inquiry. My debts to both the earlier and later Dewey are most obvious in the second set of essays in this book.

In the 1980s, with my quest in high gear, I found Richard Rorty, another fan of Dewey, on my own. By foregrounding issues of values and ethics in human inquiry, Rorty's brand of neopragmatism contributed a robust quality to the epistemology of the earlier pragmatists. Moreover, Rorty's characterization of social science as continuous with imaginative literature represented a validation of a previously marginalized form of context-sensitive and value-laden human inquiry. The aim of storytelling, noted Rorty, is to find meaning in experience, a purpose later also identified by Jerome Bruner with the narrative mode of knowing. My appreciation for (and appropriation of) Rorty's views of narrative and the novel as useful and legitimate modes of inquiry are apparent in the two essays in Section 3.

I first read John-Paul Sartre as an undergraduate, long before I had felt a need to comprehend the nature of human inquiry. My later rediscovery of Sartre would mean exploring a new subtheme in my life narrative, the one reflected in the articles in Section 4. This subtheme concerned issues of politics and audience in research texts.

Sartre helped me to reconcile the apparent conflict between my own growing attention to the political dimensions of research and the disregard for audience I found in many of the writings of those "generous intellectuals" (Greene, 1978) who were enacting Jurgen Habermas's notion of a critical science. In that regard, the greatest attraction of the (by then) maturing Tom Barone was (and is) for the early and (in certain regards) optimistic Sartre. This was the Sartre still infatuated with the possibilities of a socially committed literature as a means for promoting critical awareness. Such writing avoided the discursive features of critical theory in favor of others capable of calling attention to quite specific social conditions in need of redressing. Exhibiting an accessibility that flows out of an appreciation of vernaculars, this kind of writing could serve as an effective vehicle for persuading a broad, general audience of the need for human solidarity and social justice in particular times and places.

And then there was/is Mikhail Bakhtin: the older, postmodernist Barone chides the younger, more modernist, for his failure to focus on the works of this amazing theorist. Ultimately, however, Bakhtin's contributions to my professional identity would primarily concern the dialogical nature of existence, of history, of language, and especially of imaginative literature. From Bakhtin's ideas I extrapolated the notion that good educational inquiry, like a good novel, must provide space for a polyphonic dialogue, one between writer, characters, and reader, one in which open displays of "otherness" can promote the kinds of epiphanies that advance the story of one's self by uncovering new clusters of questions to pursue.

I am, at the time of this writing, still pulling insights from Bakhtin—and from the hundreds of others with whom I have engaged in dialogues about the nature of education and inquiry. Once heard, these other voices have never abandoned me, and, hopefully, they never will—as long as my drive to make sense of educational inquiry continues, and my own self survives in more than the reminiscences of others. The articles included here were written in the past, but my quest directs me forward, toward the additional voices that will shape future versions of who I am. As Ricouer noted, narratives, seemingly focused on the past, are in fact deceptively teleological:

> [A]mong the facts recounted in the past tense we find projects, expectations, and anticipations by means of which the protagonists in the narrative are oriented toward their mortal future. . . . In other words, the narrative also recounts care. In a sense, it *only* recounts care. This is why there is nothing absurd in speaking about the narrative unity of a life. (1992, p.163)

Among the things I care about is educational virtue—making education and schooling more life-enhancing for youngsters of all sorts and for the culture at large. Perhaps you, the reader, are on a quest with a similar theme. If so, I invite you, oriented toward your own mortal future, to join in the dialogue here. Maybe your old self will be sufficiently puzzled into growing a new one, even as its project remains constant.

And some readers may have already begun the conversation. For all of the writings contained herein have been on public display elsewhere. They have existed as pieces of my self scattered about, reproduced in books and journals, tucked away on the shelves of offices, studies, and libraries. Now gathered together in physical proximity to each other, these moments in my story may speak to each other, offering readers (I hope) a richer intratextuality, a fuller engagement with theme and subthemes, a heightened understanding of the nature of the quest that binds them together.

If the reader does indeed benefit from this offering, it is due to the graciousness of Joe Kincheloe and Shirley Steinberg, editors of this series. I thank them for inviting me to publish in it. I also thank the untold numbers of others—colleagues, friends, family members, and acquaintances—whose words and deeds have, in ways recognizable and not, enabled me to be who I am, personally and professionally. Above all, there is ultimately (in addition to yours truly) one central character in my life story, the one who has remained nearby throughout thickenings of the plot, the only one who may be rightfully called its co-author: Margaret Burke Barone. This book is dedicated to her.

References

Greene, M. (1978). *Landscapes of learning.* New York: Teachers College Press.

Greene, M. (1995). *Releasing the imagination: Essays on education, the arts, and social change.* New York: Jossey-Bass.

Ricouer, P. (1992). *Oneself as another.* Chicago: The University of Chicago Press.

Roth, P. (1988). *The facts: A novelist's autobiography.* New York: Farrar, Straus, & Giroux.

SECTION I

BEGINNINGS: ELLIOT EISNER AND LITERARY NONFICTION

The first article in this section is the result of an invitation to write about the experience of studying with Elliot Eisner. Prepared for a book on distinguished twentieth-century professors of education, this 1996 essay is included here because it is only partly about my mentor. Largely autobiographical, it reveals much about the origins of my interest in arts-based forms of qualitative research, and the formation of my professional identity.

The next three chapters address the potentials of literary forms of nonfiction for writing about educational matters. Chapter 2, published in 1980, is a slightly modified version of a central chapter of my dissertation. Chapter 3, written two years later, explores the nature of theory in this kind of writing. And, returning to an autobiographical format, Chapter 4 documents the emergence of my postmodern awareness of the ambiguous relationship between fact and fiction.

Chapter 1

From the Classrooms of Stanford to the Alleys of Amsterdam: Elliot Eisner as Pedagogue (1996)

On that first morning in Holland we awoke, Margaret and I, to a delightful surprise. Peering out of our third-floor window we could hardly believe our eyes. Overnight, the rooftops of Utrecht had, against the odds, been powdered with snow. Late March serendipity!—for native New Orleanians even January snowfalls remain minor miracles. We dressed hurriedly and crawled down the steep and narrow stairway to share our discovery with our hosts. Along the way Margaret suggested that the Eisners, having endured the Dutch weather since January, would not be as impressed. But I guessed correctly that they would be pleased for us. "And it won't interfere with our sightseeing," said Elliot, as if he had expected the unexpected.

Ellie Eisner had accompanied her husband to the Netherlands, where he was spending the spring semester of 1985 as visiting professor at the University of Utrecht. My wife and I had decided to "spring break" in Europe and had accepted the Eisners' generous invitation to stay in their typically narrow, vertical Dutch townhouse. Upon our arrival from Paris the previous evening, the Eisners had helped us sketch the outline of our itinerary for the next three days. On this, our first day, we were to "do" Amsterdam. And as Elliot guided the two of us (Ellie would run daytime errands and join us for dinner) toward the train station, I did not yet understand the snowfall as a harbinger. I could not have foreseen how this singular day would be studded with serendipitous occurrences, or how later it would come to encapsulate *for me the essence of the Elliot Eisner—the mentor, the friend, the teacher/critic, the connoisseur of life—that I, before and since, have grown to admire and appreciate.*

* * * * *

Eleven years earlier, no snow had greeted Margaret and me as we arrived in Palo Alto on Labor Day. The warm weather was not unexpected. Indeed, anticipating my Stanford experience, I had researched many facets of my graduate student setting—the Bay Area, the campus, the doctoral program, and the writings of the man who would be my advisor. No big surprises, thank you. Even as I had attempted to decide a year earlier on the doctoral programs in curriculum to which I would apply, I had sequestered myself in the Tulane University library to pore over publications of potential mentors. I was keenly aware that my own non-technicist educational philosophy—not to mention my preferred "literary" style was not currently in fashion. Understanding (somewhat, even then) the potential threats to the intellectual integrity of disempowered doctoral students, I was searching for an established scholar with similar inclinations who might provide a safe place for honest, but apparently somewhat dangerous, work. After reading a few articles by Eisner (I best recall "Educational Objectives: Help or Hindrance?," on the limitations of the then-sacrosanct objectives movement), I decided to apply to Stanford in hopes of studying with him.

By that late summer of 1974, when I first met Eisner in person, his career was impressive—even, to a starry-eyed doctoral student, intimidating. Most of his early articles contain evidence of two primary passions, the arts and education. Elliot had already begun to explore in his writing intersections of the two, including the relationships among the arts and curriculum, teaching, and evaluation. For Elliot, embarking upon an educational project is much like beginning a painting, play, sculpture, or story. One must use intelligent and informed judgment throughout both artistic and educational projects in order to maximize meaning. But neither in education nor in making art can ultimate outcomes be foreseen: final visions arise only well into the process of give-and-take between artist and material, teacher and student, student and curricular content. The artist travels with aspirations in hand but *sans* detailed blueprints. Along the way, the artist welcomes chance intrusion, entering into negotiations with emergent qualities of experience, incorporating them into the construction of an ultimate vision. So does the good teacher. So does the active student. Indeed, as Elliot would ask, isn't this always the way we negotiate with the world when we are fully alive?

* * * * *

It certainly was the way we lived that day in Amsterdam. Heavy, wet flakes were falling as we disembarked from the express train. Our plans for the day promised varied emotional tones, from a visit to Anne Frank's House to time in the renowned Ryksmuseum. The first was a solemn and moving experience. Much respectful silence all around. Later, as we entered the museum, I expected Elliot Eisner, Stanford Professor of Education and Art, to hold forth as teacher/critic/docent to the quite tutorable. Instead, no lessons, more silence. And for Margaret and me the pressure was on. Left alone to ferret out Meaning, we strained under the intensity of the occasion, attempting to focus all our intellectual and emotional energies, all that we had ever learned and experienced, on hundreds of dark and weighty masterworks. After a couple of hours, weary of the burden of teaching myself, I finally (but still rather bravely, I thought) mumbled something about art museums and cognitive overload. To which Elliot, looking relieved, responded, "Me, too. Let's go."

Go where? Outside the snow had stopped but we were soon to find its equivalent nestled in between the lines of the day's formal itinerary. The real serendipity, it turned out, lurked in the narrow moments between our planned stops. The day's biggest surprises, its teachable moments, were awaiting us in, of all places, boutiques and antique shops.

* * * * *

Ultimately, in any worthwhile doctoral program, a student will experience a similar silence, one accompanied by an inevitable loneliness as he or she struggles with shaping the contours of a personal contribution to the future of a chosen field of study. The only alternative, after all, is the fraudulent one wherein a dissertation advisor talks explicitly and narrowly: we know of lesser figures in academia who dispense to underlings prepackaged, paint-by-number dissertation topics designed to be colored in as pieces of a larger study. But mentors worth their salt know the importance of absenting themselves from the private site of intense dissertation generation, emerging only occasionally as critic and respondent to the work-in-progress. Of course, much conversation, a lot of teaching and learning, precedes the loneliness of the long-distance thesis author. And some of it occurs, of course, in formal classroom settings.

My first course with Elliot at Stanford was entitled "Curriculum Theory and Curriculum Change." Designed as an introduction to the field, the course included discussions of readings from each of the major curriculum orientations identified in the book he had co-edited with another of his students, Elizabeth (Beau) Vallance. The second course, taken a year later, was devoted to exploring issues surrounding arts-based forms of qualitative research, a relatively new passion of Elliot's. For each of the courses Elliot taught, prearrangements were minimal. Never producing anything resembling a detailed itinerary, map, or script, he would, alone or in consultation with a few doctoral students, sketch out a syllabus by identifying relevant topics and issues and selecting relevant readings. The ensuing journey consisted then of conversation, occasionally (in the form of a monologue crafted for and rehearsed on other occasions) one-sided, but nearly always intellectually provocative and characterized by unexpected (for both professor and students) side trips down interesting ideational alleyways.

But the highlights of my experiences with Elliot at Stanford were to be found not in catalogued courses but in less formal gatherings where all participants *really* traveled without a map. The Qualitative Research Study Group consisted of Elliot Eisner and five or six interested doctoral students who met weekly to discuss important issues related to arts-based forms of qualitative inquiry, especially art criticism and educational criticism. Alfred Schutz, Clifford Geertz, Susanne Langer—the scholars whose works we examined were a varied lot, most selected by Elliot, some by students. But there were rarely any "close readings" of their texts, and any attempts to discover "correct" interpretations were interspersed with movements toward establishing intertextual connections with our own ongoing projects. Indeed, some sessions were set aside solely to break the silence on our own work, to secure critical feedback from peers and professor. Elliot presided over, moderated, or better, facilitated the discussions of the Study Group, but the twists and turns of an unfettered exchange of ideas were omnipresent in these sessions.

* * * * *

Working without a map in Amsterdam can be as challenging, but also as rewarding, as a freewheeling study group. Traveling with a map means moving more expeditiously toward your predetermined destination. Without it you are more observant, more likely to find yourself in a richer conversation with your surroundings. You are more tempted to turn down intriguing alleyways. Elliot had walked through Amsterdam before and was convinced that he didn't need a map to guide us smoothly from site A to site B. Soon, however, it appeared that we were lost.

But "lost" is, of course, a relative term. One might say that the three of us were "lost" only in relation to our original destinations of the Anne Frank House and Ryksmuseum, just as one can be "lost" in a scholarly reading or discussion only when one aims toward a correct, predetermined, final understanding. One is never lost, however, if the experience of reading, discussing, traveling is an inherently vital and educational one. And we three tourists were certainly not lost in terms of the myriad of interesting sights on all sides of us. Especially the antique shops.

It began almost immediately on the first crooked leg of our trip, as we moved from the train station to the Anne Frank House. But it continued between there and the cafe where we paused for lunch, between lunch and the museum, and after the museum on the way to dinner. Elliot would glance down a narrow street and, like a hawk who spots the slightest movement in the distant underbrush, spy a shop with potential for providing a certain form of nourishment. "Let's see what they have in here," he would say, and in we would go. And lo and behold, inside were delights that Margaret and I could not have anticipated. What we found were things of excellence from cultures around the globe. We also found a lover of beautiful artifacts, a collector with seemingly encyclopedic knowledge of art from every inhabited continent, who was willing and eager to talk.

* * * * *

One of the books we confronted most intensely in our Qualitative Research Study Group, a favorite of Elliot's then, and of mine ever since, was John Dewey's *Art as Experience* (1934). Among the insights in this major work on aesthetics are those about art criticism. Since "criticism," wrote Dewey, "is judgment," to understand the nature of criticism one must first understand judgment. Bad judgment is, said Dewey, "judgment that is final, that settles a matter, [and] is . . . congenial to unregenerate human nature," while good judgment is

> development in thought of a deeply realized perception. The original adequate experience is not easy to attain; its achievement is a test of native sensitiveness and of experience matured through wide contacts. A judgment as an act of controlled inquiry demands a rich background and a disciplined insight. It is much easier to tell people what they should believe than to discriminate and unify. (p. 300)

Especially on those occasions when we explored Elliot's favorite texts (Langer's *Problems of Art*, for example) did he model for us the kind of criticism—judgment—of which Dewey wrote. His method was a mixture of a loose version of Socratic maieutics (disciplined questioning designed more to provoke controlled inquiry than to reach foregone conclusions) and insights drawn from a native sensitivity toward and wide contacts with the subject matter. As we, his students, strained to acquire an "original adequate experience" with these masterworks, Elliot would bring his judgment to bear, rarely telling us what to think about a text but more often providing the kind of criticism that first calls attention to particular ideas in and qualities of a text and then places them into wider contexts.

But here is the most intriguing fact about those sessions: Of all the activities in which Elliot could have engaged on a Tuesday night, this was what he chose to do. Participation in the Study Group was voluntary for all, certainly for the instigator. Elliot must have initiated the sessions out of love. But a love for what? The ideas in the readings? Us, his intellectual progeny? Without, I hope, sounding overly ponderous or pretentious, I want to say that Elliot, like the rest of us, participated in those Tuesday evening sessions out of a love for life. Because the experiences there made him feel alive. Dewey, after all, insisted that heightened vitality was the hallmark of true experience:

> Instead of being shut up within one's own private feelings and sensations, [experience] signifies active and alert commerce with the world; at its height it signifies complete interpenetration of self and the world of objects and events. . . . Because experience is the fulfillment of an organism in its struggles and achievements in a world of things, it is art in germ. (1934, p. 19)

I certainly recall experiencing such fulfillment as we wrestled with the brawny ideas in those readings and discussions. But an additional dimension of those sessions that contributed to fulfillment for Elliot was, I think, the opportunity to play the role of critic/teacher. One final excerpt from *Art as Experience* helps to explain:

> [A good critic is already] keenly sensitive to the unnumbered interactions that are the material of experience. . . . [But] critical judgment not only grows out of the experiences of objective matter, and not only depends upon that for validity, but has for its office the deepening of just such experiences in others. (Dewey, 1934, p. 324)

I think the Study Group was born out of a desire for an opportunity to arrange and chaperone a *rendezvous* between us and some of Elliot's favorite subject matter, to be (actively) present with us as our own intellectual awareness was expanded and our judgment honed through contact with those materials. I think it was born out of a need to travel with others who had not yet seen the sights that he had seen, to subtly steer them toward the kind of significant experiences, the "deeply realized perceptions," that made his own professional life worth living. For Elliot the connoisseur of excellent "subject matter," being alert to qualities in the world, being able to perceive them deeply, appreciate them broadly, experience them fully, makes life worth living. But Elliot the critic/teacher lives to give others those greater reasons to live.

* * * * *

The most enduring image that I retain of our jaunt into that Amsterdam winter-spring is of Elliot against a window inside a shop, backgrounded by the lightly falling snow, focusing joyously and intently, through touch and sight, on a Japanese Buddha. His precise words are gone now, only vague recollections of certain qualities in his utterances remain. These were the familiar ones of delight and earnestness, a seemingly contradictory mix of emotional tones I had come to associate with the Elliot of our Study Group. Elliot was once again in his connoisseur-and-critic mode, deeply absorbed not in scholarly treatises but in beautiful artifacts from everywhere and now eager to share his perceptions and judgments within this different field of subject matter.

Having experienced the art collection at his home, I knew that Elliot's interests in well-crafted objects were wide-ranging. But until Holland I had not realized the breadth and depth of his knowledge and appreciation. For example, with that particular Buddha and many others, Elliot would pinpoint the era and location of origin and have the information confirmed momentarily by the shop owner. And on we moved to other shops filled with African masks, and then with Chinese vases, stunning artifacts, many familiar to Elliot, that he was enabling us to see for the first time. ("Why is this piece so appealing to you, Elliot?" "Look at this quality here or that one there.") To Persian rugs. Dragging one toward the window light, he said,"You've just been to some cathedrals in France. Do you see the colors of stained glass windows here and here?" I was instantaneously returned to Sainte Chapelle. Associations made, appreciations acquired, I saw anew both rug and vibrant chapel light.

And one last burst of guided delight. Elliot saw Margaret and me admiring a watercolor of some Dutch women at the shore, and he pointed to particular areas of impressive technique. Hardly a masterpiece, but glimmers of quality here and there: the artist worked well with a good choice of materials. The painting embodied many of the soft, brooding qualities we had observed in the Dutch landscape. And, unlike other pieces we had craved, it was within our budget. The 1985 watercolor by the Dutch painter Horrix now adorns the wall in our living room, serving dual roles as objet d'art and souvenir of a special place and moment in time.

* * * * *

"Hardly a masterpiece." "Glimmers of quality." Of course, that (or any) painting cares nothing about the judgments of the critic. But what of a student and the judgments of his mentor? The metaphors of mentor-as-artist and mentee-as-artwork are hardly precise: Although he chose to work with us for the glimmers of potential he observed, we should not be considered Elliot's raw materials. We could never be molded. Human beings can never be as malleable as clay, never as predictable as stone. Although his influences on their content and style were/are often unmistakable, the signatures of his students would always remain their own.

But there were times at Stanford when it did not seem that way. Part of the struggle of the doctoral candidate involves making a unique contribution to a field even as one is being initiated into that field. But at the outset one's own professional identity awaits formation. The good notions all seem to be taken. The ideas in one's essays seem, only a day or week later, to be stale and trite and obvious or already written, better, by someone else. Even worse, that someone else may be one's mentor.

The sense of intellectual identification with an academic father figure can indeed be overwhelming, so that even the phrasing and tempo of one's writings seem to be a pale copy of a vivid original. This sense of dependency can be deepened when one is at the edge of the field, tilling soil that lies outside traditional boundaries. One is new at this, one is nervous, one's future is at stake, one is intellectually exposed, one needs to be covered from attacks by marauding traditionalists until one learns to fend for oneself. A commanding figure in the field can provide that cover. Elliot has done so for many of his doctoral students.

My dissertation defense in 1979 was not the most pleasant of experiences. A few of the examiners were, I dare say, in league with the marauding traditionalists. Much of the interrogation focused on methodological issues (for example, the meaning of validity and objectivity and subjectivity in relation to arts-based inquiry) that are still being explored today. Back then, however, the traditionalists were much more incredulous. Elliot told me afterwards that I had held my own ground, but to say that his presence there was important is to win a prize for understatement. The whole exercise unfolded within the shared understanding that Eisner gave credence to this radical notion of dissertation-as-arts-based-endeavor. His stature afforded me the necessary cover while I reloaded during that very early skirmish in what have since come to be known as the paradigm wars.

I am certain that I would have been unable to muster the courage necessary for fighting alone. But it was only years later that I fully appreciated the degree of intellectual courage demonstrated by Elliot Eisner throughout his career. Only now can I comprehend how professionally risky it is for any academic—even a tenured Stanford professor—to advance notions as avant-garde as some of Elliot's. But a sense of intellectual integrity and a responsibility to his chosen field demanded that courage.

Moreover, "fighting the good fight" can be exhilarating as well as challenging. Indeed, at the party following the defense I felt simultaneously elated and fatigued.

"Whew! It's exhausting when you swim upstream," I said.

"It's how you know you are alive," he answered.

* * * * *

In ancient Greece the pedagogue was a wise servant who would walk with a student from the privacy of the student's home to the public place of the school. At the school the student was expected to engage in the learning of various technical matters. But along the way the "slave companion" would seek out opportunities to instruct about the larger affairs of life, helping the boy to place the merely technical into the context of the wide world outside the school. This activity embodied a kind of moral education, instruction about character, teaching about how to live. If we confine ourselves to this sense of the term, then pedagogy was what was occurring in those alleys of Amsterdam. This was, to be sure, an artful, indirect form of teaching, as pedagogue and students together abandoned reliance on the rote, the mundane, the routinized, the expected, for the more complex human capacities for imagination and judgment. Pedagogue and students together practiced living more fully.

* * * * *

Of course, the centrality of these capacities of imagination and judgment in the educational process has been the focus of Elliot Eisner's pedagogical efforts throughout his life and career, with his "students" in Holland, with his students at Stanford, with his professional colleagues who have been led (some reluctantly) to understand the need to subjugate the technical elements of the activities of educational program design, teaching, research, and evaluation, to the larger dimensions of artistry and criticism.

I have pointed to courage as a hallmark of Elliot's intellectual leadership, a courage born out of a deep sense of professional responsibility. But a second hallmark of that leadership was civility. Indeed, there must reside within the soul of any true educator a respect for those whom he would educate. So while his views on educational research might have seemed contentious and revolutionary to some of his colleagues, Elliot's outlook remained consistently generous and expansive. Consider that he never attempted to advance the cause of arts-based educational research at the expense of social science. Instead, he would merely insist upon space for additional settings at the research table. Elliot knew that one does not persuade one's peers in the professoriate of the value of your own ideas by repudiating their work. The good pedagogue leads gently by the hand, accepting the experiences of the student while guiding toward new possibilities.

With courage, civility, and earnest delight, Elliot Eisner guided the field of education in this fashion. Thanks to him, members of that field who had been moving along rather predictably were presented with a delightful surprise. Through the pedagogical efforts of Elliot Eisner—embodied in his writings, in his service activities, in his presentations at zillions of podia, in untold numbers of teachable moments—members of the educational profession were persuaded to see subject matter that they never expected to see, to experience chance intrusions about which they would soon begin to exercise judgment. Thanks to the pedagogy of Elliot Eisner, the field of education has acquired greater character. So many of its members, I mean, are now more fully alive.

Note

When my wife and I travel abroad, she keeps a detailed journal that we delight in reading and rereading years later. Many of the details in this account are extracted from that journal.

Chapter 2

Effectively Critiquing the Experienced Curriculum: Clues from the New Journalism (1979)

Anyone with more than a passing acquaintance with the curriculum evaluation field—or even of educational inquiry in general—is aware of a growing interest in new sorts of approaches to such inquiry. The features of these approaches tend to place them within a more holistic, qualitative, interpretive, hermeneutical, or critical vein of empirical inquiry.[1] As such, they are meant to complement the natural-science-based, and generally quantitative, strategies that have long dominated the curriculum research/ evaluation scene.

Much of the writing by those attempting to broaden the field of curriculum evaluation has been directed toward the exploration and explication of analogies with other established disciplines such as art criticism, literary criticism, and ethnography. The thrust has been toward uncovering and publicizing the methodological heritages of these new approaches and generally attempting to establish their legitimacy for exploring the realms of educational phenomena.[2] This is, I believe, as it should be for an inquiry methodology that is, in Bob Dylan's phrase, "busy being born" (or at least being reincarnated, since many of its features bear striking resemblance to those used within related fields).

This article aspires to serve as another contribution to the work of forging sets of tools for disclosing useful truths about curricular and educational phenomena—tools that fit within the hermeneutical or critical branch(es) of social inquiry or both. This approach possesses two unique features. First, the tools envisioned here are meant for divulging information about the experiences that students live through in particular classrooms. In so doing, this approach recommends bypassing direct consideration of the intended curriculum for a focusing on what can be called the *experienced curriculum*. Second, it recommends use of the genre of literary nonfiction called the *New Journalism* because of its appropriateness for critiquing aspects of experienced events.

Evaluation and the Experienced Curriculum

The experienced curriculum consists of those events experienced by a particular student, by a set of students, or by the preponderance of students in a classroom. A discussion of the experienced curriculum does not consist of an examination of a set of plans or of chosen materials; it is a critique of the manner in which students apparently perceive various aspects of classroom situations and events, and of how they respond to, and help shape, those situations and events.

Why this focus on the student? Why does this approach recommend an indirect concern with other aspects of the classroom scene such as the quality of the teaching, or the composition of the learning materials? The answer is that by directing our focus on student experiences, we may become more aware of the intricate interplay between students and the features within their environments. An experience, after all, consists of a dialogue between an actor and his or her surroundings. It is an interactive process, composed of continuous transactions between a person and the shifting and shifted environment. One cannot study the experiences of students in a classroom without also attending to the significant qualities of the educational landscape (see below). We may thereby come to understand the character of the interactions between students and their environments, and the significance of these interactions for their educational lives. Such understanding, it may be reasonably assumed, should lead ultimately to sounder judgments on the part of educational practitioners.

Traditional curriculum and educational evaluation has in fact generally aimed at the measurement of student status and progress, although in a radically different sense than that intended here. The task of the evaluation specialist has too often been the construction, administration, and normative interpretation of achievement test scores. Only within the past two decades have we witnessed any interest in the relationship between the "quality of instruction" and "pupil achievement." Stake (1967) cites Cronbach's (1963) article "Course Improvement Through Evaluation" as the first step in this direction for evaluators. The shape of curriculum evaluation has, of course, evolved since that time, with the sophistication

in strategies and instruments for evaluating educational programs, curriculum materials, and "instructional effectiveness" having increased greatly.
And yet, as we know, the trend in many quarters is once again toward the
measurement of program value, teaching performance, and student outcomes in terms of achievement test scores. Indeed, the present accountability movement often equates teaching ability with the amount of learning measured by those scores.

While recognizing the student as the raison d'être of the educational
enterprise, the approach developed here for inquiring into the experienced curriculum avoids the simplistic notion that test scores, or narrow
slices of behavior, supply us with the only valid information about student
progress, or (even more simplistically) about the worth of a teacher or
program. Instead, emphasis is placed upon interpreting that behavior in
terms of the meaning it holds for the student, and assessing its significance in terms of educational criteria.

An experience is a complete reaction of a whole self to a situation
confronting it, a qualitative response composed of intellectual and emotional and willful elements. And aspects of a present experience are understood in terms of previous ones—within, that is, a whole psychological, autobiographical perspective. Experience is *holistic*, therefore, in terms
of both the individual's particular present experience and in the relationships of elements within this present experience to the entire life-process
of the individual. An evaluator of the experienced curriculum must come
to know and understand these experiences. What is required, first, is
empathic understanding, the vicarious participation in a form of life as
manifested in a particular pattern of actions. It is the achievement by the
inquirer of a degree of intersubjectivity (always a degree), an approximate
re-creation of another point of view through "interpreting the real world"
as Schutz (1962) put it, "from the perspective of the subjects of his investigation" (p. 7).

But evaluators must do more than empathize; they must assess the
significance of classroom experience for the educational lives of students.
Evaluators must not only participate in the qualities of experience seen by
the students but they must place them within their own (presumably)
broader, more refined perspectives.

And then, having come to be appreciated by an inquirer, the experienced curriculum needs to be conveyed to an audience. In this phase of
the evaluative process, information about features of the classroom experiences must be divulged and commented upon in a manner that both
reveals their essence and respects their integrity. It is this phase of the

evaluative process—the phase wherein elements of the experienced curriculum are identified and assessed—to which we direct our attention here.

Literary Nonfiction and the Experienced Curriculum

Through what modes of communication, what media, what forms and formats can enlightened curriculum inquirers share with their audiences the significant qualities of experience that they have shared with students in educational settings? How can they effectively comment upon those experiences? What models are already available for our inspection, models with features perhaps adaptable for use in conveying what we learn about an experienced curriculum? I suggest that evaluators look to a certain genre of literary nonfiction for ideas about publicizing their perceptions of classroom experiences. This particular field of literary nonfiction has been referred to as the *New Journalism*.

Why the New Journalism? Two general characteristics of literary nonfiction that recommend it as a mode for critiquing aspects of the experienced curriculum are identified below. As will be shown, these features are also characteristic of aesthetic criticism. Just as art criticism is itself a form of literary nonfiction, so (I contend) the New Journalism is, in fact, a form of criticism. Indeed, it is the criticism of human events and experiences, the very sorts of phenomena that comprise the experienced curriculum of a classroom or school.

The first characteristic concerns the modes of language used in many forms of literary nonfiction, and their peculiar mix. The second has epistemological overtones, and involves the regard for the patterning of information about phenomena encountered in the research setting in ways that aim simultaneously for both accuracy and intensification of feeling.

In the process of experiencing, there occurs the qualitative response of a whole human organism to a situation. To convey information about patterns within experiences that happen to take place in a classroom, we need a means that is not merely denotative and linear, but also connotative, and somehow "holistic." One that does not totally restructure the phenomena of classroom experiences for the purpose of communicating about them, but maintains, to some extent, a structural isomorphism with the patterns of qualities that the inquirer has come to appreciate within them. This kind of conveyance occurs within the artistic mode of expression.

Allowing a foreign audience imaginary access to a scene in which such experiences occur requires an artistic revelation of the character of those experiences. Langer (1957) has rightly insisted that only works of art possess the kind of articulative power needed to truly portray the "felt" aspect of experiences:

> [Every good work of art] . . . formulates the appearance of feeling, of subjective experience, the character of so-called "inner life," which discourse—the normal use of words—is peculiarly unable to articulate, and which therefore we can only refer to in a general and quite superficial way. The actual felt process of life, the tensions interwoven and shifting from moment to moment, the flowing and slowing, the drive and directedness of desires, and above all the rhythmic continuity of our own selfhood, defies the expressive power of discursive symbolism. The myriad forms of subjectivity, the infinitely complex sense of life, cannot be rendered linguistically, that is, stated. But they are precisely what comes to light in a good work of art. . . . A work of art is an expressive form, and vitality, in all its manifestations from sheer sensibility to the most elaborate phases of awareness and emotion, is what it may express. (pp. 132–133)

Any work of art is a nondiscursive formulation—a metaphor. Rico (1976) has described a metaphor as a holistic image that focuses on the "simultaneous and integral relationships within a total structure" (p. 10). A metaphor is suggestive and connotative and qualitative, rather than methodical and denotative.

Within the realm of language, it is the playwright, the novelist, and especially the poet who create metaphors. Poetry can produce what Langer (1957) calls a *semblance*, a "composed and shaped apparition of a new human experience" (p. 48). Writers or poets can re-create in the minds of their readers a classroom atmosphere that is, say, cool, businesslike, and impersonal. They can do this, not by discursively communicating and describing separate aspects of events that transpire there, but more directly through the rhythms evoked by the structure and form of clauses, sentences, and paragraphs, by the imagery within the words and phrasing, and so on.

Likewise, part of the task of the inquirer into the experienced curriculum is to transform the subjective experiences of students into events known, to transport the audience via the power of imagination into the lived-in complexity of a classroom scene. So for inquirers to publicize their emotional and intellectual responses to the experienced "whole," their language must be, to some extent, metaphorical—artful, suggestive, figurative, evocative, literary.

Often, however, critiquing the experienced curriculum might require something besides the sheerest of poetry, and that is a form and format for conveying information which uses language that is often evocative and metaphorical, but sometimes denotative and linear as well. Such a verbal portrait would contain metaphorical, artful language to evoke a qualitative sense of the wholeness of experience, but the narrative would also require denotative interpretation, and rather explicit, straightforward assessment. These latter aspects, interpretation and assessment, often lend themselves to propositional statements.

The question then turns to the quality and manner of the blending of these two kinds of languages in a qualitative portrait of the experienced curriculum. Any of several factors may determine the nature of the composition in individual cases. These would include the talents and proclivities of the writer and the nature of the intended audiences. If the author is adept at writing in a literary style, and if the audience is both sophisticated in educational matters and sensitive to what artistic language intimates, then a qualitative portrayal may produce powerful insight. Usually though, explication is required as well; propositions must be spelled out, arguments mounted in logical/linear terms, rather than merely alluded to or suggested.

In What Sense Nonfiction?

The second characteristic of literary nonfiction concerns the sense in which it is indeed nonfictional. The basic materials of the inquirer into the experienced curriculum are pieces of evidence, particular facts collected during observations in a classroom or school. Inquirers may select, interpret, and shape this factual evidence in order to provide a forceful, coherent rendering of classroom life-honoring aesthetic criteria, among others. Artists, however, are less concerned with reconstructing the literal details of a particular incident, setting, etc.—lest (artists would say) it obscure the "truth," interfere with their powers for enlarging and intensifying the "reality" to be found therein—than are sociologists, historians, ethnographers, or educational inquirers. Guernica during the bombing appeared metaphorically, not literally, like Picasso's rendition.

But for an educational portrait to have real value, it is essential that authors use as their material the actual, particular, specific phenomena confronted in the research setting. Maxine Greene (1977) referred to this distinction in relation to art and history:

> The crucial difference is that the historian is in quest of truth in some degree verifiable; while the artist strives for coherence, clarity, enlargement, intensity. Even more important: in the aesthetic experience, the mundane world or the empirical world must be bracketed out or in some sense distanced, so that the reader, listener, or beholder can enter the aesthetic space in which the work of art exists. Captain Ahab's manic search for the whale cannot be checked in any

history of the whaling industry; its plausibility and impact have little to do with a testable truth. Thomas Cole's painting "The Ox-Bow" may look in some way like the river; but if it is not encountered as a drama of color, receding planes, and light, it will not be experienced as a work of art. An historical work —Thucydides' *The Peloponnesian War*, John B. Bury's *The Idea of Progress*—refers beyond itself to events in times past, to the changing situations in humankind's ongoing experience, to whatever are conceived to be the "facts." (p. 122)

Unlike the artist, the evaluator is therefore not entirely free to disregard literal "truth." If such an educational portrait is to be convincing, especially to those familiar with the particular research scene, then not least of its virtues must be accuracy. Its characters and setting must be actual, not virtual. Their descriptions should consist of a host of personality indicators, of physical attributes and characteristics of human behavior, in actual incidents, recorded comments, and so on.

To be sure, a pure, representational narrative of events in a classroom, unedited, unsullied by subjective interpretation, "unmassaged" by the medium through which it is conveyed—a "mirror image" of events—is as impossible as it is undesirable. "The line," said anthropologist Clifford Geertz (1974), "between mode of representation and substantive content is as undrawable in cultural analysis as it is in painting" (p. 16).

The end-product of a qualitative evaluation of student experiences in a classroom is the result of both an observational process involving focusing, interpreting, and understanding by the evaluator and a writing process whereby the evaluator/author selects, shapes, and conveys the material secured. And as much as Geertz's anthropological writings, such evaluative portraits:

> are, thus, fictions; fictions in the sense that they are "something made," "something fashioned"—the original meaning of *fictio*—not that they are false, unfactual, or merely "as if" thought experiments. To construct actor-oriented descriptions of the involvements of a Berber chieftain, a Jewish merchant, and a French soldier with one another in 1912 Morocco is clearly an imaginative act, not all that different from constructing similar descriptions of, say, the involvements with one another of a provincial French doctor, his silly, adulterous wife, and her feckless lover in nineteenth century France. In the latter case, the actors are represented as not having existed and the events as not having happened, while in the former they are represented as actual, or as having been so. This is a difference of no mean importance . . . indeed, precisely the one Madame Bovary had difficulty grasping. But the importance does not lie in the fact that her story was created while Cohen's was only noted. The conditions of their creation, and the point of it (to say nothing of the manner and the quality) differ. But the one is as much a fiction—"a making"—as the other. (Geertz, 1974, pp.15–16)

Geertz is persuasive in his insistence upon a radical definition of the term *fiction* in describing anthropological writings. And curriculum portraits of the sort envisioned here are, likewise, more "made" than they are objective documentations of classroom events. But within our culture, isn't the most commonly accepted standard for distinguishing between fiction and nonfiction different from that espoused by Geertz? The Dewey Decimal System operates on different premises. If an ethnographic account is as much a "making" as a novel, why are they so often located on different floors of the library? And why are popular biographies not found on the best-seller lists of the *New York Times* under "fiction"?

As usual, however, reality prankishly resists such neat compartmentalization. For in fact, no inquiry endeavor—not even those within the natural sciences—can entirely escape from Geertz's tightly woven definition of what is "fictional." All are human endeavors, and so despite the presence of rigorous safeguards for insuring their veracity, all at their bases necessarily require large dollops of invention and judgment. Even measurers must decide what is worth measuring. Furthermore, just as works usually classified as "nonfiction" are fashioned, so can "fictional" works be truthful. Is *Up the Down Staircase* (Kaufman, 1965), for example, fiction or nonfiction? A librarian would say "fiction," but for some purposes the question is irrelevant. Its vivid truths about life in a certain kind of school situation transcend consideration of that question. We do indeed learn things from novels.

And what criteria are appropriate for categorizing Norman Mailer's *Armies of the Night* (1968a), an account of a protest march on the Pentagon that was subtitled "The Novel as History; History as the Novel"? Or Truman Capote's *In Cold Blood* (1963), which the author called a "nonfiction novel"? Or Elizabeth Hardwick's acclaimed "autobiographical novel," *Sleepless Nights* (1979)? Why did the Pulitzer Prize Committee need to devise an entirely new category in order to honor Alex Haley's *Roots* (1976), a work that Haley himself described not as "fact," nor as "fiction," but as "faction"? These and other such works point up the dilemma in attempting to cleanly bisect what is actually a fiction/fact continuum.

Is the kind of verbal portrait crafted by an evaluator of the experienced curriculum, therefore, fictional or nonfictional? It is a bit of both; thus, the term *literary nonfiction* does seem apt. The portrait, on the one hand, is something "made," and in a somewhat different sense than, say, an experiment within an established scientific paradigm is "made." The inquirer here, for example, must adhere to fewer (and of course different) canons of procedure than the "normal" scientist, and may even confront his or her materials without pre-established guiding principles for selecting and arranging them. Invention pervades every phase and aspect of this kind of project, even if this invention has parameters of its own.

On the other hand, more artistic, less restrictive, approaches may indeed value intensity and enlargement over accuracy of detail. The kind of inquiry endeavor recommended here serves other purposes that are perhaps more immediate (and more practical), and these demand reference to actual lived-in experiences. For this reason, the inquiry process should be one in which meaning is ferreted out of the complex social phenomena at hand; wherein the evaluator adequately refers to these phenomena in order to unmask the intricate complexities of events in which they are located. Details provided should be accurate reflections of existing phenomena. The inquirer-author chooses not to produce composite characters, for example, or to distort incidents to further a theme, or to invent dialogue, or even to suggest that certain activity of a particular child is typical if it is in fact unusual. This is so because in our brand of literary nonfiction, the actors in the work are represented as actually having existed and the events as actually having happened (Geertz, 1974). Once we accept the charge of referring to real events beyond the work itself, rather than creating a virtual experience, then the shape of our responsibility to our audience is dramatically altered.

Literary Nonfiction, Art Criticism, and the New Journalism

Where can we find suitable examples and models of such literary nonfiction? Is there an existing body of work that might suggest styles, techniques, and so on, for more effectively conveying information about the experienced curriculum? One field to consider is the area of art criticism. Various educators have, I believe, clearly established the appropriateness and usefulness of looking to various modes of criticism for portraying educational phenomena. I am arguing here that we might also look to criticism (though of a special sort) for revealing and evaluating the experiences lived through by students.

The experienced curriculum, as a kind of educational phenomenon, is distinct from or, better, broader than such features of the educational enterprise as teacher actions or curriculum materials. Regarding the latter, Vallance developed (1975) and applied (1977) guidelines drawn from the works of critics of the plastic arts for use in describing curriculum materials. Unlike paintings and sculptures, however, the "objects" of concern here have a form that is four-dimensional—played-out, I mean, spatio-temporally—and so are perhaps more like dances or plays. Even further, in contrast to those art forms, the happenings and characters involved here are real, not virtual. The authors of our events are all of the person-ages who produce and live within and through them. These occurrences are not the outgrowth of a single mind, but emerge out of the complex interactions of a whole community of organisms, each of which perceives the ongoing events from his or her own existential perspective and re-sponds accordingly. Is there, then, a branch of criticism concerned with actual events, that is especially adaptable to the portrayal of this kind of phenomena?

I propose that we investigate the promise that a certain genre of liter-ary nonfiction holds for writing about the experienced curriculum. This modern school of literary nonfiction has been identified as the *New Jour-nalism* (Johnson, 1971, p. xv).[3] This style of assessing and reporting events emerged in the 1960s in certain magazines such as *The New Yorker* and *Esquire*, and in books by Truman Capote, Norman Mailer, Hunter Thompson, Tom Wolfe, and others.

The past has produced other forms of literary nonfiction. Tom Wolfe (1973) argued that the antecedents of the New Journalism can be found in the travel literature of the eighteenth century, in some forms of autobi-ography, in British literary criticism from 1820 to 1840, and in other diverse places. But as we shall see, certain features of the more recent writings seem to make them relevant for criticism of student experiences.

That these modern authors of literary nonfiction, the New Journalists, function as critics of events is clear. In practice, they accept the charge that Dewey presents to the critic, namely, the re-education of the percep-tion of the audience. These writers do indeed often allow the reader, through vivid description and other literary techniques, to vicariously par-ticipate in the events described. Their language is often evocative and metaphor-laden. Instead of adopting the traditional role of the "objec-tive," "factual," detached reporter who (borrowing Ryle's term, cited in Geertz, 1974) "thinly" describes events, these writers seek to penetrate the personalities of real characters, unveil aspects of their experiences, explicate the social meaning underlying important events in an artful, powerful manner that is at once literary and realistic. This kind of New Journalist, states Johnson (1971):

> would be governed by a sense of how the events he encountered were constellated,
> how they affected his own feelings and thinking, and how they constituted a

concrete human experience for him and other people involved; and he would then make a "journal" of the event, a novelistic or impressionistic reconstruction, or an extended and thorough document. (p. 46)[4]

Furthermore, these modern writers of literary nonfiction not only vividly describe events, but interpret and present them from a particular point of view as well. Criticism, said Dewey, is judgment, and the New Journalists do indeed appraise their subjects. Works by writers such as Michael Herr ("Khesanh," 1969) and Tom Wolfe ("The 'Me Decade' and the Third Great Awakening," 1976) assess the significance of cultural events and the workings of American institutions, as do many others. The mix of their language styles resembles that described above as appropriate for portraying the experienced curriculum.

Exploring Features of the New Journalism

Although experienced events are the "objects" critiqued by these modern novelistic journalists, none have turned their attention to life in schools.[5] Yet exploration of some features of the New Journalism would be useful for curriculum critics. The discussion below centers on the treatment of broad facets of content and style, aspects that seem most applicable to writing about the experienced curriculum. Four such facets are theme, landscape, character, and plot. What are some New Journalistic writing styles and devices that possess the power for effectively portraying each of these aspects?

Theme

In developing an approach to evaluating the experienced curriculum, one issue of concern is the focus. To which classroom experiences should the evaluator attend while investigating and writing? What will determine which phenomena are attended to and talked about?

This particular approach can be concerned with similar experiences undergone by the preponderance of children in the class (Is there a general air of boredom during the math activities? Are reading lessons tackled vigorously by most of the children? Is there a rigid sameness evidencing a lack of inventiveness in their artwork?), or the experienced curriculum of an individual child may be portrayed. In either case, evaluators should be asking themselves about which experiences are most likely to plant the seeds for profound and lasting consequences. Is the experience either a "peak" experience of solitary significance, or (more often) a member of a set of experiences bearing familial resemblances that, like the mineral-laden drops of water falling to the floor of a cave, steadily and persistently form their own protuberances in the life-spaces of the students?

Either of these types of experiences is likely to significantly increase the ability—or disability—of the children to direct the course of subsequent experience (Dewey, 1963, pp. 89–90). Which experiences—or sets of experiences—are severely limiting to the power of the students over their futures? Which are expansive and liberating? Which greatly facilitate growth? Which maximally retard it? Which are highly educative? Which are deeply miseducative? The evaluator of the experienced curriculum should tend to those. In ascertaining the importance of these experiences for the children, evaluators will engage in a reciprocity of perspectives, at once viewing the meaning of the experiences (as much as possible) through the student's perspective, while assessing the potential impact on the student's growth through their own perspective.[6]

The quest for the important qualities of experience that pervade the particular classroom scene can at some point yield up to the inquirer a theme around which to erect the superstructure of an inquiry. A theme is a central insight or controlling idea that gives unity to the complex operations of appreciation and disclosure in an investigation of this kind. It is a unifying concept, a means for ordering the experience of the inquirer, that provides focus in seeking out and writing about the otherwise chaotic jumble of classroom phenomena, and that (along with whatever sub-themes come into play) accounts for all of the details of the piece. All other elements of the portrayal—including characterization, description of the psychological landscape, plot, and so on—are subordinate to this central idea that is being articulated.

Used in this sense a theme closely reflects its traditional definition as the controlling idea in a piece of fiction such as a short story, novel, film, drama (see, for example, Perrine, 1959, pp. 137–144), or piece of New Journalism. Such a theme is an abstraction that can be stated concisely, perhaps in sentence form, and exists as an idea or concept that is embodied and vivified in the particular work. There is, however, another, related sense of theme that is also pertinent to our discussion: a theme can be a grand, dominating concept of an age that seeps into the works of artists and scientists even while transcending those individual efforts. Such grand themes are analogous to the scientific paradigms of which Kuhn (1970) has written. They lie at the heart of the style of working that pervades a period of history—styles such as naturalism, realism, classicism, and so on. Nisbet (1976) has noted that such "master themes" give rise to more specialized themes in each of the various fields of inquiry. In sociology, for example, from the grand themes of order, the individual, freedom, and change, have emerged the themes of community, authority, status, the sacred, and alienation. These are the themes that have channeled the intellectual energies of masters of the human studies such as Tocqueville, Marx, Durkheim, Weber, Simmel, Mead, and Cooley.

While these grand themes are, in fact, conceptual imperatives, or cultural categories that comprise part of the perspective of the individuals in the culture, they do not fully account for the entire perspective of an individual in a particular existential situation. They are actually corrigible schemata (like Piaget's *cognitive structures*), amenable to reconstruction, to being refreshed and further articulated in each new expression of them by individuals within the culture. Each new work of art, for example, interprets life for us in a unique way, offering new insights or refreshing and extending old ones. As such, each makes its own central statement, a variation, perhaps, on a grander theme—but nevertheless a theme of its own.

What are we saying, then, about the notion of theme in relation to this sort of curriculum criticism? At least two things:

1. Within each work, there will be evidence of the influence (even if unintended by the author) of certain grand themes that relate to the study of human beings—such as growth, alienation, community, or the like.

2. Within each work, there should be a central, controlling idea, concept, or question-turned-statement that lends coherence and integrity to the narrative. There may, in fact, be a cluster of themes, or a series of subthemes interwoven within the portrait.

Characterization

The second facet of this writing concerns the portraits of the children who are highlighted in the piece. Imagine educational inquirers writing about real people! In a portrait of classroom experiences, the main characters must be developed to show their complexity. To some extent, their inner thoughts and feelings must be disclosed, the prevailing motives and reasons for their actions laid bare. Why? So that the reader may come to know and judge the quality of their experiences, their particular approach to the classroom scene.

Sketching the personalities of real people has been a significant feature of much literary nonfiction; often characterization of a particular personality is the central purpose of a piece of work, its raison d'être, in a sense, its theme. There are, of course, the traditional fully developed biography and autobiography, each aiming to unravel the life story of a public figure. Much of the so-called New Journalism form of literary nonfiction is likewise biographical in essence, so much so, in fact, that some works classified as New Journalism would be labeled as biography had the former term never been coined. *The Autobiography of Malcolm X* (1965) is an example.

John Hollowell (1977) has, in fact, noted that the lives of celebrities and personalities comprise one of the four main subject-matter categories of the New Journalism.[7] Gay Talese, in *Fame and Obscurity: Portraits by Gay Talese* (1970), has lent a new sophistication to the "star interview." And other New Journalist writers such as Joan Didion center on the relationships of individual personalities to the times in which they live. See, for example, her pieces on John Wayne ("John Wayne: A Love Song") and Howard Hughes ("7000 Romaine, Los Angeles 38") in her book *Slouching Towards Bethlehem* (1969).

I noted above that qualitative educational inquiry may aim at portraying the unique personality of an individual child in a classroom. Or the focus can be somewhat broader: we can seek to bring into sharper view the character of the classroom atmosphere, the general style of living and learning that pervades the scene. Nevertheless, this wider concern does not negate the possibility (and even the necessity) of attending to one or several particular children, in order to provide a more intimate sense of the experiences. Educational critics of student experiences may, in fact, avail themselves of any of several strategies in this regard: a variety of classroom characters may enter and exit throughout the piece, serving the needs of a particular theme, as protagonists, perhaps, in especially revealing "indicator incidents"; or writers may choose to make a point about the educational provisions in a classroom by examining the life process of a single child who in crucial respects typifies the other children in that setting; or they may focus on several children, each of whose *modus vivendi* is also somewhat common to a significant portion of the other children there—even though each is portrayed with his or her own idiosyncratic personality intact.

Whatever part characterization may play within a piece of qualitative reportage, it is important that the personalities be vividly portrayed in splendid complexity, that the peculiar nature of each individual life become etched into the mind of the readers.[8] This restoration of life to the characters that inhabit a classroom scene, as opposed to reducing them to a set of traits, or providing thin recitations of behavioral patterns, is one faculty of this approach for disclosing new kinds of information about the experiences of schoolchildren. It is a faculty shared with the New Journalism. Tom Wolfe (1973) has in fact suggested that the New Journalists have borrowed a powerful literary device from the social realism novelists:

> This is the recording of everyday gestures, habits, manners, customs, styles of furniture, clothing, decoration, styles of traveling, eating, keeping house, modes of behaving toward children, servants, superiors, inferiors, peers, plus the various looks, glances, poses, styles of walking and other symbolic details that might exist within a scene. Symbolic of what? Symbolic, generally, of people's status lives, using that term in the broad sense of the entire pattern of behavior and possessions through which people express their position in the world or what they think it is or what they hope it to be. (p. 32)

In other words, in order for the reader to inhabit and share the status world of a character, it is important that the New Journalist vividly detail these action patterns and possessions so that a degree of empathy can occur. In terms of the experienced curriculum of schoolchildren, these symbolic details seem to belong to three genera: *comportment* (what students do), *commentary* (what they say), and *products* (what they make). In reading modern literary nonfiction, it is apparent that New Journalists have used these three kinds of evidence of "status lives" to portray lifestyles. How might the critic of the experienced curriculum also use each?

Commentary. First, how have the New Journalists used in their writing what people say as a means for provoking a deeper understanding of their lives and for revealing their character? And what might educational critics learn from them? These writers have, we mentioned, borrowed certain literary devices from novelists and shaped them to meet their own needs. One of these techniques involves the inclusion of swatches of dialogue actually uttered by the characters in the scene.

For New Journalists, the recording of dialogue in full required a quantum leap from the traditional "straight" news story in which the most supposedly important quotations appeared out of context, near the "top" (Hollowell, 1977). When dialogue is fully developed, however, and when it is situated within a developing story line or plot, parenthesized by and/or interspersed within descriptions of the locale, the ambiance of the setting, the accompanying activities of the characters, and so on, then it can penetrate to the very core of the personalities being heard from. It can transport the reader into intimate encounters with these other people as we see how they handle themselves verbally in particular social situations. And there are at least two facets of someone's commentary that can teach us things about the individual: the content of what is said, and the style and form of the delivery.

What is said? How it's said?

I got off the plane around midnight and no one spoke as I crossed the dark runway to the terminal. The air was thick and hot, like wandering into a steam bath. Inside, people hugged each other and shook hands . . . big grins and a whoop here and there: "By God! You old bastard! Good to see you, boy! Damn good . . . and I mean it!"

In the air-conditioned lounge I met a man from Houston who said his name was something or other—"but just call me Jimbo"—and he was here to get it on. "I'm ready for anything, by God! Anything at all. Yeah, what are you drinkin'?" I ordered a Margarita with ice, but he wouldn't hear of it: "Naw, naw . . . what the hell kind of drink is that for Kentucky Derby time? What's wrong with you, boy?" He grinned and winked at the bartender. "Goddam, we gotta educate this boy. Get him some good whiskey . . ."

I shrugged. "Okay, a double Old Fitz on ice." Jimbo nodded his approval.

"Look." He tapped me on the arm to make sure I was listening. "I know this Derby crowd, I come here every year, and let me tell you one thing I've learned—this is no town to be giving people the impression you're some kind of faggot. Not in public, anyway. Shit, they'll roll you in a minute, knock you in the head and take every goddam cent you have."

I thanked him and fitted a Marlboro into my cigaret holder.

"Say," he said, "you look like you might be in the horse business . . . am I right?"

"No," I said. "I'm a photographer."

"Oh yeah?" He eyed my ragged leather bag with new interest. "Is that what you got there—cameras? Who you work for?"

"Playboy," I said.

He laughed. "Well goddam! What are you gonna take pictures of—nekkid horses? Haw! I guess you'll be workin' pretty hard when they run the Kentucky Oaks. That's a race just for fillies." He laughed wildly. "Hell yes! And they'll all be nekkid too!"

I shook my head and said nothing; just stared at him for a moment, trying to look grim. "There's going to be trouble," I said. "My assignment is to take pictures of a riot."

"What riot?"

I hesitated, twirling the ice in my drink. "At the track. On Derby Day. The Black Panthers." I stared at him again. "Don't you read the newspapers?"

The grin on his face had collapsed. "What the hell are you talkin' about?"

"Well . . . maybe I shouldn't be telling you . . ." I shrugged. "But hell, everybody else seems to know. The cops and the National Guard have been getting ready for six weeks. They have 20,000 troops on alert at Fort Knox. They've warned us—all the press and photographers—to wear helmets and special vests like flakjackets. We were told to expect shooting. . . ."

"No!" he shouted: his hands flew up and hovered momentarily between us, as if to ward off the words he was hearing. Then he whacked his fist on the bar.

"Those sons of bitches! God Almighty! The Kentucky Derby!" He kept shaking his head. "No! Jesus! That's almost too bad to believe!" Now he seemed to be jagging on the stool, and when he looked up his eyes were misty. "Why? Why here? Don't they respect anything?"

The excerpt is from the beginning of Hunter S. Thompson's article, "The Kentucky Derby Is Decadent and Depraved" (1973, pp. 172–173), and it serves as an example of the effective use of dialogue as a device for disclosing personality. Thompson never directly describes Jimbo's physical appearance, lifestyle, or state of mind. Instead he merely allows Jimbo to barge into the reader's mind through his talk, and Jimbo encourages us to surmise certain things about himself. We learn, among other things, that he is crudely jocular, earnestly and self-consciously macho, brash, boisterous, and grandly gregarious, with a back-slapping friendliness that resembles a packet of Cup-a-Soup—add only water: the nearest living soul. Jimbo (don't you think?) is a high-liver, with much more than a toehold in the establishment (perhaps a Houston oilman?), as well as an obviously deep aversion toward those less entrenched in the system than he.

Reporting what Jimbo said is important for telling us indirectly about his lifestyle and attitudes, but we also learn about him by noting what he does not say. Of particular interest is his reaction to the possibility of rioting and shooting at the Kentucky Derby: he appears less concerned with the degree of potential violence than with the hallowedness of the protest site. His response is not "Why the need for violence?", but rather, "Why here?" Hasn't the enemy been contained within the campuses and the ghettos? But "God Almighty! The Kentucky Derby!"

And Jimbo's style of delivery is almost as important as what he is saying. Thompson conveys the inflections of Jimbo's speech through the basic device of punctuation marks—dashes, dots, exclamation points, and so on, as well as a liberal dose of italics. The tempo of the conversation also shines through. And the spelling of "nekkid" in Jimbo's dialect is a very informative touch.

It is not always necessary to include chunks of dialogue to reveal a character, of course; brief but crucial utterances can also be quite revealing. Short quotes can be used as typical examples of the verbal exchanges that occurred during the course of classroom activities; others can help to unveil the unique personalities of primary characters. For example, during the course of my stay as a researcher in a second-grade classroom, one typically disgruntled little girl told me her feelings about her pony: "I wish I could bring him to school. If I could I'd let all my friends ride with me, and I'd trample over (the teacher) and everyone else."

The inquirer should be constantly on the lookout for such commentary—whether in long bursts or in snippets—that expresses or indicates the beliefs, attitudes, feelings, and values of the subjects being studied. For as Tom Wolfe (1973) has stated, "Realistic dialogue involves the reader more completely than any other single device. It also establishes and defines character more quickly and effectively than any other single device" (p. 30).

Another device used by a few New Journalists is the technique Hollowell (1977) calls *interior monologue*. It involves reporting what a subject has said (in an interview) that he thought he thought in a particular situation. Quotation marks are eliminated, and the reader learns of the subject's apparent feelings and thoughts without a disruption of the flow of the piece. For example, John Sack (1973) in "M" reported the thoughts and feelings of some American soldiers in combat to heighten the dramatic impact of the action itself:

> this first operation of M's had come to its melancholy close, and M's tired battalion was to kill, wound, or capture no other Vietnamese, communist or otherwise, estimated or actual, in the day-and-a-half remaining. Some of M [Company] was truly ashamed about the seven-year-old. Sullivan was annoyed with her, *dammit*, he thought, *she should have known we didn't want to hurt her. Why was she hiding out?* Much of M agreed with him, *ignorant people*, they thought. A lieutenant of the cavalry had no misgivings, thinking, *these people don't want us here anyhow, why should I care about them?*, a thought he bitterly volunteered in conversation. (p. 300)

This technique relies on the introspection of the subjects, of course, and on their willingness to reveal personal thoughts and feelings to the inquirer. Such a device, even when used, as in "M," to reveal such a morally malformed set of conscious rationalizations, can be a powerful means for projecting the reader into the perspective of the character, for promoting empathy with, and understanding of (though not necessarily condoning), the character's attitudes and outlook.

Products. Another genus of indicators of what characters are like involves what they produce. Student "makings" range from written seatwork and homework, to art objects, to science projects, even to desk contents and decorations. (The grumpy young lady quoted earlier plastered her desk with cut-outs and stickers of ponies.) This category of "symbolic details of people's status lives" might include possessions either self-made or chosen, such as styles of furniture and clothing. The idea is that what people make, what they choose to possess and emplant in their physical surroundings—that these things (taken in conjunction with comportment and commentary) can reveal character, and that this character can, in turn, be revealed to an audience through vivid description of these products and possessions.

For models of criticism of this sort of artifact, especially in terms of what they say about the educational life of the makers, the reader might look perhaps to critics of the plastic arts. New Journalists have not specialized in this area, being more directly involved with personalities, settings, and events. If, however, we are interested in writing about how people express themselves through their grooming, clothing, and other material adornments and possessions, then New Journalism is rife with appropriate examples.

There is in my judgment, however, one Grand Master among the New Journalists whose speciality is transforming perfect strangers in their jewelry, makeup, and platform shoes, into people you have always known. For example, if you weren't introduced to the following folks at Leonard Bernstein's fabulous bash in the 1960s, you're meeting them now, thanks to Wolfe's *Radical Chic and Mau-Mauing the Flak Catchers* (1969):

[Cheray Duchin] is not alone in her thrill as the Black Panthers come trucking on in, into Lenny's house, Robert Bay, Don Cox the Panther's Field Marshal from Oakland, Henry Miller the Harlem Panther defense captain, the Panther women—Christ, if the Panthers don't know how to get it all together, as they say, the tight pants, the tight black turtlenecks, the leather coats, Cuban shades, Afros. But real Afros, not the ones that have been shaped and trimmed like a topiary hedge and sprayed until they have a sheen like acrylic wall-to-wall—but funky, natural, scraggly . . . wild . . .

These are no civil-rights Negroes wearing gray suits three sizes too big—no more interminable Urban League banquets in hotel ballrooms where they try to alternate the blacks and whites around the tables as if they were stringing Arapaho beads.

—*these are* real men!

Shoot-outs, revolutions, pictures in *Life* magazine of policemen grabbing Black Panthers like they were Vietcong—somehow it all runs together in the head with the whole thing of how beautiful they are. Sharp as a blade. The Panther women—there are three or four of them on hand, wives of the Panther 21 defendants, and they are so lean, *so lithe*, as they say, with tight pants and Yoruba-style headdresses, almost like turbans, as if they'd stepped out of the pages of *Vogue*, although no doubt *Vogue* got it from them. All at once every woman in the room knows exactly what Amanda Burden meant when she said she was now anti-fashion because "the sophistication of the baby blacks made me rethink my attitudes." God knows the Panther women don't spend thirty minutes in front of the mirror every morning shoring up their eye holes with contact lenses, eyeliner, eye shadow, eyebrow pencil, occipital rim brush, false eyelashes, mascara, Shadow-Ban for under-eye and Eterna Creme for the corners . . . . And here they are,

right in front of you, trucking on into the Bernsteins' Chinese yellow duplex, amid the sconces, silver bowls full of white and lavender anemones, and uniformed servants serving drinks and roquefort cheese morsels rolled in crushed nuts—
   But it's all right. They're white servants . . . (pp. 8–9)

Wolfe's style of writing is worthy of emulation, of course, but it is unique. Krypto-Wolfes are clearly recognizable as having no style of their own. Better that he, and other huge talents like him, serve as inspirations for others to also develop their own styles. Still, his work does clearly demonstrate (among other things) the possibility of sketching real characters through the conscious statements made via their physical appearances and adornments.

Comportment. We learn much about people from how they act in specific situations. Many New Journalists, by vividly describing the behavior of their characters, have created apertures into their thought processes through which the reader is allowed to peek.

Norman Mailer is particularly adept at revealing character through descriptions of a person's style of action. In a memorable passage from *Miami and the Siege of Chicago* (1968b), Mailer finds in Richard Nixon's artificial style of gesturing an underlying mentality, an attitude toward others, and he even speculates on its source:

The crowd had been enthusiastic without real hurly-burly or hint of pandemonium. More in a state of respectful enthusiasm, and the hot patriotic cupidity to get near the man who is probably going to be the next American President. The office, not the man, is moving them. And Nixon passes through them with the odd stick-like motions which are so much a characteristic of his presence. He is like an actor with good voice and hordes of potential, but the despair of his dramatic coach (again it is High School). "Dick, you just got to learn how to move." There is something almost touching in the way he does it, as if sensitive flesh winces at the way he must expose his lack of heart for being warm and really winning in crowds, and yet he is all heart to perform his task, as if the total unstinting exercise of the will must finally deliver every last grace, yes, he is like a missionary handing out Bibles among the Urdu. Christ, they are filthy fellows, but deserving of the *touch*. No, it is not so much that he is a bad actor (for Nixon in a street crowd is radiant with emotion to reach across the prison pen of his own artificial moves and deadly reputation and show that he is sincere) it is rather that he grew up in the worst schools for actors in the world—white gloves and church usher, debating team, Young Republicanism. Captive of Ike's forensic style—as an actor, Nixon thinks his work is to signify. So if he wants to show someone that he likes them, he must smile; if he wishes to show disapproval of Communism, he frowns; America must be strong, out goes his chest. (pp. 40–41)

The analysis is most perceptive and informative. In order to write it, Mailer had to observe Richard Nixon carefully over a period of time, to project himself into Nixon's world-view, to locate the wellspring of his motives (some of which Nixon himself may have been aware). This understanding provides the foundation for Mailer's appraisal of Nixon's actions. This kind of analysis could be the gift of critics of the experienced curriculum to their readers as they characterize the lives of children in classrooms.

Landscape

The third aspect is the *educational landscape*. Landscape is not merely the sum of the features that comprise the social and physical environment, but rather a fictive—i.e., fashioned—picture of the human and material surroundings that help shape and (since experiences contain an active as well as passive element) are shaped by the educational lives of the children.

Thus, the dictionary definition of a landscape: "a portion of natural scenery, usually extensive, that may be seen from some special viewpoint." As Nisbet (1976) has noted, the last three words are crucial; each landscape is seen from a particular perspective. In portraying an educational landscape, information is presented about those aspects of the cultural terrain deemed by the writer to be educationally important and thematically relevant. And this information is given a form that contributes to the "esthetic unity" of the piece. What should emerge, then, is a very personal picture of the classroom milieu.

This kind of picture requires, rather than a detached, flavorless description of the environment, instead, a "thick" description that captures the mood of a place and its people and that provides a backdrop for the unfolding events. It involves a careful detailing of the intrusion of place into the lives of people and vice-versa. The character of a setting reflects the character of the people who live in it, who help shape the character of the setting. In my judgment, few New Journalists are as talented in their approach to disclosing the intricate collusion between landscape and the lifestyle of people as is Joan Didion (1969):

> This is a story about love and death in the golden land, and begins with the country. The San Bernardino Valley lies only an hour east of Los Angeles by the San Bernardino Freeway but is in certain ways an alien place: not the coastal California of the subtropical twilights and the soft westerlies off the Pacific, but a harsher California, haunted by the Mojave just beyond the mountains, devastated by the hot dry Santa Ana wind that comes down through the passes at 100 miles an hour and whines through the eucalyptus windbreaks and works on the nerves. October is the bad month for the wind, the month when breathing is difficult and hills blaze up spontaneously. There has been no rain since April. Every voice

seems a scream. It is the season of suicide and divorce and prickly dread, wherever the wind blows.

The Mormons settled this ominous country, and then they abandoned it, but by the time they left, the first orange tree had been planted and for the next hundred years the San Bernardino Valley would draw a kind of people who imagined they might live among the talismanic fruit and prosper in the dry air, people who brought with them Midwestern ways of building and cooking and praying and who tried to graft those ways upon the land. The graft took in curious ways. This is the California where it is possible to live and die without ever eating an artichoke, without ever meeting a Catholic or a Jew. This is the California where· it is easy to Dial-a-Devotion, but hard to buy a book. This is the country in which a belief in the literal interpretation of Genesis has slipped imperceptibly into a belief in the literal interpretation of Double Indemnity, the country of the teased hair and the Capris and the girls for whom all life's promise comes down to a waltzlength white wedding dress and the birth of a Kimberly or a Sherry or a Debbi and a Tijuana divorce and a return to hairdressers' school. "We were just crazy kids," they say without regret, and look to the future. The future always looks good in the golden land, because no one remembers the past. Here is where the hot wind blows and the old ways do not seem relevant, where the divorce rate is double the national average and where one person in every thirty-eight lives in a trailer. Here is the last stop for all those who come from somewhere else, for all those who drifted away from the cold and the past and the old ways. Here is where they are trying to find a new lifestyle, trying to find it in the only places they know to look: the movies and the newspapers. The case of Lucille Marie Maxwell Miller is a tabloid monument to that new life style. (p. 304).

An educational critic who could gain as much insight into the character of a classroom as Didion has of this region of the country, and who could render it with such forcefulness and clarity, would, I believe, be performing a fine service to education. Note that Didion is not interested in finding a positive relationship between, say, the prevalence of a hot, dry wind and the incidence of suicide, or wind and divorce, or wind and "prickly dread" (however that might be operationally defined!). Experience is an interactive process; the needs of people and the press of their environment act upon and shape each other. So, far more than merely isolating environmental variables for the purpose of linking causes within an active, stimulus-filled environment with their effects on passive people, Didion, Mailer, and other such writers are probing into the character of the complex and dynamic interface between personalities and a particular setting, whether that setting be a region of the country, city, or schoolroom.

There is, furthermore, within this kind of work, an intimate connection between educational landscape and theme. The depiction of the landscape must both feed and be fed by the theme. For example, if alienation in the classroom is the thematic concern, then the atmosphere of isolation as perceived and felt in the physical surroundings—as it is reflected in the feeling of aloneness in the activities—can be described. Even educational theory and history can be used in portraying the educational landscape.

Finally, one of the prime outcomes of this kind of writing about classroom experiences may be a set of terms that will characterize various sorts of educational landscapes. Nisbet (1976) has written about the concepts that sociologists-as-artists contributed to that field in the nineteenth century:

> Not quantitative, empirical science following any of the contrived prescriptions of current textbooks in methodology or theory construction, but the artist's vision, lies behind such concepts as mass society, *Gemeinschaft*, *Gesellschaft*, social studies, authority, the sacred and the secular, alienation, anomie, and other signal reactions to the European social landscape in the nineteenth century that we properly associate with the development of sociology. (p. 43).

The New Journalism has also provided us with conceptual handles for grasping the world we live in. Tom Wolfe's label for the 1970s—the "Me Decade"—accurately characterizes a large portion of the present social landscape. Likewise, one of the goals of the New Journalism can be to help increase the articulateness of educators in their talk about learning environments by inventing terminology for environmental features not yet focused upon. But before this can come to pass, educational inquirers must pay more attention to educational landscapes.

Plot

The next facet is the *plot*, or the sequence of events of which a piece is composed. A theme allows for a rigorous selection of insights that advance the central intention of the portrait. But writers must arrange as well as select; they must place their observations in an order that contributes to artistic unity. There should be a sense of progression in the arrangement of descriptions and interpretations of characters, landscape, and theme.

The order need not be entirely chronological, of course, but inasmuch as events observed do occur over time, a predominantly chronological approach is one possibility for the sequencing of information. Wolfe (1973) has noted that avoidance of "sheer historical narrative" in favor of "scene-by-scene construction" of events is a basic device which, having been borrowed by the New Journalists from realistic novelists such as Dickens and Gogol, distinguishes the New Journalism from traditional journalism

(p. 31). Scene-by-scene construction consists of "telling the story by moving from scene to scene," usually in a fully chronological order. The reader is thereby given the feeling of actually living through events such as those in many of the works of Mailer, Capote, Wolfe, Thompson, and others.

Often only a semi-chronological framework is used: While events proceed in order of their occurrence, there are diversions, ramblings, or flashbacks that allow for the demonstration of important connections, or the addition of interpretations and assessments of the significance of events. *Miami and the Siege of Chicago* is such a semi-chronology. Mailer plots the political conventions of 1968 as they unfolded, using a loosely chronological superstructure. In the course of describing and analyzing events, situations, and personalities, he shifts backward and forward in time, relating present occurrences to others in the past, and generalizing freely. He pauses to sketch the lives of characters ("But let us leave the convention with a look at Reagan," p. 70), to place events in the context of current American history, and even to sociologize ("There have been few studies on the psychological differences between police and criminals and the reason is not difficult to discover," p. 174).

Similar approaches are used by Tom Wolfe in many of his works, by Capote in his *In Cold Blood* (1963), in Hunter Thompson's *Fear and Loathing* books (1973a, 1973b), and in works by Mailer. And even more vaguely chronological plots are used: In *Of a Fire on the Moon* (1970), Mailer rambles more freely and broadly, including, for example, a whole chapter on "The Psychology of Machines," before returning to the Apollo moonshot, the event-at-hand.

There is a difficult question about how to gracefully and effectively place interpretations and theoretical analysis within the sequence of lived-in events without damaging the mood of the piece. The New Journalism provides little help here, for unlike what is envisioned for criticism of the experienced curriculum, it contains very little explicit analysis or global theorizing. It is usually preoccupied with the particular and seldom escapes through generalization from what has been called the tyranny of the single case.

When the particular is transcended, it most often happens in a long piece, especially a book, where the problem of smooth shifting is less acute: chapters or chapter sections provide natural boundaries between holistic description and analytical interpretation. Shorter pieces from the New Journalism seldom transcend the scene-at-hand.

Educational critics of student experiences are free to experiment, therefore. They may segregate, placing the evocative, literary-style description in the first half of a piece and the more discursive interpretation and analysis in part two. An example of this approach is found in Gail Sheehy's *Hustling* (1974). Chapter 1 is devoted to a sociological overview of the issue of prostitution; the next eight chapters are character studies of typical prostitutes of various kinds and of other characters, such as pimps and madams, associated with prostitution. Sheehy supplies us with a somewhat more integrated model in *Passages: Predictable Crises of Adult Life* (1977). Theories about the developmental stages of adulthood provide the framework for the plot. The passage to each succeeding stage is illustrated by a close-focus study of an individual moving into that life phase. The book is an interesting blend of sociological theory and vivid portraits of individual personalities, and as such is of keen interest to us.

Another device used by the New Journalists to move gracefully across the chasm between two drastically different forms of writing is the journal format. "Natural" boundaries, analogous to chapter breaks or section divisions in lengthier works, are thereby made available for shifting between metaphorical, suggestive, literary descriptions and the more linear, theoretical analysis.[9] Of course, educational critics need not necessarily structure their writings in this way; a journal format is simply one of many already available and of many others yet to be conceived. Writers may, indeed, prefer a totally nonchronological approach for plotting purpose. In sequencing their insights, as in other aspects of this writing about classroom experiences, authors can be daringly experimental and inventive while attempting to match subject matter with appropriate and powerful means of conveyance.

Closure

In this article, I have approached the question of how educational inquirers can discover and effectively convey what happens in schools. I suggested that inquirers might focus on the actual experiences of students in classrooms. In order to convey the essence of these experiences and to spell out their significance for the educational lives of students, I maintained that a certain kind of literary nonfiction should be helpful. The New Journalism was pointed to as a body of work already on hand that could be profitably mined for examples of useful writing styles, devices, techniques, and formats.

As a further point, I am not contending that any one style is the best style for verbally portraying the experienced curriculum. Existing examples of New Journalism should not be taken as precise models for approaching curriculum criticism. Certainly many styles should be experimented with in order to ascertain their power for imparting insights into these qualitative phenomena.

Perhaps the greatest benefit to be derived from examining such writings in the context of curriculum inquiry is in their inspirational value. The experiences of schoolchildren are quite complex, with manifold layers of meaning. We can take heart in seeing how other inquirers have successfully probed into the delicate tissues of human experiences, and provided us with remarkably insightful and sensitive critiques of public events and institutions. We in the curriculum field should be encouraged to do likewise.

Notes

1. See, for example, Hamilton et al. (1977) and Willis (1978).

2. See Kelly (1975), Eisner (1979), Willis (1975), Vallance (1975), and McCutcheon (1976).

3. I am not the first to consider the New Journalism in the context of curriculum evaluation. At the Cambridge Conference on Case Study in Educational Research and Evaluation (1975), Rob Walker discussed the New Journalism in these terms. See also a SAFARI (Success and Failure and Recent Innovation) report by Rob Walker cited in Barry MacDonald's "Portrayal of Persons as Evaluation Data," SAFARI papers (in press).

4. The danger always exists, of course, that one might learn more about an author from such a "subjective" reconstruction than about the phenomena it intends to portray. Poorly documented interpretations, distortion of events to fit a certain writing style or belief system, and rash general statements that attempt to stand without any buttressing by real-world referents—all tend to focus our attention more on the mentality of the author than on the empirical phenomena of the classroom supposedly being revealed. To be sure, it can be interesting and helpful for an author to forthrightly divulge relevant aspects of his or her value system. This practice would stand, I believe, in refreshing contrast to many traditional inquirers who vainly attempt to purify themselves of any taint of bias by using "objective" observational devices such as checklists and the like. But portraits of the experienced curriculum must be written primarily for the purpose of illuminating audiences about educational matters, and only indirectly about the human instrument who has fashioned the information about those matters into a comprehensible form. The best New Journalists, for this reason, include meticulous detail in their descriptions and interpretations. In the laying out of these details, the reader is in fact drawn into greater "truth." As Dan Wakefield (1966) argued, referring to Capote and Wolfe's style of New Journalism, "Such reporting is 'imaginative' not because the author has distorted the facts, but because he has presented them in a full instead of a naked manner, brought out the sights, sounds, and feel surrounding these facts, and connected them by comparison with other facts of history, society, and literature in an artistic manner that does not diminish but gives greater depth and dimension to the facts" (p. 67). This "subjectivity" issue is complex and important and concerns nearly all forms of qualitative educational inquiry. The reader is further referred to Eisner's (1979) discussion of referential adequacy and structural corroboration in educational criticism.

5. An exception, in some ways, is Jonathan Kozol's *Death at an Early Age* (1967). I have also written two New Journalism pieces that portray portions of the experienced curriculums in first- and second-grade classrooms; see Barone (1978, 1979).

6.   This "reciprocity of perspectives" requires both empathy and evaluation. The inquirer must acquire the perspective—to a degree—of the student by "reading" the manifestations of experiences found in what the student does, says, and makes. The inquirer may thereby develop (to a greater or lesser extent) an empathic understanding of the student's experiences, understanding them as the student understands them. The inquirer must also interpret these clues according to his or her own personal theory, against the backdrop of previous encounters with similar phenomena, and even in terms of theoretical notions borrowed from various fields in the social sciences. In so doing, the inquirer attempts to evaluate the significance of the experiences for the child.

7.   The other three are the youth subculture; "big events" such as conventions, anti-war protests, criminal cases; and general social and political reportage.

8.   Note that the aim is characterization, not caricature. Reducing a complex personality to traits representative of a particular class or group, is indeed a form of reductionism. Reductionism in this kind of qualitative approach is especially dangerous, for there is the suggestion of a representation of complex, empirical reality. The readers may be drawn into such a facile characterization, their critical faculties blunted by a highly detailed appearance of reality. It is the responsibility of the author to avoid such reductionism. My thanks to Nel Noddings for this point.

9.   For an example of the use of this journal format, see Rogers's (1977) fascinating diary of the events surrounding a total eclipse of the sun in Mauritania.

References

Barone, T. (1978). *Inquiry into classroom experiences: A qualitative, holistic approach.* Doctoral dissertation, Stanford University, 1978.

Barone, T. (1979)."Of Scott and Lisa and other friends." In Elliot W. Eisner (Ed.), *The educational imagination: On the design and evaluation of school programs* (pp. 240–245). New York: Macmillan.

Capote, T. (1963). *In cold blood: A true account of a multiple murder and its consequences.* New York: Random House.

Cronbach, L. (1963). Course improvement through evaluation. *Teachers College Record, 64* (8), 672–683.

Dewey, J. (1958). *Art as experience.* New York: Capricorn Books.

Dewey, J. (1963). *Experience and education.* New York: Collier Books.

Didion, J. (1969). *Slouching towards Bethlehem.* New York: Delta Books.

Eisner, E. (Ed.) (1979). *The educational imagination: On the design and evaluation of school programs.* New York: Macmillan.

Geertz, C. (1974). *The interpretation of cultures.* New York: Basic Books.

Greene, M. (1977). Toward wide-awakeness: An argument for the arts and humanities in education. *Teachers College Record, 79* (1), 119–125.

Haley, A. (1976). *Roots.* Garden City, N.Y.: Doubleday.

Hamilton, D., Macdonald, B., King, C., Jenkins, D., and Parlett, M. (Eds.) (1977). *Beyond the numbers game.* London: Macmillan.

Hardwick, E. *Sleepless nights.* New York: Random House, 1979.

Herr, M. (1969). "Khesahn." *Esquire, 72* (3), 118–123.

Hollowell, J. (1977). *Fact and fiction: New Journalism and the nonfiction novel.* Chapel Hill: University of North Carolina Press.

Johnson, M. L.(1971). *The New journalism: The underground press, the artists of nonfiction, and changes in the established media.* Lawrence: University of Kansas Press.

Kaufman, B. (1965). *Up the down staircase*. Englewood Cliffs, N.J.: Prentice-Hall.

Kelly, E. F. (1975). Curriculum evaluation and literary criticism: Comments on the analogy. *Curriculum Theory Network, 5* (2), 87–106.

Kozol, J. (1976). *Death at an early age*. New York: Houghton-Mifflin.

Kuhn, T. (1970). *The structure of scientific revolutions* (2nd ed.). International Encyclopedia of Unified Science 2, (2). Chicago: University of Chicago Press.

Langer, S. (1957). *Problems of art*. New York: Charles Scribner's Sons.

McCutcheon, G. (1976). *The disclosure of classroom life*. Doctoral dissertation, Stanford University.

Mailer, N. (1968a). *Armies of the night: History as a novel, the novel as history*. New York: New American Library.

Mailer, N. (1968b). *Miami and the siege of Chicago*. New York: New American Library.

Mailer, N. (1970). *Of a fire on the moon*. Boston: Little, Brown.

Nisbet, R. (1976). *Sociology as an art form*. New York: Oxford University Press.

Perrine, L. (1959). *Story and structure*. New York: Harcourt, Brace and World.

Rico, G. (1976). *Metaphor and knowing: Analysis, synthesis, rationale*. Doctoral dissertation, Stanford University.

Rogers, M. (1977). "Totality: A report." In Paul Scanlon (Ed.), *Reporting: The Rolling Stone style* (pp. 170–189). Garden City, NY: Anchor Press.

Sack, J. (1973). M. In Tom Wolfe (Ed.) *The New Journalism* (pp. 292–303). New York: Harper and Row.

Schutz, A. (1962). *The collected papers, volume I* (B. Natanson, Ed.). The Hague: M. Nijhoff.

Sheehy, G. (1974). *Hustling: Prostitution in our wide-open society*. New York: Dell. Sheehy, G. (1977). *Passages: Predictable crises of adult life*. New York: Bantam Books.

Shulman, L. (1970). Reconstruction of educational research. *Review of Educational Research, 40* (3), 371–396.

Stake, R. (1967). The countenance of educational evaluation. *Teachers College Record,* 68 (7), 523–540.

Talese, G. (1970). *Fame and obscurity: Portraits by Gay Talese.* New York: World Publishing.

Thompson, H. (1973a). *Fear and loathing in Las Vegas.* New York: Popular Library.

Thompson, H. (1973b). *Fear and loathing on the campaign trail.* San Francisco: Straight Arrow Books.

Thompson, H. (1973c).The Kentucky Derby is decadent and depraved. In Tom Wolfe (Ed.) *The New Journalism* (pp. 172–187). New York: Harper and Row.

Vallance, E. (1975). *Aesthetic criticism and curriculum description.* Doctoral dissertation, Stanford University.

Vallance, E. (1977). The landscape of "The Great Plains Experience": An application of curriculum criticism. *Curriculum Inquiry, 7* (2), 205–228.

Wakefield, D. (1966, June). The personal voice and the impersonal eye. *Atlantic,* 86–90.

Willis, G. (1975). Curriculum criticism and literary criticism. *Journal of Curriculum Studies,* 7 (1), 3–17.

Willis, G. (Ed.) (1978). *Qualitative evaluation: Concepts and cases in curriculum criticism.* Berkeley, Calif.: McCutchan.

Wolfe, T. (1969). *Radical chic and mau-mauing the flak catchers.* New York: Bantam Books.

Wolfe, T. (1973). *The New Journalism.* New York: Harper and Row.

Wolfe, T. (1976, August). The "me decade" and the third great awakening. *New West Magazine,* 30.

Chapter 3

Insinuated Theory
from Curricula-in-Use
(1982)

In this essay, I would like to propose a kind of curriculum theory, and to give one specific example. The sort of theory I have in mind is not generated through application of the social science model for curriculum building. I do not share the enthusiasm of the conceptual empiricists for the idea that science is the sole source of curriculum knowledge.

Nor will the curriculum theory to be defined here resemble the brand of curriculum theory usually served up by those writers known as *reconceptualists* (although it may, in a way, serve to complement their work). Indeed, a case might be made that writers like William Pinar and Dwayne Huebner often function more as curriculum philosophers than curriculum theorists. This is not, of course, meant to disparage their valuable contributions: it is important (in the words of James MacDonald, 1975, p. 6), to "develop and criticize conceptual schema in the hope that new ways of talking about curriculum, which may in the future be far more fruitful than present orientations, will be forthcoming."

But there are still those of us liberal enough to believe that curriculum theory can also serve a somewhat more traditional purpose: that is, to be more directly helpful to practitioners in planning and using actual curricula. Such theory may be generated in a variety of ways, but the approach suggested here will involve inquiry into individual programs and materials. One result of this approach can be theory that links features of those specific curricula with the lives of the people who use it. It is theory that arises from criticism of curricula-in-use.

Criticism of individual curricula, as an inquiry approach, is a rather recent phenomenon, and so the number of published critiques is small. The few existing examples of materials criticism (as those by Vallance,

1977, and Munby, 1979) have examined curriculum documents apart from an educational setting—critiqued them much as an art critic would critique a painting or a piece of sculpture—as completed works, static artifacts. More appropriate for our purposes here is an approach to criticism that looks at the process as plans and programs are implemented, that investigates facets of the curriculum as integral parts of a usually complex educational landscape, and that attempts to ferret out the educational meaning in the transactions between curriculum and users.

More specifically, the kind of criticism of curricula-in-use I envision contains three characteristics that can lead to useful curriculum theory:

1. The criticism enables the reader to view (to some extent) curriculum transactions from the perspectives of the students.
2. The criticism provides an interpretation and assessment of those experiences from the viewpoint of the evaluator/critic.
3. The criticism divulges common or typical qualities in the interactions of students with facets of the curricula, as well as idiosyncratic patterns of interactions.

Published critiques of curricula-in-use that satisfy these three criteria are rare indeed. In fact, I suggest that the most enlightening example of this kind of criticism of a program-in-use produced so far—the most extensive, most masterfully composed, the most fascinating, and potentially instructive work—was accomplished by someone outside of the field of education. The program critiqued is the early NASA (National Aeronautics and Space Administration) Space Program. The work is a book of literary nonfiction written by Tom Wolfe entitled *The Right Stuff* (1979).

In previous writings I have pointed out the similarities between the genres of modern literary nonfiction and art criticism (Barone, 1980). This form of nonfiction as practiced by writers like Joan Didion, Norman Mailer, and Truman Capote clearly satisfies John Dewey's definition of the aim of all art criticism, i.e., the reeducation of the perception of an audience. The objects critiqued are usually public events and institutions and the lives of public figures. But *The Right Stuff* explores the interaction between a planned program of activities and the lives of those engaged in that program. It describes, interprets, and assesses in language often quite vivid and evocative, the meaning of the space program for the early Mercury astronauts. It is—no matter that the author has probably never heard of the term!—a piece of curriculum criticism.

It is, furthermore, a critique of curriculum-in-use which exhibits the three characteristics mentioned above, and one that serves up an excellent example of curriculum theory. I will, therefore, refer to it often for purposes of illustrating what a curriculum theory might look like and the process through which such theory can emerge.

Concerning the first characteristic: The kind of curriculum theory I envision will arise from the real qualities of students' experiences of, and their interactions with, the ongoing activities, and from the meanings that facets of the curriculum hold for them. It is important, therefore, that the criticism (to some degree) view the curriculum from the students' perspectives, and expose the meaning of the activities for their lives. For example, in *The Right Stuff*, Wolfe promotes understanding of some of the realities of the space program by transporting us into the world of the astronauts. We come to know the astronauts as people. Wolfe does not portray the astronauts as "Flying Saints" (as the press often presented them), but as full-blooded human beings, the "first American single combat warriors" (as he calls them) who confronted and altered both the tedious and the death-defying activities prescribed for them. And this is done through a style of prose so vivid as to evoke a strong sense of what it felt like to be an astronaut. His recreations of their experiences through language promotes, at points, an empathic identification with the astronauts. In the following passage, Wolfe describes some of the early training of the astronauts in the Navy, learning to land on the decks of aircraft carriers. Notice the point of view:

> To say that an F-4 was coming back onto this heaving barbecue from out of the sky at a speed of 135 knots . . . that might have been the truth in the training lecture, but it did not begin to get across the idea what a newcomer saw from the deck itself, because it created the notion that perhaps the plane was gliding in. On the deck one knew differently! As the aircraft came closer and the carrier heaved on into the waves and the plane's speed did not diminish and the deck did not grow steady—indeed, it pitched up and down five or ten feet per greasy heave— one experienced a neural alarm that no lecture could have prepared him for: This is not an airplane coming toward me, it is a brick with some poor sonofabitch riding it (someone much like myself!), and it is not gliding, it is falling, a fifty-thousand-pound brick, headed not for a stripe on the deck but for *me*—and with a horrible smash! it hits the skillet, and with a blur of momentum as big as a freight train's it hurtles toward the far end of the deck—another blinding storm— another roar as the pilot pushes the throttle up to full military power and another smear of rubber screams out over the skillet—and this is normal!—quite okay!— for a wire stretched across the deck has grabbed the hook on the end of the plane as it hit the deck tail down, and the smash was the rest of the fifteen-ton brute slamming onto the deck, as it tripped up, so that now it is straining against the wire at full throttle, in case it hadn't held and the plane had "boltered" off the end of the deck and had to struggle up into the air again. And already the Mickey Mouse helmets are running toward the fiery monster.

And the candidate, looking on, begins to feel that great heaving sunblazing deathboard of a deck wallowing in his own vestibular system—and suddenly he finds himself backed up against his own limits. He ends up going to the flight surgeon with so-called conversion symptoms. Overnight he develops blurred vision or numbness in his hands and feet or sinusitis so severe that he cannot tolerate changes in altitude. On one level the symptom is real. He really cannot see too well or use his fingers or stand the pain. But somewhere in his subconscious he knows it is a plea and a beg-off; he shows not the slightest concern (the flight surgeon notes) that the condition might be permanent and affect him in whatever life awaits him outside the arena of the right stuff. (pp. 26–28)

Of course no one can ever directly experience a situation or event as another person does, and so no writer (not even one as masterful as Wolfe) can recreate a scene precisely as viewed by another. But we human beings do have the capacity for some empathic understanding of others. And how do we achieve that understanding? We do it by attending to and interpreting the outward physical manifestations of inward thoughts and feelings—by looking and asking for clues about existential status. I believe that a dual strategy of observation and interviewing can provide the clues needed by a curriculum critic to create empathic understanding with students.

Engendering empathy is not the only task of the curriculum critic in search of curriculum theory. Again, let us look at what Tom Wolfe does for the readers of *The Right Stuff*. We do indeed get to know the astronauts very well. Yet even as we begin to experience the training and the launches and the touchdowns and the press conferences through the eyes of the astronauts, nevertheless we sense that it is Tom Wolfe who is editing and shaping and even commenting upon those experiences. There exists what Alfred Schutz calls a "reciprocity of perspectives" as we see through the eyes of the astronauts through the words of the author. But that is not all. For then the author helps us to make sense of what we have seen. A good example is his explication of precisely what is meant by "the right stuff":

As to just what this ineffable quality was . . . well, it obviously involved bravery. But it was not bravery in the simple sense of being willing to risk your life. The idea seemed to be that any fool could do that, if that was all that was required, just as any fool could throw his life away in the process. No, the idea here (in the all-enclosing fraternity) seemed to be that a man should have the ability to go up in a hurtling piece of machinery and put his hide on the line and then have the moxie, the reflexes, the experience, the coolness, to pull it back in the last yawning moment-and then to go up again the next day, and the next day, even if the series should prove infinite—and, ultimately, in its best expression, do so in a cause that means something to thousands, to a people, a nation, to humanity, to God. Nor was there a test to show whether or not a pilot had this righteous quality. There was, instead, a seemingly infinite series of tests. A career in flying was like climbing one of those ancient Babylonian pyramids made up of a dizzy progression of steps and ledges, a ziggurat, a pyramid extraordinarily high and steep; and the idea was to prove at every foot of the way up that pyramid that you were one of the elected and anointed ones who had the right stuff and could move higher and higher and even—ultimately, God willing, one day—that you might be able to join that special few at the very top, that elite who had the capacity to bring tears to men's eyes, the very Brotherhood of the Right Stuff itself. (p. 24)

Wolfe accomplishes here what all good curriculum critics should at least attempt. He serves as a perceptive outsider who is revealing things he has discovered about the inside actors. He is providing a fresh interpretation of the "rules of the game" which (he says) were only implicitly understood (or at least never verbalized) by the players themselves. He is rendering things coherent, making them more real. In doing this, he does not merely present his reactions to aspects of the program, nor does he simply hold up a mirror to the thoughts and feelings of the characters as they interact with or reflect upon the program. He does portray "student" experiences, but also, in an attempt to disclose their educational significance, he perceptively comments upon those experiences from another vantage point.

This interpretation of significance by the critic contributes one of the essential ingredients needed for good curriculum theory. Indeed, the kind of theory I am proposing is itself implied in the description of a set of students using the curriculum and in the critic's interpretations of the educational import of those experiences.

Is, then, the description and interpretation of that quality called "the right stuff" an example of a curriculum-in-use theory? No, "the right stuff" is of course a personality trait, not a curriculum theory. It is only when Wolfe characterizes the results of the rendezvous of that proclivity for intelligent valor with the prescribed activities that a curriculum theory is fully implied.

Here is what happened in the early space program: The astronauts, as former test pilots, resented the passive role of riding in, instead of flying, the capsules. Even a monkey could do (and had done) that! It did not require the right stuff. So using the clout derived from their national prestige and prominence, they were able to alter that role, and in the process, the program. First, nomenclature changed. The Mercury "capsule" became a "spacecraft." Then the program hardware changed. A window was placed in the spacecraft; and a hatch they could open themselves after splashing down. Why? "Because pilots had windows in their cockpits and hatches they could open on their own." Finally, they wanted manual control of the rocket. NASA was aghast, but control would be granted in several forms, including as "over-rides"—when the booster rocket engine was malfunctioning, the astronaut, like any pilot, could take over and guide it himself. If the NASA curriculum was to have an impact upon the lives of its learners, the learners would also influence the curriculum.

But let us return to one aspect of the description above of what constitutes this kind of curriculum theory: Is it necessary that the experiences of a *set* of students be involved? Could such theory not emerge from the observation by an inquirer of an individual child?

Certainly individual educational biographies are legitimate focal points for curriculum criticism. Pinar's (1975) quest, for example, through his autobiographic method, is to locate and publicize the important biographic moments lived by individuals. His approach, in its emphasis on the unique character of individuals, is reminiscent of the approach of several child specialists in the 1930s such as Jean Carew. Their approach was also holistic and qualitative and steeped in inferences about the meaning of experience. Their aim, like Pinar's, was to explore ideographically the totality of a person's existence, in order to understand actions in terms of previous experiences. Such studies of individual children, while perhaps useful for some educational purposes, do not offer much information about the patterns of interactions that pervade a classroom community of youngsters or a portion of one. They do not attempt to discover—and so have little to say about—the commonalities within the experiences of students as they interact with features of particular curricula. Commonalities do, of course, exist. Alfred Schutz (1962) is correct when he insists that although the individual defines the world from his own perspective, he is nevertheless a social being, rooted in an intersubjective reality. A shared reality based upon a common humanity and a common culture or subculture provides an overlap in the perspectives of individual students. Particular configurations of qualities in the experiences of individual children using a curriculum can often be located in the experiences of many other children in the same classroom and in other classrooms.

One strategy curriculum critics can employ is to focus carefully upon one or more children whose comportment reflects these general configurations—students whose patterns of interaction with the curriculum are in some ways typical. What I mean here by "typical" is close to what Wilhelm Dilthey, the famous nineteenth-century philosopher of the human studies, called the *ideal type*. For Dilthey, the *type* is a configuration of values or motives, and the attendant meanings, in a particular situation. The type, therefore, can exist only in context, and so it stands in contra-distinction to the nomothetic kind of generalization which expresses a general relation in nature. The typical, said Dilthey, is that which presents the general in a particular case (Tuttle, 1969, p. 86). The typical exhibits patterns in particular situations that are similar to—though never quite identical with—patterns in other times and places.

For example, in one classroom where I observed, elaborate avoidance strategies were evidenced by one fourth-grader whenever he was asked to engage in exercises from a certain workbook. These actions were typical of (but not identical with) the patterns of comportment of an entire set of students under similar conditions. A curriculum critic could suggest the general pattern of comportment of these students in the presence of their workbooks through a vivid portrait of the particular actions of one pro-tagonist. She might thus provide a more intimate sense of the experi-ences shared by the students, as well as alert readers to the possibility of students in other places interacting similarly with the workbooks.

In *The Right Stuff*, Tom Wolfe introduces us to several individual astronauts. They are not caricatures. Their complex personalities are fully developed. We see the impact that the space program had on each of their lives, as well as the influence their own personalities had on the space program. But we are led to perceive some commonalities as well, including the exhibition of that quality Wolfe called "the right stuff" as it interacted with the program script. As Wolfe focuses on specific instances of this trait interacting with the curriculum, the abstract personality trait is given "flesh-and-blood"; it is made tangible, made real. And vice versa: because he has revealed this typical pattern of interaction, we are able to appreciate more fully the individual lives of the astronauts and their ac-tions in relation to the activities planned for them. The typical and the specific are engaged in a dialectic, and as a result, our understanding of each is enhanced.

In such manner is curriculum-in-use theory born. By now, however, it should be obvious that this sort of theory exhibits characteristics quite unlike traditional social science theory. It is theory from within the critical and/or hermeneutical tradition of social inquiry, not the positivist. Be-cause of its careful attention to experienced phenomena, the kind of in-quiry that yields such theory is highly empirical, but at the same time, it is phenomenological in its regard for viewing the curriculum from the per-spectives of those for whom it was designed. Ours is theory of a transparent sort: we can see its inside as well as its outside. It aims to foster understanding as much as it attempts to explain.

Such theory does not rearrange the relationships between complex phenomena into a propositional form, but attempts to represent them in their full complexity and to discern recurring patterns of qualities in them. In interpretive studies, as Clifford Geertz notes (1974, p. 25), theory is less stated than it is insinuated. This is because "what generality it contrives to achieve grows out of the delicacy of its distinctions, not the sweep of its abstractions." Such theory is "close to the ground," nestled in elaborate webs of meaning spun in specific contexts. The author/critic may depict transactions between children and the curriculum that are typical across certain contexts, but it is left to the reader to judge whether any generalities can be safely transported to foreign situations.

The theory insinuated in the text of *The Right Stuff* has served us well as an example, but it differs in one respect from what I believe criticisms of curricula-in-use will usually be like. The primary goal of the space program was clear and agreed-upon: to place men on the moon without loss of life. If the training of the astronauts was a task more problematical than originally thought, it nevertheless remained tightly focused on one clearly perceived end. Wolfe's purpose in his book is to detail the impact of the program on the lives of the astronauts and vice versa, but not to make direct judgments about the values underlying the program's rationale. I respect his judgment—his purposes are, after all, his purposes. The book is still terrific. But in the world of education, larger questions are more difficult to ignore. How much simpler would life be (and how much less interesting) for curricularists if their greatest concerns really were technical ones? Discourse that makes judgments about values, attitudes, or behavioral norms taught intentionally or tacitly in individual programs, or that places transactions between curriculum and user in sociopolitical or historical context, is an important ingredient of some curriculum-in-use theory.

So, with some of the reconceptualists, I too deplore ahistoricality and atheoreticality in curriculum writing. But I also suggest that the power of our texts would be enhanced by grounding our meta-talk in specific examples and by speaking to practitioners instead of to just ourselves. I do not believe that such conversations must necessarily cloud a curriculum philosopher's visions of what curriculum could be. Indeed, whether there is to be a cultural revolution in education or just incremental improvements, will not practitioners need to be involved?

The kind of theory envisioned here is for thoughtful practitioners. It will hopefully aid in improving the design, selection, and implementation of programs and materials, and ultimately in providing more profound and liberating educational experiences for students.

Such theory does not predict—at least not in the strict sense of that term—but it can educate about possibilities. The text of *The Right Stuff*, for example, documents what did happen, and therefore suggests what can happen. Planners reading such critiques of educational programs should be more informed about the nature and value of the experiences being recommended to students in their own programs. Likewise, a teacher presented with a set of portraits of the transactions between materials being considered for adoption and students in other classroom settings would presumably be in a position to make a wiser decision.

There is, of course, always the danger that this approach will not yield portable theory at all, but only information so contextual in nature that it hinders rather than aids the judgments of practitioners concerning the appropriateness of the program or materials for their students. I don't think this will occur, at least not when the critiques are done well. But we need (I believe) to be as empirical in our attempts to ascertain the capacity of the theory generated from this approach to enlighten as the approach is itself in studying and portraying curricula-in-use. And so, a research agenda for interested parties: to insinuate such theory in portraits of curricula-in-use, to provide these critiques to practitioners, and to carefully watch what happens.

References

Barone, T. (1980). Effectively critiquing the experienced curriculum: Clues from the "new journalism." *Curriculum Inquiry, 10* (1), 29–53.

Geertz, C. (1974). *The interpretation of cultures.* New York: Basic Books.

Macdonald, J.B. (1975).Curriculum theory. In Pinar, W.F. (Ed.), *Curriculum theorizing: The reconceptualists* (pp. 2–11). Berkeley: McCutchan.

Munby, H. (1979). Philosophy for children: An example of curriculum review and criticism. *Curriculum Inquiry, 9* (3), 229–249.

Pinar, W.F. (1975). Currere: Toward reconceptualization. In Pinar, W.F. (Ed.), *Curriculum theorizing: The reconceptualists* (pp.396–414). Berkeley: McCutchan.

Schutz, Alfred. (1962). *The collected papers. Vol. 1.* Edited by B. Natanson. The Hague: M. Nijhoff.

Tuttle, H.N. (1969). *Wilhelm Dilthey's philosophy of historical understanding: A critical analysis.* Leiden, Netherlands: E.J. Bril.

Vallance, E. (1977). The landscape of "The Great Plains experience:" An application of curriculum criticism. *Curriculum Inquiry, 7* (2), 87–105.

Wolfe, T. (1979). *The Right Stuff.* New York: Farrar, Straus, Giroux.

Chapter 4

Ambiguity and the Curriculum: Lessons from the Literary Nonfiction of Norman Mailer (1991)

All great literature, I think, lures those who experience it away from the shores of literal truth and out into uncharted waters where meaning is more ambiguous. Some would-be readers are reluctant to board the boat. For on the solid ground are planted these confident, reassuring texts— from scientific treatises to journalistic reports—that offer apparently dependable, trustworthy, helpful accounts of how things really are. We call these texts factual, nonfictional, and the words they contain seem to correspond directly to actual phenomena, to real world objects that are guaranteed to be there when we reach for them.

So we may embark upon the reading of a literary text with some trepidation. What if, entranced by the formal beauty of the story, we lose sight of the shore? With all grounding gone, drifting aimlessly into a realm of fantasy where nothing is anchored down? Or maybe we will be swept down through a *gap* in the nonliteral text. This is the literary critic Wolfgang Iser's (1974) term for the deliberately positioned blanks in the narrative which the active reader must fill in with personal (and so indeterminate and ambiguous) meaning. I the reader must, Iser insists, imaginatively construct my own reality of what I read. But if, in squinting my eyes while trying to read between the lines of the text, my imagination fails me, won't I fall like Alice down into a nonsensical world where all is fluid belief and nothing is hard evidence?

Others among us may refuse to abandon the land because the open waters are simply no place to conduct daily commerce. Art, we believe, is for its own sake, while we need (to borrow a current phrase) "news we can use." So we may consent to leave port only at night. It is dark on shore then, reality having receded into a single shadow. With classes dismissed, why not venture, leisurely and harmlessly, out into the dreamy, romantic realm of the fictional text?

We work, therefore, on the land by day with what we think are the facts and tell playfully ambiguous stories as we drift on the dark waters of night. I confess that once, as a child of my culture, I felt reassurance in the tidiness of this conventional demarcation between fact and fiction. As a teacher I could not imagine learning anything substantial or useful from a text offering anything less than the literal truth. As a reader, I did not yet grasp how good literature really works; how it urges us to place the minutiae of daily life in an imaginary context, thereby estranging us from them; how it urges us out to a place just far enough offshore to turn and recognize these phenomena as features of what the aesthetician Susanne Langer (1957) calls a *virtual world*, how this imaginary world then stands against, and comments upon, the familiar qualities of life-at-hand, allowing us to see them in a new light.

Ultimately, I erased the boundary between the realm of the text which purports to give only the facts and that of the metaphor-laden story which dares to (as Sartre once put it) lie in order to tell the truth. But I did so haltingly, and not in a single confident stroke of understanding. Indeed, my insight came only gradually, after confronting a form of writing that aims to straddle the boundary between actual and virtual worlds, one foot firmly planted in each. These works are hybrids of textual species, essays/stories written in a literary style but shelved (curiously) in the nonfiction section of the library.

In 1963 Truman Capote claimed to have originated this new literary form. A *nonfiction novel* is what he called his chilling tale of two mass murderers, *In Cold Blood.* Capote later accused Norman Mailer of falsely claiming paternity of the genre. Mailer had subtitled his *Armies of the Night* (1968), an awarding-winning account of a protest march on the Pentagon, as follows: *History as a Novel, the Novel as History.* Works such as these, which reported on public events in a personal, literary style, soon came to be known as the *New Journalism*, and they proliferated in the 1970s. Tom Wolfe (1979, *The Right Stuff*, 1969, *Radical Chic and Mau-Mauing the Flak Catchers*), Joan Didion (1969, *Slouching Towards Bethlehem*), and Michael Herr (1968, *Dispatches*) were among the most talented at critiquing important social events in a powerful manner that was at once artful and realistic.

My awareness of the form first arose during that heated moment of history, the late 1960s. Then the frenzied flow of world events thrust upon journalism a new significance, while simultaneously causing consumers of the news to cast a suspicious eye upon traditional claims of objectivity. Weren't the media's claims to an unbiased presentation of raw information somewhat debased by their penchant for passing on, unchallenged, the establishment's version of the day's stories? The New Journalism would, instead, intentionally suit up in an unabashedly personal style, presenting the facts, as proponent Dan Wakefield (1966) suggested, "imaginatively . . . in a full instead of a naked manner . . . in an artistic manner that does not diminish but gives greater depth and dimension to the facts" (p. 87). A style, as it were, for land and sea.

And even though the New Journalists never got around to fully exploring my own professional bailiwick, the high school classroom, it was what they had to say, the substance of their commentary, as much as their stylistic vitality that wrought changes in my personal and professional consciousness. In hindsight, it seems that two of these texts in particular helped me to navigate out there in those uncharted waters. Both books were written by that master of literary nonfiction, Norman Mailer. The first may now be recommended reading for (am I really this old?) an American history class. The focus of *Miami and the Siege of Chicago* (1969) was on the events surrounding the Republican and Democratic presidential conventions of 1968.

Recently rereading this book, I was reminded that the potential of a literary text will remain just that when the reader is unprepared to unleash it within a reading experience. In my initial (youthful) reading, I was not prepared to hear ambiguity in Mailer's voice. With many of my fellow baby-boomers, my political self was just being born and Mailer (along with non-storytelling philosophers such as Nietzsche, Niebuhr, and Marx) was serving as a kind of intellectual midwife. The sources of my outrage were those of the time; civil wrongs and the stupid, immoral war. And soon my heroes were the dead ones, martyrs whose souls my fellow mourners and I were impelled to claim and share. In this most fertile soil the seeds of our frustrations had sprouted and yielded, as if overnight, the perfectly formed fruits of ideology, dogma, and moral certainty. We partook and were fortified for collective action, for righteous confrontation. It was the age of a new positivism, an outlook that offered the moral equivalent of the old scientific truth-mongering. We were a new breed of landlubbers, the kind that worked the soil for justice. How comfortable and secure were we in our knowledge that our actions were so ethically, well, grounded. Our complete contempt for the patently evil and ignorant establishment precluded the kind of doubts that arise upon cool, distanced contemplation out in a rowboat.

Certainly, as a novice high school social studies teacher my daytime mission seemed crystal-clear. My curriculum platform, that nexus of personally held beliefs about what is educationally good, true, and beautiful, was as rigid as it was narrow. With George Counts and other right-thinking educational progressivists known as *reconstructionists*, I would dare, through my teaching, to build a new social order. Under my tutelage, the Roman Catholic teenagers of middle- and upper-class conservative parents in New Orleans, Louisiana, would be transformed into first-generation, ideologically correct McGovernites.

In retrospect the depth of my naiveté was (as you've already noticed?) stunning. We believed, I and my liberal-to-socialist peers (suspected of having infiltrated classrooms from coast to coast), that we could, by sheer dint of will, levitate above, and thus avoid becoming stuck in, the viscous contingencies pervading the institutionalized environment of the school. The righteousness of our cause would enable us to reshape the hearts and minds of the next generation in accordance with our own precious utopian vision. And if I, for one, could do that, how comparatively easy to will an interpretation on a text! For how else, save for blindness from the Light, can I explain my failure to treat Mailer's book as a work of art rather than as propaganda? What else could account for my missing, for example, the reserve in the authorial voice as it described my heroes, the leaders of the nonviolent New Left in somewhat less than flattering terms? ("They were," Mailer wrote, "ideological in their focus—which is to say a man's personality was less significant than his ideas" [Mailer, 1969, p. 134].) And although my primary affections and allegiances always remained with the Kennedy most recently slain, Mailer's subtle characterization of Eugene McCarthy would have been, back then, disturbing if fully absorbed. McCarthy was, in Mailer's eyes, both supremely intelligent and a romantic "who dared the incalculable wrath aroused in Lyndon Johnson" by his challenge to the President. But McCarthy was also gravely flawed, an aloof man, a hard man, and bitter in adversity: "too bitter even to express his bitterness, it leaked out of the edges of his wit, turned as punishment upon his own people . . . and leaking, seemed to get into the very yellow of his skin, his single most unattractive feature" (Mailer, 1969, p. 121).

Today, the distance afforded by time allows for greater appreciation of the nuances in Mailer's text. A less passionate rereading offers the balance of cognition and emotion that characterizes a true aesthetic experience. This is not, of course, because the text has changed; rather, because I have evolved with the times. But only somewhat. For I remain deeply appreciative of the opportunity for coming of age in an irreverent, socially committed era like the 1960s, a time which fostered sensitivity to the imperfections of society, which opened our eyes to the plight of the less fortunate around us, to the groups of disenfranchised—including (since my eyes are still open) today's public school teachers whose professional autonomy and status have steadily eroded within our increasingly bureaucratized and depersonalized system of schooling.

So if today's rereading of *Miami* does not evoke in me the deep anti-establishment revulsion it once did, I am yet reminded that Mailer, more than any other literary craftsman I confronted in my youth, gave to me a permanent gift: He gave me a direction in which to travel, if not, as I once thought, a final destination. His gift was a kind of moral compass to help me navigate responsibly across the ethically featureless ocean of the 1980s (and, I hope, beyond). Or perhaps these later years deserve a crueler metaphor. Maybe they are more like a sea of land, a parched and barren bed of sand devoid of moral signposts. The Great American Desert? This shift in metaphor seems apt because it is the very one that Mailer, in a triumphant work written in 1979, near the onset of the current moral drought, employs to characterize a significant part of the American landscape. (Recall that it was a Western president who brought the desert to so many of us. It was Palm Springs' Ronald Reagan whose simple and apparently sincere faith in mirages ["Over there! A Shining City on a Hill!"] was so seductive to many of my countrymen.)

The book is *The Executioner's Song* (1979) and the protagonist of Mailer's "true-life novel" (as he called it) was one Gary Gilmore. In 1977 this Utah native was executed for committing a set of heinous murders. In over a thousand pages Mailer painstakingly recreates the last nine months of Gilmore's life, from his murderous acts to his death in the electric chair. But like all great literature, Mailer's text—even while reciting the minutiae of a single life—transcends those seemingly isolated particulars. While meticulously introducing us to the actual conditions of Gilmore's world, Mailer suggests that we also view his life metaphorically. His story is, therefore, only ostensibly about one man's life and death.

By filling in the gaps so artfully arranged by Mailer, the reader can recognize features of the soul of Gary Gilmore within the larger cultural landscape. Gilmore's crimes were literally senseless; free of purpose, devoid of meaning, they merely happened. Crimes of convenience. Observing the actions of Mailer's Gilmore, we gain a glimpse of what it means to engage in an extreme form of moral relativism, an amorality, that is, which represents the very antithesis of the dogmatic, tightly ideological posture affected by us 1960s types. We had envisioned reconstructing the world, the neighborhood of mankind, using very specific blueprints. But Gilmore, like many children of the 1980s, was merely an opportunist devoid of moral grounding and so incapable of withstanding the slightest breezes of circumstance. Of course, Gilmore lashed outward, in violence. His whims were indulged within a bizarre theater of the cruel, while our present-day self-indulgence is less obviously harmful. These days the sins of choice are those of omission, as, for example, the plight of society's less fortunate is ignored through a narrowing of the definition of who really are our neighbors.

But Mailer implies that vestiges of the westernness of Gary Gilmore remain within us. We are all, he suggests, sons of the pioneers, hyper-pragmatic and self-reliant (so the myth goes) frontiersmen, self-absorbed individuals undisturbed by the common condition. Joan Didion (herself a true master at disclosing the essence of life in the modern American West) articulated most eloquently Mailer's theme in her review of *The Executioner's Song*:

> The authentic Western voice, the voice heard in *The Executioner's Song*, is one heard often in life but only rarely in literature, the reason being that to truly know the West is to lack all will to write it down. The very subject of *The Executioner's Song* is that vast emptiness at the center of the Western experience, a nihilism antithetical not only in literature but to most other forms of human endeavor, a dread so close to zero that human voices fade out, trail off, like skywriting . . .
>
> When I read this, I remembered that the tracks made by the wagon wheels are still visible from the air over Utah, like the footprints made on the moon. (in Manso 1985, 607)

We Americans are indeed inhabitants of a callow culture, a nation in its adolescence, one lacking the maturity that could provide a strong sense of who we are and where we want to go as a people. This partially explains, I believe, our infatuation with the tools that science gives us. With no clearly defined vision of our own we find it convenient to partake of the half-hidden values implicated in the use of technology. Well, why not use them? As the educational sociologist Margret Buchmann (1985, p. 156) has noted, we believe that "our tools should not lie idle: where knowledge is valued for its instrumental qualities the charge to use it is almost implied." Of course this technological imperative (like our national malaise; indeed, like most of society's virtues and evils) has crept into our schools. There our shiniest tools, the ones that speak the loudest, the ones we teach to, are, of course, the standardized tests. Educators, we too are children of our culture, and have lacked the vision and the voice, the will to question where we are being led by our inventions.

Yes, the 1980s have been a chilling time for the "non-Western" teachers among us who still aspire to a restoring of the human voice to the next generation of Americans. But reading Mailer can help. Indeed, he points out to us two important signposts on the road to pedagogical (and maybe even national) maturity. The first says this: When we arrange the learning environment and select the activities in which we recommend that students engage, we are not performing a merely technical exercise. The humanities, the arts, the sciences, even "computer science," none of these areas of study are comprised of value-neutral content or thinking skills to be acquired by students in a moral vacuum. Instead, our teaching and learning encounters are, as the title of yet another book of Mailer's suggests, *existential errands*. We must take responsibility for the social and personal consequences which inevitably flow from our curriculum plans and their execution in the classroom. When we are vexed by external mandates that aim to deny us the autonomy we need to act as professionals, then we may move outside the classroom to confront the forces which presume to shape the nature of our work. But to do this responsibly we must first work toward articulating a personal vision of a more just, humane, and democratic society and begin to understand how the overt and the hidden curriculum will inevitably promote or retard progress toward that vision.

But the message on the second signpost is more cautionary: Pay attention to history, it says. Remember how, in the 1960s, some of us had such a vision? Back then we lived within the narrow lines of moral certitude, just as in the 1950s it had been the facts themselves that blinded us to the values undergirding them. Now we know that the ennui, hopelessness, and drift of the 1950s (like the malaise of today) occupy one side of a coin. On the flip side are dogmatism, intolerance, polemicism. What Mailer does is urge us not to flip the coin, not to force a choice between fact and fiction, between knowledge and values, between final truth and possible meaning. In Mailer's work, as in nearly all good literary nonfiction, such choices are not made. Instead we are enticed to pull together and to accommodate two apparent opposites.

And so might it be in our curricular efforts. Just as Mailer has probed beneath the surface of actual events, crafting them into stories whose deeper, less apparent, meanings the reader is invited to explore, so we as curriculum designers must avoid awkward attempts at bluntly imposing on our students our facts and dogmas, our preformulated performance objectives, our own personal visions, no matter how fully crystallized and dearly held. We should know by now to, instead, invite our students into that dangerous vessel which will float them away from the safety of literal truth and the twin seductions of ethical sloth and moral intolerance. We must do, that is, what the good storyteller does. We must design activities that entice them into paying careful attention to the social and empirical world around them. But we must leave gaps for students to fill in, holes which encourage them to actively intervene in the proceedings, to assume responsibility, to think critically about the significance of that which they have experienced, to wonder about how it fits into their own maturing outlooks on the world, to share their tentative thoughts with teachers and each other, to tear down and construct again any conclusions reached, and then to act.

Only then will our lessons for them be like Mailer's for us: Stay open, tuned in to the world and ready to change it. Use your judgment in considering how to make it better, even while avoiding any final pronouncements about its constantly evolving status. And so become accustomed to the doubts and anxieties inevitably involved in the exercise of that judgment. Learn not to submit to imperialism or tyranny in any guise—political, intellectual, technological, moral. Do not seek to escape from the responsibilities of freedom. Instead, why not get into the boat?

References

Buchmann, M. (1985). What is irrational about knowledge utilization. *Curriculum Inquiry, 15* (2), 153–168.

Capote, T. (1963). *In cold blood: A true account of a multiple murder and its consequences.* New York: Random House.

Didion, J. (1969). *Slouching toward Bethlehem.* New York: Delta Books.

Herr, M. (1968). *Dispatches.* New York: Avon Books.

Iser, W. (1974). *The implied reader.* Baltimore: Johns Hopkins University Press.

Langer, S. (1957). *Problems of art.* New York: Charles Scribner's Sons.

Mailer, N. (1968). *Armies of the night: History as a novel, the novel as history.* New York: New American Library.

Mailer, N. (1969). *Miami and the siege of Chicago: An informal history of the Republican and Democratic conventions of 1968.* New York: New American Library.

Mailer, N. (1979). *The executioner's song.* New York: Warner Books.

Manso, P. (1985). *Mailer: His life and times.* New York: Simon and Schuster.

Wakefield, D. (1966). The personal voice and the impersonal eye. *Atlantic, 278* (6), 86–90.

Wolfe, T. (1969). *Radical chic and mau-mauing the flak catchers.* New York: Bantam Books.

Wolfe, T. (1973). *The new journalism.* New York: Harper and Row.

Wolfe, T. (1979). *The right stuff.* New York: Farrar, Straus and Giroux.

Section II

DEWEYAN INFLUENCES: THE AESTHETICS OF THE EVERYDAY

The three chapters in this section reflect major concerns of John Dewey. Chapter 5 was originally an essay commissioned by the Rockefeller Brothers Fund as part of a program related to excellence in arts education, and was published in a 1983 issue of *Daedalus* devoted to the Arts and Humanities in American schools. It is not another argument for the use of portraiture as a form of educational inquiry, but an actual case study in the style of Sarah Lawrence-Lightfoot (Lawrence-Lightfoot & Davis, 1997), an example of program evaluation as literary essay. And the prevailing theme of the essay is Deweyan: the folly of dichotomizing between art and craft.

The next two chapters display my affinity for the Deweyan brand of progressivist education. Chapter 6 is another case study (1987), this one in the form of a critical biography, a life story framed lightly within social reconstructionist theory. The protagonist is a student teacher who shared Dewey's antipathy toward traditional forms of education.

Chapter 7 is a reprint of an essay (1993) which explains how anesthetic forms of educational assessments (i.e., standardized tests) can diminish the aesthetics of everyday life in schools, sapping the capacity of students for composing their own unique life stories. This text, too, is haunted by the spirit of John Dewey.

Chapter 5

Things of Use and Things of Beauty: The Swain County High School Arts Program (1983)

It is clear that children should be instructed in some useful things . . . [but] to be always seeking after the useful does not become free and exalted souls.
                                                                    —Aristotle[1]

Weaving, hit's the prettiest work I ever done. It's asettin' and trampin' the treadles and watchin' the pretty blossoms come out and smile at ye in the kiverlet.
                                            —"Aunt Sal" Creech of Pine Mountain, Kentucky[2]

The Appalachian mountains of western North Carolina are aging gracefully. Millions of years ago (geologists tell us), they possessed the kind of brittle, angular, energetic majesty of the Rockies. But with an infinite patience, Nature has rounded their formerly pointed peaks into gentle curves and cushioned them with a lush green canopy. Underneath this blanket of vegetation, one can observe the aging process up close, as the mountain streams etch wrinkles into the face of the earth. The centuries of erosion have worn down this land, but strength and dignity clearly remain: even at their age, they are still able to lift themselves into the grandeur of the clouds.

Somewhere within these ancient hills lives a young man named Donald Forrister. Every weekday morning around half past seven, he leaves his wooden frame house, climbs into his pickup truck, and heads north. Down a narrow dirt road to the highway, he rambles, to the town of Bryson City, and a few miles later, into the parking lot of Swain County High School.

Forrister is an art teacher—the only art teacher—at the school, and the old Smoky Mountains provide, in many ways, an apt metaphor for what he has accomplished here. Slowly, carefully, patiently, Forrister has succeeded in shaping formless adolescent talents into aesthetic sensibilities of impressive maturity. Almost single-handedly he has created a high-school arts program that is not only outstanding, but—perhaps even more remarkable—cherished by both the school and county communities. Any such embrace is, we know, quite rare in an era in which the arts are often treated, in Jerome Hausman's phrase like "unwelcome boarders in a burgeoning household."[3] So even though the story of the Swain County High School Arts is, in many respects, a singular one, I believe we might learn from its telling much that is pertinent to the general survival and flourishing of the arts in our schools.

Introduction to the Program

It was a spring morning in 1982 when I first met the central characters in the Swain story: the students. That morning, as usual, they flowed down from the mountains like individual drops of dew that coalesced into a stream. Along the way they were joined by Don Forrister, members of the Swain administration and staff, and me. Together we poured through the school doors.

The mountains looming above the school provide a sense of locale—but move inside, and where are you? Many places you have been before—the more or less standard Modern American School Plant, circa 1978. The building's right-angled innards seem familiar: the variously sized cubicles of space that stare blankly at the newcomer, the prolonged rectangular corridors that invite one, without a hint of destination. I am surprised to find here in rural North Carolina a school building similar to those where I live, in the Cincinnati suburbs, partly because of my preconceptions about the level of financial support for education in a county so rural and with so small an economic base. But there it is: the same charmless modernity, the refreshing lightness of the glass and brick, the airiness of the pleasingly massive open chamber that dominates the heart of the building and serves primarily as a reading area and media center. But a startling difference, so crucial to our story, becomes vividly apparent: from the boldly executed 5- by 5-foot abstract expressionist painting hanging on the brick wall near the lobby to the administrative offices, to the cloth wall-hangings (stuffed tubes intertwined playfully into serpentine knots) dangling above the stairwells, to a remarkable set of drawings near a side entrance (one, a carefully composed and brilliantly colored still life of red and green apples)—there is art. To be sure, there is room for many more pieces, but the presence of any student artwork of such quality adorning the inside of a high school is unusual and exciting, and serves to whet one's appetite for learning more about these students and their arts program.

The student body of Swain County High School averages about five hundred, of which eighty usually elect to take art. During their freshman or sophomore year (in Art I class), students are introduced to what Forrister considers the foundations of aesthetic awareness: line, form, design, and color. These concepts are explored not only through examination of the works of major artists, but also through a number of individual projects completed under the critical eye of the teacher. The forms of arts and crafts offered in Forrister's program include macramé, pottery, fibers, weaving, drawing, photography, silk-screening, papermaking, batik, stitchery, quilting, lettering, and airbrushing. According to Forrister and his students, it is from this exposure to a smorgasbord of possibilities that a student will sense proclivity toward one or more areas, in which he or she then selects a set of major projects for Art II and III. It seems probable that the range of activities enhances the overall success of the program.

But training in every area of the arts is certainly not provided in the program. The emphasis is on the visual: the development of musical talent is under the aegis of the school band, while students with a literary or theatrical bent must look to the English Department for training. And that many of the visual art forms, including all forms of painting, are missing is owing to the program's primary financial source: supplies, equipment, and the services of Don Forrister are paid for largely by federal vocational funds. Hence, the emphasis on the commercial arts and crafts (although not a totally exclusive one, as we shall see) provides the program with a strong, local Appalachian flavor. To paraphrase Oscar Hammerstein, the hills are alive in the Swain County High School Arts Program—which accounts for some measure of the program's success as well as its local support. This vital link with the community deserves documentation, and to do that we move back outside into the hills.

Community Context: Natural Richness/Economic Poverty

Swain County, North Carolina, is by and large a national park—or more precisely, over half of the county is situated in the Great Smoky Mountains National Park, and over half of the park is in Swain County. About

one half of the Cherokee Indian Reservation, including the town of Cherokee, is also within the county lines, but, like the park to the north, is
outside the county's governmental jurisdiction. Since the federal government controls 82 percent of Swain only 18 is left for local taxation.

In the lower third of the county sits Bryson City, the county seat by
default, and hardly a city at all; it is a town of fifteen hundred people, and
except for Cherokee, the only municipality in the county. The texture of
life in Bryson City is of course influenced to some degree by its locale, but
in other ways seems quite typical of small-town America. There are, no
doubt, some of the same qualities that Carol Kennicut found so dismaying
in turn-of-the-century Gopher Prairie: a self-satisfied provincialism in values and mores, perhaps; a cultural bleakness that even rules out most
forms of public entertainment (save a games arcade and one "last picture
show"), certainly.

Rebutting this notion, a local newspaper asserts: "Bryson City ain't
very fancy, but it's real."[4] And if that sounds like a cliché, it also has the
ring of truth. I observed among the populace a genuinely courteous and
friendly demeanor, with no hint of pretense. And though much of the
town's commercial property is incessantly drab, many of its houses exude
a homemade charm lacking in the dour architecture of Gopher Prairie.

And unlike the folks of *Main Street,* one can detect a curious ambivalence among some of Bryson City's natives concerning its small-town
status. The local press may insist: "If you're looking for a place with a lot
[of] neon, fast-food restaurants and crowds of people, don't come to Bryson
City"—and rightly so, for Bryson City has indeed managed to escape
some of the cultural blight of the twentieth century. But there is a note of
false bravado, perhaps even thinly disguised desperation, in that quote.
For one thing, there is an unmistakable feeling of pride among the locals
in their newly opened Hardee's, the first national fast-food chain to locate
a franchise in Bryson City. But, more important, the quote comes from
the *Smoky Mountain Tourist News*[5]— so its seeming disdain of crowds
is in reality an open plea for carloads of tourists and a suggestion that in
coming to Bryson City they will somehow manage to escape from one
another. No doubt there are those in Bryson City who would love to see
it swell to the size of Gatlinburg, Tennessee, the overwhelmingly commer-
cialized tourist Mecca over across the Park—no matter that Bryson City's
major selling points are the very virtues (the peaceful isolation, the wilderness sanctuary, the small-town charm) that Gatlinburg has chosen to
prostitute. But since the Bryson City area is on the edge of the tourist
belt, miles from the nearest interstate highway, it must be carefully sought

out by vacationers for the attractions it offers: hiking, picnicking, white-water rafting, and above all, the natural splendors of the mountains.

I was not really surprised to hear Don Forrister speak one night of the spirituality he perceives in these mountains, for in them, I too experienced a rare communion with nature. Sitting on the porch of Forrister's mountain home after a twilight thunderstorm, I watched the fireflies painting in watercolor on a gigantic canvas, their speckled phosphorescent moments of light diffused and softened by the mist. I recalled a poem by William Cullen Bryant, "Thanatopsis," that I had been forced to memorize in high school long ago, but which was only now helping me to see and hear "the voice of gladness, the smile, the eloquence of beauty, the mild and healing sympathy" that is the lavish gift of Nature.

This natural richness must surely suffuse the lives of the inhabitants of these mountains and compensate somewhat for the economic poverty that pervades the county. The average per capita income in 1979 was $5,705, compared with the national average of $8,773.[6] In April 1982, when the national unemployment rate was 9.2 percent, Swain County's was a staggering 26.2 percent.[7] But poverty in Swain County has a long history—which may be why, as some Bryson City townsfolk insisted to me, "folks here is poor, but they don't feel poor." One suggested that, because of a tradition of self-sufficiency—including vegetable gardening, canning, building one's own furniture and often one's own home—hard times in these hills are less painful than in the city or suburbs. Perhaps. It is a sociological truism that the poor have less to lose to a depression. But many from the middle class are also out of work in Swain County, and the testimony in a local newspaper article of several of the jobless, concerning their emotional shock and alienation, sounds like an echo from far-off Detroit or Akron.

Of the four thousand in Swain County's labor force who *are* employed nearly half are either tradesmen or workers in furniture and clothing factories. (A blue-jeans factory closed in early 1982.) Most of the others work at some level of government or in service-related businesses, the motels, gas stations, cafes, and gift shops that cater to the tourist dollar. The tourist business is seasonal, of course, but still important to the Swain County economy.

The Craft Heritage: Aesthetics and Functionality

Tourists are lured by the wilderness of the mountains, and once there, attempt to preserve their memories by purchasing souvenirs of the mountain culture. The countryside is speckled with craft and gift shops—the River Wood Craft Shop, the One Feather Craft Shop, and (within a stone's throw of the pink-and-white Teddy Bear Motel) Miller's Groceries and Crafts. The shops contain tons of mass-produced bric-a-brac, but items handcrafted by the Cherokees and white mountaineers also abound— baskets, pottery, quilts, rugs. The genuine handiworks are a fundamental part of the Southern Appalachian heritage. Recently popularized in the series of *Foxfire* books, the crafts of the white Southern Appalachia Highlanders have evolved for generations since the arrival of the first pioneers in the late 1790s and early 1800s. By considering their cultural artifacts, it is possible, I believe, to discern several qualities of life among these people. I will suggest only three.

The first, perhaps the most obvious, has already been mentioned. It is an almost totally *self-sufficient* life-style, demanded of a people kept apart from the rest of civilization by distance and even isolated from neighbors by a rudely intervening mountaintop. Once, in these hills everything was handmade: cabin, furniture, clothing, utensils. Second, one senses the enormous *care* invested in these artifacts. It is surely a patient people who were (and are) willing to wash and straighten animal and vegetable fibers, to stretch, twist, and spin them, to dye and weave the yarn into cloth. Only someone inspired to create a thing of beauty and excellence could produce from that hard-earned cloth the intricately patterned Appalachian "Sunday" quilts. And that inspiration must surely have come, as did Bryant's, from the "various language" spoken by their natural surroundings. One senses a link between the aesthetic pleasure that must have pervaded the creation of these artifacts and the satisfaction derived from the beauty in these hills.

But ultimately, there is *pragmatism*—indeed, the traditional pragmatism of the American frontier. These early mountaineers were not artists in any full-blown technical sense; they were craftspeople. In their work, aesthetics was clearly subordinate to function. The generally harsh circumstances of their lives strongly suggested a utilitarian channel for release of any artistic tendencies: "Direct your need for the creation of beauty toward the things of survival." Thus their pride in a cabinet built or a basket woven must surely have sprung not only from an appealing form, a pleasing design, an interesting texture but also, and perhaps primarily, from the work's practical attributes, its strength, its durability, its general usefulness.

The Official Vocational Orientation

One escape route from poverty in Swain County nowadays is through the production and sale of arts and crafts. The people of Swain County are aware of this fact, and a rationale for an arts program that rested on it would, it seems, be viewed quite sympathetically, for it would be the latest manifestation of the pragmatism that has informed this region (indeed, this country) for decades. The Swain County Arts Program is in fact strongly vocational. The program is funded by the federal government and administered by the North Carolina Vocational Education Department. Its official raison d'être, therefore, is to equip students with the knowledge and skills needed to become commercial artists, artisans, and craftspeople.

Within the school, the thrust of the program is also seen as primarily vocational—Mr. Frizell, the school principal, for example, spoke of it strongly in those terms—and written documents support this notion. For example, in "Art," the Swain County High School Arts Program booklet prepared for a school accreditation process, it is stated unequivocally that "Crafts as a Vocation is an individualized program concerned with occupations in the crafts industry. (Crafts as a Vocation is taken as Art II and Art III by graduates of Art I who so choose.) The greatest portion of time is spent in laboratory activities while increased emphasis is placed on developing skills for local crafts industries."[8]

Again in the booklet's description of the Commercial Arts courses, one reads: "At least 50 percent of the allocated time for this class will be used in the lab or shop for hands-on experience, *illustrating their relevance to the work world* (italics added)." And why are the "basics"— color and line, design and layout, balance and proportion—taught in that course? "In order for the student to develop competencies relative to the occupation." Likewise, two of the major objectives of the Photography course (taken as Art III) are "to prepare individuals for gainful employment in occupations relating to photography" and "to become aware of sales potential and prepare and practice selling photographs."[9] And so it goes. One cannot escape an awareness of the program's official orientation.

The Roots of Vocationalism
This curricular pledge of allegiance to commerce is, of course, hardly novel—whether in the area of the arts or in terms of the overall agenda of

the American School. Indeed, one of the first influential Americans to suggest that schools should pay serious heed to the needs of the marketplace was Benjamin Franklin. Franklin's utilitarian approach was embodied in his plans for an academy in which classical scholarship was to become a curricular bedfellow to subjects of a more commercial interest to the newly emerging middle class: natural science and its applications, agriculture, bookkeeping, the technology, and so on.

Franklin suggested that the study of art (especially drawing) be assigned a purpose in addition to developing creative expression, namely, as a useful tool for improving the design of the work of shipbuilders, engravers, cabinetmakers, and mechanics. Franklin's academy never became a reality, but his utilitarian notions of the general curriculum—and the place of art within it—were the beginning of a lasting trend. Schooling, especially on the secondary level, would gradually divest itself of a large portion of the classical curriculum, often in favor of subjects and approaches more vocationally oriented. Several years later there appeared perhaps the original arguments for actual course offerings of handicraft art, such as embroidery, quilting, drawing, painting, and needlework, in terms of an expanded economic opportunity. These were in the form of newspaper advertisements for the private "English" schools that, in the mid-eighteenth century, many in the middle class favored over the stuffier Latin grammar schools; indeed, some of the logic in "Art" is reminiscent of such arguments.

But only in the last half of the nineteenth century was the marriage of art and industry in the school curriculum finally achieved. These were the years of robust industrial development and expansion, decades that witnessed the rise of American iron and steel, the expansion of the textile industry, and the growth in railroads and shipping that opened up both foreign and domestic markets for American goods. It was also, if we are to believe a bulletin of the U.S. Bureau of Education, a time of increased opportunity for artists willing to serve as handmaidens to the newly crowned lord of manufacturing:

> In addition to the increased competition arising from the steam carriage, new and cheaper methods of manufacture and increased productivity, another element of value has rapidly pervaded all manufacturers, an element in which the United States has been and is woefully deficient—the art element. The element of beauty is found to have pecuniary as well as aesthetic value. The training of the hand and of the eye which is given by drawing is found to be of the greatest advantage to the worker in many occupations and is rapidly becoming indispensable. This training is of value to all the children and offers to girls as well as boys opportunity

for useful and remunerative occupations, for drawing in the public school is not to
be taught as mere "accomplishment." The end sought is not to enable the scholar
to draw a pretty picture, but to so train the hand and eye that he may be better
fitted to become a bread-winner.[10]

Another indication of the importance of art training for industry during
this time was the intense lobbying by leading industrialists in Massachusetts to ensure passage into law, in 1870, of a proposal requiring all cities
with a population exceeding ten thousand to provide art instruction to
teenage boys.[11]

The last half of the nineteenth century was thus the heyday of the
vocational rationale for the teaching of drawing and the crafts in the
public school. John Dewey and the progressive education movement finally provided a rationale for the fine arts as an activity central to the
educational process, and both the justifications for, and the methods in,
courses of the fine arts and the practical (or industrial) arts disparate, as
indeed they are today.

In Swain County, according to Frizell, "it was not easy to get the crafts
and commercial art into the vocational program" back in 1973. The school
administration decided to make the attempt when the state-funded arts
teacher/counselor retired. The intercession of the state's Superintendent
of Public Instruction was required, but the Swain County Commercial
Arts and Crafts Program was finally accepted by the state Vocational
Education Department. Today, only one other such program in North
Carolina—a strongly craft-oriented one in Robinsville—also receives funding through the state from the federal government.

The Swain program must be resubmitted every year, with projections
of courses to be taught and numbers of students, along with the follow-up
studies of program graduates. This last process is crucial, for the survival
of the program depends in large measure on the percentage of Art III
graduates who choose to pursue arts or crafts, or both, as avocation or
as a major in a technical school or four-year college. The required percentage fluctuates, but according to Alice Lance, the school's vocational
guidance counselor, it usually hovers around 50 percent. "It is totally up
to the Vocational Education Department," she said. "They go by the
numbers. . . . What's saving the program is that the students have been
using . . . [their arts and crafts training] . . . but it's scary."

This number seems astonishingly high, especially considering the traditional disinclination of the region's people toward higher education, and
it stands as testimony to Forrister's profound influence on the career choices
of his students. So, despite its slightly tenuous future status, the program

has indeed proved successful in terms of its official mandate. And while that accomplishment itself is interesting, there are, I believe, even more compelling achievements in the Swain County High School Arts Program. To consider those, we need to look closer at the program in action.

Nonvocational Outcomes of the Arts Program

There are really three arts-and-crafts rooms presided over by Forrister. The main classroom is located, fittingly, in the school's vocational wing, whereas to reach the other two—the photography darkroom and the weaving room—requires considerable transit through those right-angled corridors. Forrister's classroom is L-shaped (the lap of the L is an adjoining arts material storeroom), its angularity somewhat softened by the layers of student crafts and artwork that cover the horizontal surfaces and cushion the walls. Entering this room is like exiting from the building: one leaves the nowhere-land of the school plant and slips back into Appalachian hill country. The sense of place returns, thanks largely to the local flavor of objects like the baskets woven of birch twigs, the large, intricately designed Sunday quilt, and the drawings of hill country still lifes. Many of these exhibit the same blend of the aesthetic and the functional seen in the artifacts of the Southern Highlands pioneers.

And the longer one remains, the stronger wafts the aroma of the hills, not only in the distinctive accents of the students, but also in their open and friendly demeanor, a reflection of their elders on the sidewalks of Bryson City. And certainly, the perseverance and care of the students as they tussle with their materials are the qualities one can see fossilized in the artifacts of the mountain pioneers. Does the same fuel that fired the engines of the mountain craftsmen move these students in Don Forrister's classroom? Is it indeed a struggle for economic survival that motivates them? Are the scarlet threads woven into that rug merely to supply a tangential beauty, placed there primarily to catch the eye and only secondarily to please it—not as an end in itself, but as a means of ringing the cash register?

Just what does motivate these teenagers? It is an important question, because the answer can provide a clue to the *educational* meaning and significance of the program's outcomes—the character of its impact on the lives of these students. Having spent only four days in the school, I will avoid pronouncements, and instead share my reasons for some strong suspicions. They are based on observations of student comportment, on their informal comments, on mass "whole class" discussions over which I presided, and on interviews with individual students.

An Eclecticism of Purpose

First, it is apparent that many different motives coexist here; as in most human endeavors, there are a variety of prevailing causes and reasons for actions. There is indeed a degree of the career/economic/commercial incentive, although the amount seems startlingly small in light of the program's stated intentions and sources of funding. Consider, for example, the case of Robert, the senior voted "most talented in art" by the graduating class, an adolescent whose sensitive and technically accomplished drawings are an emphatic testimony to that talent and whose family (according to Forrister) is of extremely modest means. I was quite moved by one of Robert's drawings and was interested in acquiring it, but his refusal to sell it was absolute: "I like to keep all of my drawings." Don Forrister assured me that this disinclination to part with their work, even for money, is quite common among his students—and their parents. Only a few of them (including the craftspeople) will merchandise their handiworks. More often, the creations will either adorn their homes or become gifts, providing lasting pleasure to themselves, their kin, and friends.

And their plans for future employment? The current crop of upperclassmen appear to fit the pattern of the past: of the fourteen I surveyed, eight expressed an intention to work at an arts- or crafts-related job. For some, following in the paths of former students like John Herrin, a truck driver who "moonlights" in macramé, crafts may provide a supplementary income. But for the majority of Forrister's students, different motives seem to dominate. Their interest in arts and crafts is not based primarily on the acquisition of a salable skill. Here is the question I posed to an assembly of sixteen Arts II and III students: "Suppose it were impossible to use what you have learned in this class in terms of a job. Would you still have taken this class, and would you still enjoy it as much?" A show of hands indicated a nearly unanimous affirmative response.

So while the image—among much of the Swain County public, members of the school administration and faculty, and the distant bureaucrats in Raleigh and Washington who administer and fund the program—may be of students learning to draw and weave for the primary intention of acquiring future economic self-sufficiency, reality begs to differ: the economic imperative, the prevailing practicality of their ancestors, is, for most of these students, clearly subordinate to motives more compelling. What are they?

A Personal Pride

One motive concerns a personal pride in their accomplishments. There are several facets to this pride, including a degree of vanity from the attention their talents attract. Occasionally, a sense of self-importance could be detected among some of Forrister's senior students, an awareness of a kind of privileged status usually associated with talented athletes or found among high-school thespians backstage before the senior play. This status, as far as I could tell, was certainly not flaunted—and part of it might be explained by the fact that so many of Forrister's senior students were already part of, in Philip Cusick's term, the school's "power clique."[12] But this status was also derived from the recognition of, and admiration for, their many awards and honors, which the students (as they readily admit) welcome. The elixir of victory is heady stuff; the scent from a drop or two can apparently provide the momentum for many a painstaking and time-consuming project. This attention and excitement may be particularly impressive to the large percentage of Forrister's students who are, according to Lance, less than academically able in other subjects. Can we imagine the impact on the psyche of an eleventh-grader who, after years of frustration, boredom, and perhaps even derision in math and English classes, is suddenly flown to New York to receive a national award for his drawings?

Nevertheless, many junior and senior students insisted to me that visions of plane trips to exotic locations, or even the regional trophies and blue ribbons, did not lure them into Art I. As freshmen or sophomores, they could not imagine that they might possess such talent. Just a few years later, however, the pride in creating, in their words, "a thing of excellence," or more accurately, the accolades received from those creations, does seem to explain partially the students' reluctance to sell them.

An "Expression of Their Art"

But many students are unwilling to part with their "lesser" works as well. Could this perhaps indicate a more intrinsic satisfaction in their creation? In that regard, a closer inspection of "Art" reveals this beguiling passage:

> A great many people work at crafts as a hobby or avocation and a growing number are becoming craftsmen and producing crafts as a vocation. For some, craft work is an "alternative" vocation which the craftsmen prefer above the nine-to-five job. For others, it is their sub occupation and expression of their art for which the benefits can seldom be calculated in dollars and cents.[13]

A priceless "expression of their art"? Is there really a nonvocational incentive producing outcomes infinitely more valuable when measured with the kind of economic yardstick implied in the program rationale? The phrase suggests a purpose more concerned with the needs and development of the individual, as opposed to an exploitation of the needs of the marketplace. There are, of course, many rationales for aesthetic education that pertain to the personal well-being of the individual, such as the development of artistic talent, aesthetic appreciation, the therapeutic value of the artistic process, and so on. "Expression of their art," in the context used here, however, inspires two thoughts: First, it is reminiscent of the aesthetic pleasure that was an important by-product of the time-honored process of crafts-making in these hills; second, it is a phrase that evokes a particular branch of art theory, expressivism. The theorists of expressivism see art as an embodiment of the artist's inward feelings and images into an objective, outward "expressive" form. They often speak of a subjective inner life—"the life of feeling," as Susanne Langer puts it— and the aim of art, in their view, is to promote insight into and understanding of this inner realm. As Wordsworth saw it, art is "emotion recollected in tranquillity." But according to the expressivists, recollection is also a publication: a work of art is a transmutation of personal feelings and imagery into a unique sensible form, an objectification of the subjective. Objects of art, said Langer, articulate and present "ideas of feelings" for our contemplation.[14]

But are we not placing an overwhelming burden on the shoulders of a single phrase in a single paragraph in a single program booklet? Is the development of the students' creative self-expression really a significant feature of the daily activities in Forrister's classes? The evidence, it appears, leans strongly toward the affirmative, especially for the more advanced students.

According to Forrister, the Art I students are more interested in functional items, or in decorating things to be used—like the silkscreen designs for their tee shirts. With maturity, however, expressing oneself through the creative process also becomes important: in the private conversations I had with senior students, several told me of how they inform their materials with "a part of" themselves. Perhaps most telling was a discussion with an articulate young man, son of a Baptist minister. Jim, an Art III student, was pursuing the art of papermaking, a process of sifting pulp through a wire screen, painting it with colors, often including other materials such as straw, newspaper photos, and so on, for a collage effect. In one sensitive piece, a photo of a pensive old woman in a rocking chair sits among brooding clouds of purple, green, and yellow-gray.

TOM: Why do you like papermaking?

JIM: I like to be able to . . . it's not so defined. I like the freedom of it more than anything.

TOM: What do you mean by "it's not so defined"—that you can make abstract sorts of things?

JIM: Yeah, like lots of times you'll make something that you're not sure why you're doing it, but when it gets finished, you really like it.

TOM: When you do your papermaking, do you ever think, "Well, that has a certain feeling to it," . . . like it's expressing an emotion?

JIM: Oh yeah, I think it depends on when I come into class, what kind of mood I'm in. I think that comes out in some of my work.

TOM: Like, for example, the one that you're doing now of the old woman. What kind of feelings does that express?

JIM: Kind of a lost feeling. You see, I graduate in about a week . . . and I feel kinda worried about it. I guess that's coming out in it. At least I think so.

TOM: You probably wouldn't have done that one . . .

JIM: Earlier on? No, I wouldn't have . . .

TOM: When was the first time you realized [you were expressing yourself through your art]?

JIM: Probably sometime last year when I was a junior.

TOM: But in Art I, it . . . was just techniques?

JIM: Yeah.

TOM: Do you think other art students . . . also express themselves like that?

JIM: Oh yeah, a lot of them . . . 'cause basically you [are allowed in Forrister's class] to do what you want to.

By the freedom "to do what you want," I do not believe that Jim meant the license to scratch and scrawl angrily on a drawing pad, or, in high spirits, splash paint randomly on a canvas. Such behavior is only primitively "expressive"; it is not artistic expression. In Forrister's class, the individual student is preeminent, but the individualism that develops there has a distinctly Deweyan cast to it. In lieu of a mindless outpouring of unbridled emotion, there is a considered channeling of impulses into purposeful actions. The student's artistic activity is in fact comprised of careful negotiations with the materials, ardent attempts to create forms that communicate ideas and images. Degrees of success vary, of course, but in this process, qualitative forms of intelligence can clearly develop.

"Working Hard" at Self-Expression

Several students described the process of self-expression as "fulfilling" and "enjoyable," but also insisted that it was "hard work." No question that I asked of Forrister's class was greeted with more chuckles of affirmation than this one: "Is art as hard a subject as the others you take?" Some admitted to electing Art I with hopes of coasting through with minimal effort. They apparently harbored a notion quite common in our society, the one that associates crafts like basket weaving with extremely low rates of mental taxation. But to their astonishment, these students soon found Art I, in their own words, "harder than other subjects," because they had not anticipated a "striving for perfection." Who, after all, would have expected this newfound desire to "make your next project better than your last"?

But in Forrister's class, the nature of the "work" is different from the Calvinistic notion of work implied in Weber's famous critique of the Protestant ethic, the conception that has prevailed in America's schools for centuries and that remains today the image of educational virtue held by parents, schoolteachers and administrators (including many at Swain), and much of the general public. Such "work" demands a deferment of present interests and needs for a vision of future rewards, the imposition of self-discipline to withstand the tedium of—in today's educational lingo—the "time on task." The result is said to be the development of certain personal attributes, as noted in this description of the weaving process of the mountaineers by Frances Goodrich, an early twentieth-century preservationist of the hill country artifacts: "In the younger women who were learning to weave and keeping at it, I would see the growth of character. A slack, twisted person cannot make a success as a weaver of coverlets. Patience and perseverance are of the first necessity, and the exercise of these strengthens the fibers of the soul."[15]

Patience and perseverance are indeed personal qualities helpful in overcoming the monotony of the production phase of the weaving process (or the boredom of the assembly line), for further implied in this notion of work is the mindless replication of a prototype—and thus a personal distancing, an alienation from the process. Indeed, any intellectual engagement with one's materials could be harmful to the faithful reproduction of the prototype. What is needed, instead, is skill in copying precisely—and in the arts and crafts, the "training of the mind and eye," as that U.S. Bureau of Education Bulletin puts it, might provide such skill.

It is not surprising that during the late 1800s—the period of maximum coziness between art education and industry—this image of work was most clearly reflected in the methodology of art instruction. The methods originated, as did the Industrial Revolution, in Great Britain. The British National Course of Art Instruction (or the Cole System, after Henry Cole, head of the South Kensington Training School for Art Masters) was transported to the United States, and its aim was, indeed, to train students manually in copying. According to Stuart McDonald,

> Exact uniformity was insured by the National Course of Instruction, each of which had several stages, the sum of which comprised the twenty-three Stages of Instruction. The Stages . . . were mechanical steps to the acquisition of "hand-power." Twenty-one were successive exercises in copying . . . intended . . . to be strictly initiated until Stages 22 and 23 were reached—a most unlikely eventuality.[16]

This manual training approach to drawing was brought to America by another Englishman, Walter Smith, and soon the art instruction in American schools was pervaded by these alienating exercises of meticulous reproduction of master designs.

The activities in Forrister's class, however, provide a stark contrast with the Cole System. Technique is indeed mastered there, but as a means to a greater goal rather than as an end in itself. And the students do seem to be "working," but in a sense different from that implied in the Protestant ethic. Patience is certainly present, but it often seems less imposed than arising from a more immediate gratification. The effort appears to be generated from within the activities themselves, and directed toward an original transformation of the ideas and experiences of the individual student.

One can observe in this process a dialogue between the student and the materials being shaped, a qualitative problem-solving process in which the student/worker/artist struggles with possibilities, tentatively moves on the material, encounters resistance, and manipulates the component parts. For example, at one point in "working" on his paper collage, Jim incorporated some torn pieces of white paper above the head of the woman in the rocking chair, hoping to achieve a daydreaming effect. The "product," however, spoke back to him: "Perhaps too bright, distracting the eye from the central figure." Jim listened, reconsidered, added a more yellowish cast that reflected the woman's sallow facial tones, and that skirmish ended successfully.

Thus was the aesthetic tension between creator and creation resolved, as Jim used his "freedom" to "work hard" at portraying his own distinctive ideas, feelings, values, and ends-in-view. Aestheticians are prone to words like "authenticity," "self actualizing," "liberating" and "emancipating" in describing the effects of this creative process. It is a process that celebrates individual growth, as the student wrestles with the materials in order to create meaning, to make sense of his life.

Expressiveness in Crafts

The result of this process—a result Maxine Greene has called the *recovery of the self*[17]—is a far cry from what one might expect in a vocationally oriented arts program, especially considering those of an earlier day. Nevertheless, this kind of personal unfolding occurs not only in the more obviously artistic endeavors of Forrister's students, but sometimes in their crafts making as well. There are many similarities in the processes: the same attitude of caring, the personal attachment to their products, the pleasure in their creation. In craft production, of course, the intended function or use of the object imposes limitations on shape and form. Some aestheticians would disqualify most crafts from membership in the realm of fine art on this basis: they are not (in Langer's term) virtual objects, objects whose only function is to "create a sheer vision, a datum that is nothing but pure perceptual form."[18]

Yet it is clear that crafts making can involve aesthetic judgments, as argued by Edward Mattil, who in this passage could have been speaking of the early Southern Highlanders:

> We must assume that the earliest tools and utensils of man were restricted to the considerations of utility. As their efficiency improved, there was a steady evolution of form. In any situation where people were first required to produce the necessities of life by hand, the useful concern was of prime importance and as long as impoverished or stringent conditions continued, the art quality of the object rarely exceeded the functional design of the object. However, as soon as time and skill permitted, the craftsman was fairly sure to elaborate or decorate his objects and it was at this point in mass development where the matter of choice entered into the picture. For example, when man became able to create a variety of clay bowls, each good for holding grain or water, he found himself engaged in the process of making judgments—practical *and* aesthetic—in determining form and decoration.[19]

Today's Swain County High School students also often create meaning in their crafts, arranging elements of color, form, and texture into imaginative relationships that communicate feelings. Indeed, they told me so: when I asked the assemblage of advanced students to divide into two groups—art students to the right, craftspeople to the left—no one moved. There was near-unanimous insistence that any arts/crafts dichotomy would be an unimportant one. The students whom I had observed "working" at crafts like weaving, quilting, and batik-making clearly perceived themselves as "doing art." Indeed, distressed by their inability to respond effectively to the question in a group setting, two students sought me out later for private discussions, and one of them said that while some minor distinctions may exist, nevertheless, there is "art in crafts," and that she was able to express her emotions especially in the design phase of her weaving. (I was able to extract an admission that in the production phase, there was some "work" required, as Frances Goodrich has assured us, but even that process was often filled with the excitement of seeing one's design "come to life" with one's personal qualities placed in it.)

Interestingly, the Arts Program booklet suggests that it is those once tangential, individually produced aesthetic qualities that today provide the craft products with their functional value:

> In our age of mass production where a certain "sameness" marks most products, there is a growth market for goods that are unique and distinctive. The craftsman who can design and produce articles that have aesthetic value and bring distinction to their owners, have access to a market with which mass production cannot compete.[20]

Thus the "functional" value of today's craft objects may be defined less by their utility than by their ability to persuade a prospective purchaser visually. The mountain folk of yore could have survived the winter under an ugly quilt, but today's Appalachian craftsmen must beware the frigidity of the uninterested consumer.

Recall, however, that Forrister's students are generally not interested in selling their wares, and can therefore give freer range to their own personal aesthetic values in the construction of their objects. Individual self-expression thus seems central not only to the activities of Forrister's future artists but to the crafts-making as well, and that is surely one of the sources of a profound satisfaction that attracts them to Don Forrister's class.

Here, then, is what we have learned thus far about the Swain program: that there exists within the program major non-vocationally related features, including motivational factors such as a thirst for self-esteem and a need for self-expression; and that these incentives result in program outcomes that are officially unsanctioned and therefore officially ancillary, but that are of central importance to a preponderance of the students.

These findings are especially intriguing when viewed in light of a particular ongoing dialogue among some educationists. Radical critics of schooling have long portrayed schools as extensions of the modern technocratic state, as agencies ideologically committed to the corporate social order. Through both the overt and hidden curriculum, it is said, the institution of the school transmits the dominant cultural system. Schooling thus promotes a subversion of individuality in favor of attitudes and a world view that further the mechanistic purposes of business and industry. In the rather pessimistic critique of some of the radical determinists, any piecemeal reform of this monolithic apparatus of control is extremely problematical. Teachers in particular are seen as ineffective change agents, enmeshed as they are in the technocratic superstructure of the school.

The official vocational rationale of the Swain program would seem to pay homage to this point of view, but the program in action suggests the possibility of a more complex and attractive model. Here, classroom events and activities that reflected the divergent values of an individual teacher seemed to produce liberating rather than stultifying experiences. To elucidate this further, we turn now to the history of the program and the role of its chief architect.

An Appalachian Artist Designs an Arts Program

Donald Forrister knows these hills and their people, for he is one of them. Now a tall, slim, thirty-three-year-old, he was born and raised in Appalachia and attended college at Western Carolina University, and reflections of those qualities found in the mountain artifacts, described earlier in this essay, are clearly visible in Forrister's personality. There is, for example, his strong self-reliance and independence of thought and action. These manifest themselves in a variety of ways, including personal appearance. The beard and long hair of a couple of years ago were perhaps for some of the teachers an unwanted reminder of the stereotypical mountaineer and helped to solidify Forrister's image among them (at least according to some students) as something of a "weirdo." The beard, neatly trimmed, remains today, but Forrister's consistent casualness of dress, as well as his general lifestyle and values, are reminiscent of the "back-to-nature" movement among middle-class youth in the late sixties and early seventies. (The difference may simply be that Forrister never left.)

But his independence can be seen in other ways as well. He refuses to gossip and is intentionally uninformed about the politics within the faculty and administration. Though Forrister does not seem disliked by other faculty members, some may perhaps mistake his aloofness for disdain.

For example, he often lunches with students in the cafeteria rather than with his peers—only a slight breach of the etiquette of collegiality, but surely a habit (again, according to students) deemed irregular by some teachers. These qualities of independence and a loose definition of his role status are greatly admired by some of Forrister's students and seem instrumental in gaining their trust and respect.

"Hard-working" is the trait cited most often by Swain teachers and administrators, and a large measure of his success is owing to his enormous investment of time and energy in the program. In class he is a blur of movement from student to student for seven class periods a day, and even, during some periods, from classroom to weaving room to darkroom. On closer inspection, the blur becomes a mosaic I made up of individual exchanges between Forrister and students, such as a mini-critique of a choice of subjects, a quick nod of affirmation concerning a color mixture, or a one-on-one demonstration of a new technique. An arts course consists of an untold number of such interactions, each a piece of an emerging pattern. And Forrister's dedication extends well beyond the school grounds and class time. He can be found on weekends escorting a group of students to an art exhibit in Asheville, consulting with an individual student on a photographic project, and so on.

The students prefer to use the word *caring* to describe this "hard work." But the latter, it seems to me, is simply a manifestation of the former, just as the perseverance of the early spinners and weavers followed on their desire for beautiful coverlets and quilts. That Forrister does indeed care very deeply about his program was obvious. One anecdote in particular highlights this. In attendance at a ceremony honoring the Arts program was the mother of a former Swain student who had won a $10,000 scholarship to a prestigious art institute, thanks, she said, to "that man. And when we telephoned him to tell him the news, do you know what he did?" she asked. "He cried."

Forrister admits to "getting emotional" whenever a student creates particularly beautiful work. That emotionality is touching, of course, but it is important mainly insofar as it illuminates what lies at the heart of the Swain County success story: the simple but intense mission of a single teacher to enhance the lives of his students through art. And it is a cause that was achieved not only through the unswerving dedication of that one man, but by his shrewd intelligence as well.

Which brings us to our final commonality between the character of the Appalachian people generally and Don Forrister in particular: deep-seated pragmatism. We saw that pragmatism in the hill folks' ingenious combinations of the useful and the beautiful in the utensils of everyday living. Forrister's work of art is his program, and his methods for assuring not only its survival, but also its flourishing, in terms of its own values and definition of success, are also pragmatic.

Part of what Forrister did was to make the program famous. This high visibility was achieved through active participation in a wide variety of arts-and-crafts contests. Of course, the students' talents won the awards, and the incentive produced by recognition was developed in the classroom through the teaching process I have already described. But Forrister also played a leading role in the selection of student work for entrance in competitions, a tactic that often resulted in a legitimation of his expertise. One senior described to me the growth of his respect for Forrister's judgment:

> I would want to enter one of my drawings in a contest, and [he] would say, "Why don't we try this other one," because he thought it was better. And he would tell me why he liked it more. And I would say, "Well, OK." And . . . when *he* chose the ones to put in [the contest], I would win [an award], and when I chose which ones, I wouldn't. . . . A lot of the time that happened. . . . So I figured he must really know what he's doing.

Forrister's primary aim in emphasizing competitions, I am convinced, was to heighten student interest in art, not to increase the visibility of the program. Furthermore, I believe him when he says that his students' career decisions are of secondary importance to him. Nevertheless, a significant side effect was also spawned by these two measures of success. Both the obvious vocational influence and especially the contest results greatly impressed many parents and the school's administrators. The regional and even national recognition stirred local pride and, according to Lance, has even been noticed in Raleigh. As a result, Forrister had acquired a little of the aura of a winning football coach. His job certainly seems secure: Frizell has stated that, even if the vocational funds were slashed, "we would find the money to keep Forrister here."

Such a change in funding sources would probably increase Forrister's autonomy, and a few changes might ensue (such as the inclusion of "nonvocational" art forms like painting). But these should be minimal, since Forrister already possesses the freedom to pursue his own aspirations under the existing arrangements, freedom that seems less a result of forethought than of fortune. This is how it came about. During the 1970s, said Forrister, a regional representative from the State Vocational Education Department would visit his classes to monitor the orientation of his pedagogical methods and choice of curricular content. "For one or two years I wouldn't hear anything, and then a new person would take over [in the regional office], and complain about my emphasis, and I would have to concentrate on commercial art, and lead them more into the crafts."

In the last three or four years, however, Forrister says that he has acquired greater latitude in his choice of content and methods, with more emphasis on generating intrinsic interest and less on vocational. What has brought this about? A "reduction in force," a decrease in the staffing of the regional office, which has forced the Vocational Department to rely on a less direct, more quantitative, and less informative program-evaluation procedure. I have only Forrister's word for this shift in emphasis, but the irony in such an occurrence would be rich indeed. Is there any other example of a budget cut resulting in the enhancement of artistic self-expression in students? I know of none.

Thus have the seeds sown by Forrister sprouted in the cracks of a concrete technocracy. The success of his efforts belies any notion that schools are necessarily the kinds of "total institutions" posited by some of the radical critics. Indeed, as institutions become more complex and cumbersome, their management and the monitoring of official mandates tend to become more problematical. Corporate hegemony tends to diminish, while individual prerogative is enhanced. So while Forrister's actions may in some respects resemble the kind of "resistance" in educational institutions described by Jean Anyon and others[21]—that is, an individual agent's direct contestation of the systematic imposition of the technocratic will— a metaphor less antagonistic in tone seems more appropriate, one that suggests an accommodation of aims from a variety of sources. Direct contestation is not necessary in an organizational arrangement whose unwieldiness allows for a peaceful coexistence between formally sanctioned aspirations and those held by individuals charged with conduct of the program.

Note that in the Swain County program, official criteria are indeed being met. The development of individual self-expression has not been accomplished at the expense of the mandated vocational outcomes. On the other hand, neither has Forrister allowed the vocational imperatives to overwhelm the curricular decision-making and the pedagogical processes—even though compromises (already documented) were sometimes necessary. Even early in the program's history, Forrister certainly never resorted to any methods even vaguely resembling the essentially anesthetic Cole System of training students. He has shown us that preparing students for an occupation in the arts and crafts does not today require an alienating, spiritually exhausting regimen of mindless exercises. Indeed, evidence suggests that the personal rewards flowing from creative activities often encourage a lasting devotion to the artistic process and therefore an inclination toward an arts- or crafts-related career. And it seems fitting to learn this from a native of the Southern Highlands, where functionality and aesthetic pleasure have traditionally cohabited within the arts and crafts.

On Effectively Arguing for the Arts

This demonstration of a successful eclecticism of purpose has, I believe, important implications for the manner in which those of us close to the arts argue for their inclusion in the curriculum. Too often we display—as has, for example, Jacques Barzun[22]—a tendency to dismiss the necessity of justifications that are less "rudimentary" than those involving self-expression and aesthetic appreciation. The sources of this tendency are surely noble: an acute awareness of the intense satisfaction to be derived from the aesthetic experience and a desire to enhance the capacity of members of the younger generation for engaging in such experiences. Such an acquisition might even lead, as Harry Broudy has hoped, to "the good life . . . the kind of life that finds its expressions in the so-called good works of art."[23] I would suggest, however, that it is an over-reliance on the art-for-art's sake arguments that has, regardless of their intrinsic validity, partially contributed to the sadly consistent relegation of the arts to the curricular caboose. Despite the lip service sometimes paid to the arts, the American public (including legislators and many educators) obviously does not share our devotion to a belief in their intrinsic worth. Perhaps a generally low level of aesthetic literacy prevents a sizable number from appreciating the profundity of the life-enhancing capacities of the arts; perhaps not. At any rate, the survival of school arts programs may, especially in an era of economic stringency, require emphasis on rationales more sensitive to the fundamentally pragmatic character of the American people.

How much, for example, would the people of Swain County value a program—even an award-winning program—that served, in their eyes, no "useful" purpose? Even in this region steeped in a tradition of folk art, would there be widespread and sustained enthusiasm for a program that educated solely for "worthy leisure time activities" or "aesthetic appreciation"? My hunch is that the American-style pragmatism of these economically distressed people would ultimately deem such a program frivolous and of low priority.

The Swain County example therefore suggests the judicious employment of *additional* arguments, pragmatic ones that present the arts as instrumental in, and indeed as fundamentally essential to, the development of competent individuals capable of functioning in our society. It is beyond the scope of this essay to identify and articulate all such rationales, but we should note that they include others besides the obvious career-education justifications.

One particularly intriguing and, I believe, potentially fruitful argument sees the growth of aesthetic awareness as fundamental to the development of the "basic skills" of reading and writing. According to Elliot Eisner, there exist a great many forms of public representation of privately held concepts and images. We need to increase the literacy of students in a variety of these forms by developing their aesthetic awareness and artistic expression and, therefore, a more sophisticated perceptual system, one with greater power for the imaginative perception of qualitative relationships among empirical phenomena. This is important because

> information developed out of a highly differentiated perceptual system can then be used as content for a form of representation, often in a form other than that in which the information was initially acquired. For example, consider the writer of literature. To be able to write, the writer must have something to write about. To have something to write about, the writer must be able to "read" the environment in which he lives. He must become aware of qualities of gesture and nuances of voices, he must have subtlety of vision . . . . For those who are unable to see, or to hear, or to taste, or to smell, the content of literature will be little more than something that other people enjoy. School programs that neglect developing the child's literacy in forms of representation that sharpen the senses ultimately deprive the student of the very content he needs to use well the skills of reading and writing.[24]

I wish to stress that I am not advocating a total abandonment of those rationales that point to the intrinsic delightfulness of the aesthetic experience, or that emphasize personal growth and self-expression —especially for audiences that seem, to any degree, potentially receptive of such arguments. But the approaches that emphasize the instrumental value of the study of art would seem to hold greater potential for persuading a skeptical and frugal American public (and American educators, who should already know better) that the arts are indeed worthy members of the curriculum household.

Finally, regardless of justifications engaged in, and the program's stated objectives, once a program is in place, the successful attainment of the truly fundamental aim of art education—the intellectual and emotional growth of the individual—will obviously occur only through the hard work, the dedication, the caring, the talent, and the intelligence of those in charge. Don Forrister has exhibited these qualities in fashioning a program that, although undergirded by a utilitarian rationale, nevertheless results in the flourishing of that fundamental aesthetic purpose; a program which reveals that, while caution is certainly in order, such rationales no longer need give us pause.

The discovery of that truth has been, for me, both instructive and inspirational. Indeed, I will remember that discovery—as I will the artifacts of the pioneers of the Southern Highlands and those of their descendants, the students of Swain County High School—as, itself, a thing of general usefulness and of a simultaneously singular beauty.

Notes

1 Aristotle, "Politics, Book 8," in *The Basic Works of Aristotle,* edited by Richard McKeon (New York: Random House, 1941), 1308.

2 Quoted in *Handicrafts of the Southern Highlands,* by Allen H. Eaton (New York: Russell Sage Foundation, 1937), 4.

3 Jerome J. Hausman, "The Plastic Arts, History of Art and Design: Three Currents Toward Identifying Content for Art Education," in *Concepts in Art and Education: An Anthology of Current Issues,* edited by George Pappas (London: Macmillan, 1970), 14.

4 *Smoky Mountain Tourist News*, Bryson City, North Carolina, May 21, 1982, 8.

5 Ibid.

6 "County Development Information for Swain County," Center for Improving Mountain Living, Western Carolina University, Cullowhee, NC, August 1981, 4.

7 "Swain Jobless Rate Climbs," *Asheville Citizen,* Asheville, NC, April 1982, 2.

8 Donald Forrister and Gerald McKinney, "Art," Arts Program Booklet, Swain County High School, n.d., p. 2.

9 Ibid., 7, 11.

10 Quoted by Elliot W. Eisner and David W. Ecker, "Some Historical Developments in Art Education," in *Concepts in Art and Education, p.* 14.

11 Ibid.

12 Philip Cusick, *Inside High School: The Students' World* (New York: Holt, Rinehart and Winston, 1973), p. 153.

13 Forrister and McKinney, "Art," p. 1.

14 Susanne Langer, *Problems of Art* (New York: Scribner's, 1957).

15 Wilma Dykeman and Jim Stokely, *Highland Homeland: The People of the Great Smokies*, Division of Publications, National Park Service, U.S. Department of the Interior (Washington, D.C.: Government Printing Office, 1978), 107.

16 Stuart Macdonald, *The History and Philosophy of Art Education* (New York: American Elsevier Publishing Company, 1970), p. 188.

17 Maxine Greene, "Teaching for Aesthetic Experience," in *Toward an Aesthetic Education,* A Report of an Institute, sponsored by CEMREL, Inc., Music Educators National Conference (Washington, D.C.: 1970), 41.

18 Langer, *Problems of Art*, 32.

19   Edward Mattil, *Meaning in Crafts* (Englewood Cliffs, N.J.: Prentice-Hall, 1971),
      3.

20   Forrister and McKinney, "Art," 1.

21   See, for example, the following papers presented at the symposium "Resistance
      in Education," at the American Educational Research Association Annual Meet-
      ing, New York, 1982: Jean Anyon, "Aspects of Resistance by Working Class and
      Affluent Fifth Grade Girls to Traditional Sex-Role Demands"; Nancy King,
      "Children's Play as a Form of Resistance to the Classroom"; Janet Miller, "Resis-
      tance of Women Academics to Curricular and Administrative Discrimination in
      Higher Education."

22   Jacques Barzun, "Art and Educational Inflation," in *Art in Basic Education,*
      Occasional Paper 25, Council for Basic Education, Washington, D.C., 9.

23   Harry S. Broudy, "Some Duties of an Educational Aesthetics," *Educational Theory*
      (November 1951), 192.

24   Elliot W. Eisner, *Cognition and Curriculum: A Basis for Deciding What to
      Teach* (New York: Longman, 1982), 76–77.

Chapter 6

Educational Platforms, Teacher Selection, and School Reform: Issues Emanating from a Biographical Case Study (1987)

Can schools of education hope to transform schooling from the "bottom up," through the preparation of novice teachers who will serve as effective change agents in their professional settings? Some teacher educators remain committed to the development of programs that promote critical and/or progressivist ideals in their students and the talents for realizing the ideals in the students' future workplaces (Beyer, 1984; Goodman, 1986).[1] But others have suggested that formal university training is nearly impotent in the light of more profound earlier biographical influences (Lortie, 1975; Petty and Hogben, 1980). This essay attempts to portray the nature of those influences in the life history of one exceptional pre-professional. It then suggests how progressivist teacher educators might make wiser use of resources by augmenting programmatic efforts with admissions processes that recognize these biographical influences.

Pedagogical Platforms and the Biographical Method

The subject for this study is one of several teacher candidates in the United States and Great Britain who is involved in the use of pre-professional biographies. Over a period of eleven months I engaged this future-teacher in extensive, in-depth interviews of an informal conversational type (Patton, 1980). My purpose was to elicit information concerning biographical influences on the development and early employment of her *pedagogical platform.* This notion is adapted from Walker's (1971) conception of the platform of a curricular designer. For Walker,

> the word *platform* is meant to suggest both a political platform and something to stand on. The platform includes an idea of what is and a vision of what ought to be, and these guide [the curriculum developer or teacher] in determining what he or she should do to realize his or her vision. (p. 52)

Of course a pedagogical platform may not be as fixed, enduring, or "solid" as the metaphor implies. Indeed, it may sometimes consist of a fragile nexus of vague attitudes, tentative beliefs, complex and even contradictory dispositions, and ideologies perhaps only semi-congealed. Still, in any belief and value complex, there are certain notions (or planks, if you will) more deeply entrenched and elaborately buttressed.

Ascertaining how these central planks are acquired and implemented suggests the use of a biographical approach to educational research (Berk, 1980; Butt, Raymond, McCue, and Yamagushi, 1986). In this approach the educational inquirer offers life stories to others who are also seeking more fully to understand that part of their world related to education and formal schooling. The present study, however, attempts to examine the information provided by the biographical subject in a critical light. The biographer strives for a *reciprocity of perspectives* (Schutz, 1962), first attempting to understand life events from the viewpoint of the subject who has lived them, and then analyzing and assessing them from a different, perhaps broader, perspective. Or as the hermeneuticist Hirsch (1976) might have put it, the subjective *meaning* of a life text is given *significance* as it is viewed in relation to a larger context, that is, another "mind," a wider subject matter, an alien system of values, and so on. In the present biography the life text of a teacher-to-be is considered in regard to what it might suggest about the admission of a candidate or candidates to the teaching profession.

Shelley Citoyen: A Critical Biography[2]

Each of the three sections of this biographical portrait depicts a crucial phase in the growth and initial use of Shelley Citoyen's progressivist educational perspective. First was a period of imprinting during her *apprenticeship-of-observation* (Lortie, 1975). Specifically, we focus on the elementary grades six and seven, during which Shelley experienced two widely divergent educational ideologies-in-practice. The next phase entailed an ideological maturation during which she gradually articulated a rationale to support her pedagogical perspective. Finally, there was the formulation of a strategy for acquiring the competence needed to maintain a reasonable degree of congruency between ideals and actions in a potentially antagonistic workplace.

Phase I: Foresdale versus Hillside Park

In May, 1986, Shelley Citoyen became certified to teach in Middlestate Valley, a region where the hills of the upper South collapse into the American Midwest. In 1986 while educational rhetoricians were demanding a return to traditional values and teaching methods, schools in Middlestate were, almost uniformly, already paragons of traditionalism. But Shelley's story begins in an earlier time—the late 1960s, a time of radicals and reformists extolling the virtues of alternatives to American public schooling. Popular educational writers such as Featherstone (1967), Gross and Gross (1970), and Silberman (1970) successfully publicized the source of their inspiration, the British Primary School, and legions of educators trekked to England for firsthand glimpses (Ravitch, 1983). Even Middlestate Valley was not untouched by the trend. In the following decade some schools were constructed without inside walls: a few educational ideologues found allies in economy-minded school boards who realized the potential savings in a dearth of partitions. Most Middlestate teachers, however, were reluctant, and perhaps (lacking formal reeducation) unable radically to alter pedagogical habits. Still, one school in the region did significantly modify its educational orientation. I call it Foresdale School.

In 1976 Shelley Citoyen was an eleven-year-old sixth grader at this school. She remembers her time there vividly as one of intellectual excitement sandwiched between relentlessly dreary school terms. Shelley lived her year at Foresdale within Sycamore Pod, comprised of fourth, fifth, and other sixth graders. The pod was a huge room divided into quadrants each the size of a normal classroom in which "both the kids and the teachers were constantly moving." The desks were in clusters, never in rows, and each of the four teachers who served the pods, "floating" from one section to another, had a desk in the center of the room. There was, recalls Shelley, a tremendous physical freedom that she had never thought possible in school, including travel to the lavatory and library without special permission. But the freedom at Foresdale transcended the merely physical; there was also some freedom of content choice. Each of the teachers would offer to students a unit on a topic of personal interest. In science, for example, it might have been geology, astronomy, or ecology. Thus, says Shelley, the curriculum catered somewhat to both teacher and student interests and enhanced the enthusiasm of each. Indeed, she contends that her present enthusiasm for astronomy is traceable to this formative period.

The flexibility within this nongraded and modular structure was also helpful in math. Shelley had left fifth grade at Venice Elementary deficient in math skills. She believes that a traditional classroom structure could not have afforded her the ease of "remediation" found at Foresdale. Whole group, teacher-dominated instruction probably would have exacerbated the problem. Instead Shelley was placed with students of various ages but similar ability levels, and then progressed nicely.

The project approach was also prominent in Sycamore Pod, from individual library research of past Triple Crown winners, to a group-oriented science project that Shelley cites as typical of the activities at Foresdale. Several students had heard discussions in the media about the effects of talking to plants. Intrigued, they decided to develop their own experiment:

> [The] three of us bought a whole bunch of begonias . . . and set up all these isolated conditions which had their grounding in scientific method. We wanted to see if it was just the carbon dioxide that a person exhaled on a plant while talking directly to some plants, and then we tape recorded our voice and played it to others. We had to keep logs of what times they were spoken to or played the tape. And then we had a Christmas break and the plants died. [But this didn't matter because] the point was not "do plants grow better if you talk to them?" but "can you develop a scientific experiment, can you go through that process?" (Interview, September 23, 1985)

But for seventh grade Shelley attended Hillside Park Junior High School, and the personal imagery darkens. The memories are of bloated lectures on content long since faded; of scouring the pages of authoritative textbooks for answers to questions supplied, rather incestuously, on adjacent pages; of a correspondingly harsh and barren physical setting marked by the clanking of raindrops on the corrugated tin army-barracks roof, cold and dusty tile floors, and the imperious demands made by the hard seat of the single desk that owned her, six periods a day, for the entire school year; of the hours of "heavy science fiction, 'Star Trek' especially," now serving as a retreat from the tedium and boredom (relieved only intermittently by her project-oriented history teacher) that school had become. And finally, she remembers the sensation of persevering, of "holding my breath," with hopes for a future—high school? college?—that might more closely resemble the recent past.

It was apparently this seventh-grade experience that soured Shelley on certain facets of traditional American schooling. Having once thrived in an emancipatory educational setting, Shelley found confinement to a more restrictive milieu difficult. Asked to cite the fundamental difference between the two experiences, she observes that at Foresdale, through the freedom to work on personally meaningful projects, the students were "learning to be ourselves . . . and learning that was important." She contends (in rather vague humanistic terms) that from that time on "I saw myself as an individual, and the way that carries over into my [present perspective] is that I want kids to know that . . . from the moment they walk into school . . . they're people with a lot of worth, and deserve to have someone look at them as individuals." It is clear to Shelley, therefore, that initial proclivities toward one kind of progressivist educational ideology were formed prior to any formal teacher training. But while these early experiences would prove crucial, the precise features of Shelley's educational platform would remain hazy and unnamed for several years—at least until Shelley had retraced the steps of the Silbermans and Featherstones.

Phase II: A Summer in England

Shelley had toyed with the notion of becoming a teacher since sixth grade, but it was a failure of imagination that delayed her application for entrance into the teacher education program at Middlestate Valley University until the end of her sophomore year. The educational innovations of the early seventies, rare in that valley even then, had been crushed in the "back-to-basics" onslaught of the eighties. Even Foresdale had bowed to the inevitability of "self-contained" classrooms. And even as she drifted into the program, Shelley had difficulty envisioning herself exciting and empowering future students in the manner of her sixth-grade experiences. Her hopes, she reports, were vague and dim. After admittance, however, her experiences in her professional education courses were sufficiently positive to keep those hopes alive. There were occasional introductions to practices that she labels "non-traditional." Her overall regard for her professional education coursework was therefore fairly high. Missing, however, was a theoretical framework for placing individual impressions of particular practices into a grand design. Her MVU coursework was light on philosophical foundations and educational theory, on developing a theoretical basis for discriminating between potentially transformative and merely reproductive classroom activities. Nor could a legitimation of progressivist methodology emerge through field observations and prac-

tice. Indeed, in the MVU program, beginning students (usually sophomores) observed in generally traditional public school classrooms. Junior
practicum students taught in "borrowed" classrooms of a similar nature,
guided by well-intentioned university supervisors (several progressively
oriented) but without interacting with a "master" elementary teacher whose
daily practice consistently operationalized a progressivist platform.

Fortunately, Shelley found a summer course entitled "Language and
Learning in the British Schools." Taught in England by the director of the
MVU Writing Center, the course combined visits to primary schools with
theoretical considerations of integrated approaches to the language arts.
It was during this experience that she began to articulate for herself several formerly latent platform planks, three of which were experientially
rooted in her year at Foresdale.

First were the *holistic teaching strategies*. She learned to value approaches that integrated the skills of reading and composition with important and meaningful subject matter. This whole language approach
reminded Shelley of the fulfillment experienced in many Foresdale activities—for example, reading about ancient Greece while writing and then
performing a classical style play. These thrilling memories bounced up
against the recollections of the reductionist methods of excessive drill and
rote memorization that plagued her other childhood classroom experiences.

Second was a view of the *student as an active agent* in the learning
process. In England Shelley observed students, with teachers' guidance,
creating rich classroom environments decorated with their own artwork,
books, and other artifacts. This student-centered, problem-solving approach allowed—indeed, demanded—the kind of freedom that Shelley had
reveled in at Foresdale. It correspondingly de-emphasized a teacher-im-
posed structure on classroom activities. Now Shelley realized retrospec-
tively that a different form of structure had been present in her sixth-grade
learning experience. While "it's true that you were not tied to doing this,
this, and this as in a regular classroom," a structure based on student
purposes emerged from within the activities.

Thirdly, Shelley formulated a *humanistic strategy of classroom management*. The need for threats and punishments evaporated in the light
of English schoolchildren's self-propelled involvement in individual and
group-oriented activities. In these schools, as at Foresdale, external management of student comportment was rarely necessary.

These three central planks in Shelley's platform—integrated approaches
to the curriculum, a student-centered classroom, and a humanistic orien-

tation toward pupil control—have rested at the core of at least one branch of the progressivist agenda since the time of the American Progressivist Education movement of the 1920s. Indeed the last two were among the seven guiding principles of the Progressivist Education Association (Cremin, 1961), and the project-method approach implied in the first two are traceable back to the writings of Dewey (1902) and Kilpatrick (1918). But in the 1980s, progressivist practices were not easily found in the heart of America, Dewey's native land. Moreover, the philosophical perspectives of student teachers and their classroom behavior do not always match (Tabachnick, Popkewitz, and Zeichner, 1979-80). Nevertheless, in the third phase of her pre-professional biography Shelley would develop a strategy for implementing her progressivist platform in this ideologically contrary educational setting.

Phase III: Student-Teaching at Roosevelt

How would Shelley defend, practice, and promote her progressivist platform in such a time and place? Her reasons for choosing Roosevelt Elementary School as a student teaching site reveal a strategy. She could have lessened the challenge; Waters School, although a greater distance from her home, had an integrated curriculum that more closely resembled the British progressivist ideal than did Roosevelt. Or she could have increased her burden by teaching within a traditional setting under the guidance of a stranger to her own preferred brand of pedagogy. Instead she chose a third option. She persuaded Nancy Foyer, whom she met on her trip to England, to accept her first student teacher in over twenty years of teaching. Shelley's decision was based on a belief that Roosevelt offered a unique learning opportunity. While apprenticing under an experienced and ideologically compatible "master teacher," she might simultaneously acquire some important survival strategies—the knowledge and skills helpful in maintaining her pedagogical integrity as the single "informal" style teacher within a traditional school. These coping strategies seemed particularly crucial for an insecure and vulnerable first-year teacher.

> I can't expect that in the next few months the whole world is gonna change and that all these schools are gonna teach the way I want to teach, and so I thought [that] going in as a first-year teacher it would be a better idea to know how to get around things and to institute [these progressive style practices] within my own single classroom. (Interview, August 23, 1985)

By mid-November in her student teaching term Shelley had identified three elements in a plan for achieving a relative degree of integrity in platform implementation. The first involved the assurance of an administrative support base. Shelley recognized the futility of subterfuge or mendacity during a job interview. She was prepared to declare her unwillingness to work under a school principal who would disallow the execution of the essential planks in her platform.

Secondly, Shelley began to consider means of creative resistance to extra-institutional mandates. Take, for example, the reading series required by the district. Shelley learned from Nancy the possibility of treating the mandated textbook as simply another resource "chapter book," with a "bunch of different stories in it." Only the specified lists of spelling words from the book, demanded by the school board, had to be taught.

Finally, might not other teachers feel threatened by her unusual ideas? Shelley planned to assume a defensive posture as a beginning teacher, never flaunting her beliefs: "It's not my personality and I don't think it gets results." She was learning to politely ignore comments such as, "Don't the kids get distracted by all of the clutter [art-work hanging in the classroom] so that they won't want to work?"

But after initially implementing her platform in a self-contained classroom, she imagined growing bolder in future years, armed with test scores that validated her approach. Obvious successes should gain converts, and mere autonomy protection might evolve into a more aggressive transformation of the structure of the school itself, by collaborating with like-minded teachers in forming pods similar to those at Foresdale. Upon such an occasion would a circle close, as Shelley brings to her own sixth-grade students the kind of emancipatory experiences that had, one generation earlier, changed the course of her life.

Issues of Teacher Selection

What might Shelley's biography suggest to those educational progressivists among us charged with admitting candidates to our teacher education program? Two issues arise. These concern the attributes desirable in potential teachers and a selection process that honors these characteristics.

Desirable Qualities in Candidates
Upon her full admittance into the MVU teacher education program, Shelley seemed to possess two qualities necessary for a reform-minded elementary school teacher. These were a strong motivation for transforming the structure of schooling into a more progressivist model, and a basic prac-

tical intelligence needed for professional competence in the school environment.

A Reformist Platform. Upon entrance into the MVU program, Shelley already possessed a professional direction, which had been clarified within the first two phases of a professional socialization process. Indeed, the contrasts between the early images of educational alternatives were apparently so stark, and the preference for a progressivist approach so profound, that they had remained intact over years. Shelley's experiences thus served to illustrate the depth of intensity possible in the imprinting process—an intensity that under other conditions might favor a more traditional educational world view. Given this possibility, why are educational platforms (and the competence needed to implement them) so rarely considered prior to admission to teacher education programs? Is this omission not particularly unfortunate for SCDEs at which progressive educational reform is a defined mission? Are such institutions failing to locate—perhaps even denying entrance to—a highly motivated and capable group of people in favor of others with less reform-minded outlooks? Why do such institutions often ignore the importance of pre-program platforms in favor of a vague hope that educational belief and value systems can be easily reshaped in the crucible of progressively oriented coursework and clinical/field-based experiences?

Clearly, even the most careful screening process that granted access to the most purely motivated and ideologically mature candidates would not diminish the importance of preservice programs that promote critical reflection about educational platforms and the development of a progressivist practical philosophy. Shelley's own life history suggests the importance of functioning models in the validation of an educational platform. Still, strong empirical evidence (Hanson and Herrington, 1976; Lortie, 1975; Petty and Hogben, 1980; Stephens, 1967) encourages skepticism about the potential of teacher education programs for altering biographically rooted ideological proclivities. Even Goodman (1986) reports that "not all preservice teachers valued the focus" (p. 196) of his progressivist-oriented course aimed at teaching students a critical approach to social studies curriculum design. One apparent social adaptionist (in the minority) deemed the coursework "worthless," because "as teachers, we are going to be expected to teach out of a textbook," so why "waste time developing units?" (p. 196). This quotation rings true to those teacher educators among us who perennially confront the demands of students for instruction in the basic coping skills of classroom management and didactic instruction.

Environmental Competence. A second characteristic desirable in a future educational change agent was Shelley's liberal belief in the reformability of the structure of schooling and a willingness to work for incremental change from within that structure as long as there is an adequate degree of autonomy in her own classroom. Moreover, Shelley seemed well-equipped intellectually and socially to learn how to effect such changes. Indeed, after final admittance to the teacher education program, Shelley set about honing her talents for transforming essential features of her professional environment in accordance with her platform. There were strong early indications that Shelley possessed a capacity for growth in what Newmann (1975) has labeled (in another context) *environmental competence.* By this term Newmann meant more than merely coping with one's situation in life, but rather the ability of a citizen—Citoyen was a citizen-teacher—as a moral agent effectively to exert influence on public affairs while exercising her practical philosophy. Shelley, as noted, understood the importance of diplomacy and caution in implementing her platform. She realized, moreover, that environmental competence as a progressivist readier would presume competence in teaching. Recall, in particular, her hopes for legitimizing her approach by providing a persuasive example of competent progressivist-style teaching through evidence of desirable student learning outcomes.

A Progressivist Admissions Process

How might a teacher education faculty committed to a critical/ progressivist reform of schools employ in its admissions process the criteria of a reform-minded personal platform and a capacity for growth in professional competence? One of several possible models consists of two components: self-selection by candidates, and a screening by a panel of teacher educators.

Those contemplating entrance into a particular teacher education program should be equipped to make intelligent judgments about its suitability for their purposes. This requires information—about the nature of the program, and about themselves. Students, therefore, would enroll in a pre-admission introductory course wherein the reformist intentions of the program are carefully and forthrightly articulated. This course would expose students to progressivist rationale and critical educational theory. If possible, students would confront examples of reformist theory-in-practice directly in the field. Additionally, university teachers might consider the development and use of case studies of progressively oriented student teachers and practicum students in situations demanding environmental competence. These studies would describe actual situations confronted by students in later program courses (see below). Upon completion of the first course, students should be cognizant of (a) the progressivist orientation of the program, (b) its degree of compatibility with their own educational belief and value systems, and (c) the strength of their own commitment to transforming a part of the world of schooling. Those compatible with the vision offered would then apply for provisional program admission. Those looking for an adaptionist program aimed primarily toward the technical pedagogical competencies needed to adjust to the "real world" of schools—one oriented toward what Katz (1974) has called *excessive realism*—should carefully reconsider.

Self-selection would be augmented by a counseling process. Students would share important biographical information with a committee of teacher educators. Journals required in the introductory course would describe personal reactions to course experiences and insights into course content. These writings would serve as a source for questions to be asked in biographical interviews designed to elicit information similar to that related by Shelley in this study. If a degree of harmony between professional goals and program orientation is apparent to the committee, provisional admittance would be recommended.

Full admittance would be considered only after at least one additional course, primarily field-based but taken prior to student teaching. In this course students would begin to exercise their progressivist practical philosophies. On the university campus students would plan a three- or four-week unit in conjunction with observations in a primary or secondary school classroom where the unit would later be taught. Ideally, students would be placed in practicum situations similar to Shelley's student teaching site, that is, with progressivist cooperating teachers; in predominantly traditional schools. When these are scarce, students may be placed with cooperating teachers who are less progressivist minded, but not entirely unsympathetic to nontraditional teaching approaches. Placements in homogeneously progressivist schools should be avoided, for this course should aim not only at enhancement of progressivist teaching ability but also at the development of abilities to resist non-progressivist institutional constraints creatively.

To this end, students would be introduced on campus to a variety of progressivist/critical approaches to planning (Kohl, 1976; Egan, 1985; Rachelson and Copeland, 1983) and teaching, but would need to negotiate with cooperating teachers or administrators concerning the ideological complexion of their actual practice (Goodman, 1986). On-campus seminars would also consider potential strategies for implementing progressivist platforms with the limitations of the practicum settings at hand.

Meanwhile student assessment by university supervisors would focus on the degree of environmental competence demonstrated in (a) student bargaining with teachers and administrators and (b) the quality of student planning and its execution. The latter means, of course, success in progressivist-style teaching. Specific criteria for judging such success would vary from institution to institution, but some might reflect Shelley's platform planks mentioned earlier: good use of holistic teaching strategies, ability to motivate students using intrinsic motivation, and student-centeredness in activities. High priority for program admittance would be accorded to students whose environmental competence in each of these areas enabled them to bring progressivist ideals to bear upon classroom realities.

The Hazards of Traditional Criteria

For progressivists this admissions proposal holds advantages over the traditional use of GPAs and test scores. First, such scores seem less likely to predict a potential for professional competence than direct, context-bound observations of transactions within a teaching environment. Secondly, standardized test scores are ideologically loaded in a non-progressivist direction. For critical theorists they are features of a capitalistic system of schooling with sorting functions that serve to perpetuate class inequalities (Bowles, 1972). Neo-progressivist reformers and open-school advocates have (Shelley's willingness to compromise on this point notwithstanding) long bridled at the dehumanizing and trivial nature of the "objective test" (Barth, 1972; Gardner, 1967; Morrison, 1966; Silberman, 1970). Nevertheless, if early "success" in a system subtly promotes an ideological bias toward a reproduction of the conditions associated with those "positive" experiences, then those whose academic "superiority" has been certified by test scores and high GPAs might tend to regard with special affection the educational premises that support these forms of evaluation. In using these measures as admission criteria, progressivist teacher educators may be, despite enlightened programmatic efforts, unwittingly serving to perpetuate the educational status quo. Therefore, the alternative process outlined here is not unusual and/or unfair in establishing an ideological litmus test for gaining entrance to the profession. As professional gatekeepers, we must be alert to the fact that no admissions criterion can be ideologically neutral in a field so permeated by values as is education.

Conclusion

Is it possible to overestimate the challenge of reforming education in institutions so resistant to change as the American public schools? I think not. Can, then, progressivist/critical teacher educators afford to continue to ignore the apparent impact of early acquaintances with schooling on the professional platforms of candidates for their programs? We have done so in the past. I suggest that we now concern ourselves with more than attempts to educate or reeducate future teachers towards a progressivist/critical pedagogy. We must also recruit and select environmentally competent teachers-to-be whose life experiences have brought them to a passionate yearning for a critical transformation of schooling in America.

Notes

1 Theoretical distinctions are sometimes made between the perspectives of progressivist philosophers such as John Dewey and modern critical theorists such as Michael Apple. However, Goodman (1986) notes that in practice a "more eclectic stance which allows one to draw ideas associated with a general orientation rather than a singular point of view" (p. 182) is possible. The progressivist/critical orientation employed here is generally social reconstructionist in nature, as opposed to the social adaptionist. Adaptionists favor teacher education programs that emphasize classroom coping skills and traditional methods that tend to reproduce the educational status quo.

2 Names of the protagonist and places and institutions associated with her are fictitious.

References

Barth, R. S. (1972). *Open education and the American school.* New York: Schocken.

Berk, L. (1980). Education in lives: Biographic narrative in the study of educational outcomes. *Journal of Curriculum Theorizing, 2* (2), 88–154.

Beyer, L. E. (1984). Field experience, ideology, and the development of critical reflectivity. *Journal of Teacher Education, 35* (3), 36–41.

Bowles, S. (1972). Getting nowhere: Programmed class stagnation. *Society, 9* (8), 1–7.

Butt, R., Raymond, D., McCue, G., & Yamagushi, L. (1986). *Individual and collective interpretations of teacher biographies.* Paper presented at the annual meeting of the American Educational Research Association, San Francisco.

Cremin, L. (1961). *The transformation of the school: Progressivism in American education.* New York: Knopf.

Dewey, J. (1902). *How we think.* New York: D.C. Heath.

Egan, K. (1985). Teaching as storytelling: a non-mechanistic approach to planning reaching. *Journal of Curriculum Studies, 17* (4), 397–406.

Featherstone, J. (1967). Schools for children. *New Republic, 15* (7), 17–21.

Gardner, D. E. (1967). *Does progressive primary education work?* London: Association for Childhood Education International.

Goodman, J. (1986). Teaching preservice teachers a critical approach to curriculum design: A descriptive account. *Curriculum Inquiry, 16* (2), 179–201.

Gross, B., & Gross, R. (1970). A little bit of chaos. *Saturday Review, 53* (21), 77–85.

Hanson, D., & Herrington, M. (1976). *From college to classroom: The probationary year.* London: Routledge & Kegan Paul.

Hirsch, E. D., Jr. (1976). *The aims of interpretation.* Chicago: University of Chicago Press.

Katz, L. (1974). Issues and problems in teacher education. In B. Spodek (Ed.), *Teacher education: Of the teacher, by the teacher, for the child* (pp. 1–19). Washington, DC: National Association for the Education of Young Children.

Kilpatrick, W. H. (1918). The project method. *Teachers College Record, 19* (4).

Kohl, H. (1976). *On teaching.* New York: Schocken.

Lortie, D. C. (1975). *School teacher: A sociological study.* Chicago: University of Chicago Press.

Morrison, P. (1966). Tensions of purpose. *ESI Quarterly Report,* (Issue No. 2). Newton, MA: Education Development Center.

Newmann, E. (1975). *Education for citizen action.* Berkeley, CA: McCutchan.

Patton, M. Q. (1980). *Qualitative evaluation methods.* Beverly Hills, CA: Sage.

Petty, M., & Hogben, D. (1980). Explorations of semantic space with beginnlng teachers: A study of socialization into teaching. *British Journal of Teacher Education, 6,* 51–61.

Rachelson, S., & Copeland, G. (1983). Webbing: A humanistic approach to curriculum development. *Journal of Humanistic Education, 7,* 6–8.

Ravitch, D. (1983). *The troubled crusade: American education 1945–1980.* New York: Basic Books.

Schutz, A. (1962). *The collected papers, Volume I.* The Hague: M. Nijhof.

Silberman, C. E. (1970). *Crisis in the classroom: The remaking of American education.* New York: Random House.

Stephens, J. (1967). *The processes of schooling.* New York: Holt, Rinehart, Winston.

Tabachnick, B., Popkewitz., T, & Zeichner, K. (1979–80). Teacher education and the professional perspectives of student teachers. *Interchange, 10,* 12–19.

Walker, D. E. (1971). A naturalistic model for curriculum development. *School Review, 80* (1), 51–69.

Chapter 7

Breaking the Mold: The New American Student as Strong Poet (1993)

Because the Bush administration was destined to leave us with few substantial accomplishments in the field of education, educational historians and theorists are reduced to studying its rhetoric. "Breaking the mold" was one of the catch phrases its members fondled repeatedly as they promoted the reformation of schools without additional funding. The phrase can be traced back to the unveiling in April 1991 of President Bush's America 2000 plan for educational reform. The initiative included a strategy for enlisting communities in "devising their own plans to break the mold and create their own one-of-a-kind high-performance schools" (U.S. Department of Education 1991, p. 15). A New American Schools Development Corporation (NASDC, whose Board of Directors consisted primarily of the chief executive officers of many of the largest American corporations) was established to award contracts to "high-risk, break-the-mold" design teams whose efforts at school invention are "outcome-oriented" and "establish benchmark measures" for assessing their progress toward attaining "world class standards" (New American Schools Development Corporation 1991, pp. 50, 51). In the first round of NASDC competition, 11 projects were selected out of 686 proposals (see Mecklenburger, 1992, for a description of the winners).

Now, it is hard to argue with the premise that the rigid, omnipresent, traditional organizational structure of the American public schools needs rethinking. But in this essay I want to suggest that the New American School proponents did not fully understand the nature of the "mold" they professed a desire to "break." Indeed, I will contend that the kind of school designs sought by NASDC (perhaps unintentionally) ensure the continuation of pedagogical practices aimed at molding American students into a standardized product.

It is hardly news to note that the American school is patterned after the industrial workplace. The literature detailing the analogies between various organizational features of school and factory (or, in an updated if still business-based image, the corporate workplace; see Berliner, 1991) is abundant, comprehensive, and sophisticated. I can only scratch its familiar surface here. But we know that in the school-as-factory-or-business metaphor teachers are portrayed either as workers on an assembly line or as executive managers, and are charged with the efficient mass production of a finished product. This product, the school graduate, should match as closely as possible a prototype usually designed by planners removed from the school or factory plant. Features of the prototypical school graduate are implicit in curriculum requirements and standardized instruments of assessment mandated from outside the institution of the school. These standardized measuring instruments (usually pencil-and-paper tests) also serve to gauge the effectiveness of the workers/teachers in molding the raw materials/students into products that match the prototype.

The Bush educational plan was careful to maintain this emphasis on product standards. Even as it solicited divergent organizational designs, the NASDC Request for Proposals stipulated that "designers set high performance objectives (standards)" for students in the school programs. While the document did at one point suggest that "assessments may be based upon existing or new tests or may use quite different forms of assessments" (p. 51), NASDC's explicit hope was nevertheless for school designs that enabled all students to acquire the common skills and knowledge necessary to be "effective members of American society" (p. 51). What did this mean? Specific formulations of the desired outcomes were being developed:

> A number of efforts are now underway to develop national consensus standards in the core subject areas. . . . a number of professional organizations have sought to establish frameworks that might be the basis for national standards. (p. 48)

NASDC's focus on common skills and knowledge and their insistence upon an end product molded to meet predetermined, measurable standards honors a critical element of the traditional school-as-factory model. The school designs they solicited preserved the tendency for pedagogy to be driven by high performance on standardized assessment tools, even if those tools were "quite different ones." Their New American Schools were destined to be cast within the Old American School mold.

In my view the Bush/NASDC obsession with standardized educational outcomes served to weaken incentives for the fundamental educational quest, namely, the development of each student's uniqueness as an individual human being. Indeed, now that the term "breaking the mold" has been withdrawn from the national political landscape, I intend to play with it in the relative privacy of this journal article. Moving beyond facile rhetoric, I want to explore its meaning for designing schools that are sensitive to certain *aesthetic* impulses that lead to good educational practice. The public relations specialists who coined the phrase "break the mold" would surely greet with dull surprise my observation that it does indeed suggest an aesthetic basis for the educational enterprise. Nevertheless, here is the line of argument I take in this essay:

Standardized schools with standardized visions of success tend to produce standardized human beings. New American Schools that truly broke the mold would proffer no such standardized vision of success. Instead, they would offer students and teachers the autonomy of the artist who works toward an end that is emergent, and not yet in view. They would be concerned less with molding students in accordance with "national consensus standards" than with providing the growth of unique, powerful, integrated identities. They would support a process wherein teachers assist each student in the weaving (and reweaving) of profoundly educational, aesthetic experiences into a narrative, or story, of a unique and responsible *self*.[1]

The Aesthetics of Everyday Life

The possibility of discovering aesthetic qualities within a commonplace activity such as education would have once seemed absurd. Until fairly recently art was equated by the prevailing formalist critics with "high art," a process wherein an elite corps of aesthetes created beautiful, self-contained objects to be admired from a distance. Back then, art had little to do with experiences outside of the theatre or museum. It was John Dewey who led the rescue of art from its imprisonment in an "aesthetic remove" distanced from the affairs of everyday life. Especially in *Art as Experience,* Dewey (1934/1958) articulated a vision of art as coterminous with being in the world, as "prefigured," he said, "within the very process of living" (p. 24). For Dewey, aesthetic experiences are not confined to the contemplation of high art, but arise from within the interaction of a human organism with her surroundings. Dewey denied the dichotomy between "ethereal things" and "live creatures," and pointed instead to bio-

logical commonplaces that reach to the roots of the aesthetic in experience. Aesthetic qualities such as balance, harmony, rhythm, tension, and
form are to be found in the most elemental activities of the human animal. Wrote Dewey (1934/1958):

> Life itself consists of phases in which the organism falls out of step with the
> march of surrounding things and then recovers unison with it. . . . [But] if life
> continues, and if in continuing it expands, there is an overcoming of factors of
> opposition and conflict; there is a transformation of them into differentiated as-
> pects of a higher powered and more significant life. The marvel of organic, of
> vital, adaptation through expansion . . . actually takes place. Here in germ are
> balance and harmony attained through rhythm. Equilibrium comes about not
> mechanically and inertly, but out of, and because of, tension. . . . Form is arrived
> at whenever a stable, even though moving, equilibrium is reached. (p. 14).

Consider Dewey's example of how a unified structure is achieved within
one particular event of ordinary life, the experience of a storm aboard a
ship at sea. As passengers on a boat we anticipate a storm's wrath with
apprehension, and prepare for it both physically and psychologically. Our
whole selves react with tension to the storm's presence as it reaches a
crescendo; we adapt to the conditions it imposes, and move to "recover
the unison" with the environment that has been momentarily disrupted.
With the passing of the storm we feel tired, but satisfied that we have
overcome and survived the disequilibrium. We have had what Dewey would
call an *aesthetic experience*, an event that emerges out of, but distinguishes itself from, the inchoate and formless general stream of experience. It is an experience that is, as Dewey (1934/1958, p. 39) put it,
"rounded out . . . because it possesses internal integration and fulfillment
reached through ordered and organized movement."

Dewey was the primary tiller of the soil in which latter-day theorists
would plant their ideas about the place of one particular kind of art form
in the lives of ordinary human beings. This art form was the story, and
the prominence of episodes of storytelling in the course of living has
lately been reaffirmed within the field of literary criticism. And locally,
within the field of education, discourse about stories has become a virtual
cottage industry, thanks to the work of educationists such as F. Michael
Connelly, D. Jean Clandinin, William Pinar, Kieran Egan, Jan Nespor,
Madeleine Grumet, Ivor Goodson, Nel Noddings, and many others. Most
helpful for our purposes here have been those authors (educationists and
others) who have expanded the meaning of storytelling beyond the
commonsensical notion of story-as-episodic-event, to include the process
wherein an individual makes sense of the totality of her singular life. What

follows is one version of the thesis that the entire life of a human being can be construed as a kind of story, and the argument that personal identity is achieved through a kind of storytelling.

Life Story as Self Construction

Human beings do not view time as a series of isolated moments, each one disconnected from the other. Instead we tend to make sense of the moments of our lives by placing them within the context of all previous instants of awareness. Similarly, each action taken by ourselves or by those with whom we come into contact is not an independent happening. Rather, it is what may be called a *life assertion*, dependent upon accumulated memories of prior activity for its meaning, and contributing to the meaning against which future actions will be regarded. In order to make sense of each action, we must *interpret* it in a manner which assumes the presence of an agent, a unified being who is performing the action in the light of a previous history of activities and because of a personal involvement with the world. This process of interpretation is therefore a *hermeneutical* activity. It is not unlike the act of interpreting each new passage in a story text in light of what has already been encountered within and outside of the text. As Polkinghorne (1988) explained:

> Narrative is the form of hermeneutic expression in which human action is understood and made meaningful. Action itself is the living narrative expression of a personal and social life . . . and its organization manifests the narrative organization of human experience. Acting is like writing a story, and the understanding of action is like arriving at the interpretation of the story. (pp. 142–43)

The narrative that is written as a human being constructs herself through action is the story of the self. What do I mean by *self?* The pragmatist philosopher George Herbert Mead (1934) described personal identity as neither a material substance nor a spiritual soul, but as an *idea* that is constructed by a conscious human organism. This idea is developed and modified over the course of a lifetime, as the person interacts with the various features in her physical and (especially) her social environments. Moving forward onto the environment in accordance with personal needs and desires, the actor finds that people and things within it will respond in various and complex ways. The person will construct a coherent self-identity out of these interactions by interpreting them, and integrating them into a historical unity, an idea of "who-I-am-as-one-who-acts-in-relation-to-others-in-the-world." Therefore, "I" am not some sort of existential isolate who arrives at a static self-identity, but rather my identity is an *achievement*, gained and modified through a process of moving upon and experiencing a world in which others are simultaneously achieving their own identities.

A story is composed out of various events in one's experience. These scattered events are gathered together into a meaningful whole that reveals their relationship to each other. For Ricoeur (1981) this relationship is the *plot* of a story; indeed, the plot makes events into a story. The plot of each story that we tell about ourselves, like the plot of all stories, possesses the kind of unified structure or internal integration ascribed to one of Dewey's "aesthetic experiences." Indeed, found within a life narrative are Aristotle's famous three stages of a story: a beginning, a middle, and an end. As Polkinghorne puts it: "The self is that temporal order of human existence whose story begins with birth, has as its middle the episodes of a lifespan, and ends with death" (1988, p. 152).

Of course the author of a self-narrative is writing a story that is not yet finished. She is not merely fashioning together particles of information confronted in the past about who her "self" *must be*. Since she is still alive, her text is, to some extent, open-ended; she is still constructing who it is that she wants to become. Are some people more successful than others in constructing their selves? The question of what constitutes quality in living is the question of just what is a good life. There are of course no correct answers chiseled somewhere in granite. But this question is central to the value-saturated enterprise of education. I suggest that it must be confronted if we are to clarify our aspirations for our students, to comport ourselves well as educators, and to design the kinds of school environments that support students in the process of constructing their selves. I will, therefore, offer a necessarily abbreviated, unapologetically personal, but hopefully persuasive, response.

Schools as Communities of Strong Poets and Storytellers

In responding to the question of what is a good life, I draw sustenance from the work of philosophers Charles Taylor, Richard Rorty, Harold Bloom, and Friedrich Nietzsche. Each has considered the question of which life stories are most worthwhile. All agree that, no matter how similar the contingencies of their lives, no two individuals can ever compose identical life stories. The complexity and richness of the transactions between each singular agent and her environment negates the possibility of duplicate human identities. Of course, a person may still more or less plot out her life story in passive accordance with someone else's notion of who she should be. Nietzsche saw this unfortunate tendency as the result of a lack of self-understanding and identification, of insufficient knowledge of oneself as a unique individual. This was the failure, explained Rorty (1989),

> to see oneself as [truly] idiosyncratic, [but rather as] a specimen reiterating a type, a copy or replica of something that already has been identified. [It was]. . . for Nietzsche, to fail as a human being . . . to accept someone else's description of oneself, to execute a previously prepared program, to write at most, elegant variations on previously written poems. (p. 28)

For Nietzsche, a good life is like a good original story or poem insofar as disparate thoughts and actions are consciously shaped into a narrative unity, an aesthetic form. The admirable person is able to provide this coherence, not out of weakness and imitation, but through will and automony. Such a person has what Nietzsche called *style* (cited in Polkinghorne, 1988, p. 154). And style, it seems to me, is the primary attribute of what the philosopher Harold Bloom (1973) called a *strong poet*. A strong poet is someone who refuses to accept as useful the descriptions of her life written by others. Instead, the strong poet is a strong storyteller, continuously revising her life story in the light of her own experience and imagination. The strong poet constantly redescribes her past interactions with the world around her, constantly reinvents her *self*, so that she may act in the future with ever greater integrity and coherence. The strong poet plots her life story toward her own emergent ends and purposes.

These ends and purposes are not developed in solitary confinement. A strong poet is not a disengaged esthete who composes her life story in a kind of existential isolation. Instead, she is necessarily a social being and a moral agent, a responsible citizen of a shared community. The growth of the self, as Charles Taylor (1991) has emphasized, must take place within "a moral space, a space in which questions arise about what is good or bad, what is worth doing and what is not, what has meaning and importance . . . and what is trivial and secondary" (p. 28).

But this moral space defines a realm that is simultaneously personal and social. In this view, personal integrity and responsibility toward others need not be conflicting dimensions of one's being. To the contrary, an individual contributes to communal growth whenever she successfully redefines herself; and conversely, an individual is fulfilled only through enlarging the community's sense of what is possible. Of course, as Dewey

(1944/1966) reminded us, the renewal of self and community is best facilitated within a *democratic* culture. The more equitable the distribution of power in a society, the more likely that strong poetry will be shared and composed.

Now, what if the New American Schools adopted the notion of the strong poet as the ideal student? What if the New American Pedagogue aspired to being present with students who continuously integrate the content of the disciplines (the content of life) into a coherent and personally relevant world view? What if educators aspired to empowering students within a democratic school setting to act with a sense of personal integrity, responsibility, and autonomy? In other words, as designers of the educational environment, and as pedagogues, what educational moves could we make toward realizing our hopes for students who have style? I will suggest two such moves, two phases of the educational act, each of which must, to be successful, exhibit certain aesthetic attributes. In the first of these the teacher "reads" that portion of the life text of the student that has already been composed and lived. In the second the teacher invites the student into the having of aesthetic experiences that offer wondrous options for the future. I will describe the second move first.

Pedagogy, Storytelling, and the Aesthetics of Self-Creation

As I have suggested, each student is, like each of the rest of us, a person in the midst of writing and rewriting her own life story. Each is comparable to an artist in the middle of a creative process that moves toward a resolution that is not preformulated, but gradually emergent. The end of the story of each living human being is yet to be encountered. The uncertainty that accompanies this process of self-creation is, therefore, as the literary critic Frank Kermode (1967) noted, the source of much human anxiety. This is the anxiety of the artist, the poet, the storyteller, the schoolchild, who has dared to begin a work of art (here, her life) without a clear sense of how to bring it to meaningful closure. With the knowledge that death will someday end the writing, we are eager for clues as to how to compose the next chapter of our personal histories. We may each wish to create the best possible self, the strongest, most autonomous, most expansive, most "rounded out" of possible life stories, but to imagine the final version of that story is usually beyond our capabilities. It would mean imagining how we choose to describe ourselves at the story's ending, at the time of our own death. Those of us—children, adolescents, and adults—who are continuously *redescribing* ourselves stand in awe of the gap between our present life position and where we might someday finally rest. We struggle to transform at once so much dissonance and tension into the kind of stability, consonance, and equilibrium that marks an aesthetic closure to a life. Given the formidable nature of the task, how can we bring ourselves to act at all? Kermode (1967) described how we all rely upon the stories of others for guidance in writing our own.

Reading a story to its conclusion can provide for us what Kermode (1967) called "the sense of an ending." Some stories are *authoritative*: they tell us in a grand and dogmatic fashion how to live our lives; they identify purportedly correct ends and purposes for living. These include eschatological religious stories of apocalyptic prophecy. But others are much more tentative and localized, more heuristic, provocative, and ambivalent in their suggestions about the meanings of specific, familiar incidents and events. These are the daily anecdotes we tell to ourselves and to each other, as well as stories of fictional and nonfictional literature. Each of these stories partakes, more or less, of Aristotle's aesthetic form. At the outset the reader recognizes a familiar dilemma and is pulled into an intriguing situation. The plot thickens until the central crisis is resolved. And the story ends, while the reader lives on. This closure is, of course, like the rest of the story, ersatz, virtual, not actually lived. Still, it can offer the reader a degree of comfort. The release that is felt upon reaching a story's end resembles the tired satisfaction experienced at the end of Dewey's storm at sea. Like all aesthetic experiences the story is structurally analogous to a fully lived life, and the formal "rounding out" of a story can soothe us in its intimations of endings satisfactorily achieved. It suggests that advancing toward a meaningful closure to the story of one's self is not an insurmountable task.

Literary tales can also be comforting in another sense. As readers of the text we are enticed into participating vicariously in a storied world. Literary critics have called this fashioned world (whether "true" or imaginary) the *virtual* world of the story. Entering this realm enables us to distance ourselves from our daily lives, making it easier to apprehend everyday realities that are easily taken for granted. (A philosopher of science once remarked that water was not discovered by a fish.) So stories can provide a means for the student/reader to observe life from a safe distance, as a voyeur who can ponder the suitability of the strategies of the story's characters as options for action in her own life.

Sometimes, however, the reader/voyeur feels challenged to act in a disturbing new way. Good stories can pose a threat to our equilibrium in their capacity gently to persuade us of the wisdom of choosing a life course dramatically different from the one down which we have been traveling. Stories, I mean, can be, as Foucault (1977) put it, *transgressive*. Some transgressive stories challenge the reader to critique the taken-for-granted values that have paved the path of her life, or call into question her attitudes about prevailing social practices. Others go further: they transgress against *what is* by evoking *what can be*: they adumbrate more enticing visions of, suggest more expansive options for, the future. But all worthwhile stories are, said Foucault, "gestures fraught with risks" insofar as they challenge absolutes considered sacred and beyond interrogation. Good stories can thus offer radical alternatives for thinking about the world and acting within it. They can provoke redescriptions of the lives of students who read them, stimulate novel readings of their life texts, offer new interpretations of self-identity, even alter life directions. They can promote greater degrees of integrity and coherence in a student's autobiography. They can promote the creation of more integrated and responsible selves. They can embolden students to become more powerful poets.

The (Truly) New American Educator will understand the value of placing powerful stories within the proximity of her students. But she will not only entice students into the virtual realms of stories portrayed in books, on stage, on television. She will also encourage them to write stories about events in their own lives and in the lives of others. Reading, hearing, and discussing the stories of other people is one kind of activity that promotes the reconsideration of one's own life story. *Composing* stories is an additional mode of sense-making that offers practice for the imposing task of living. And finally, students need to be invited into constructing the kind of aesthetic experiences that are not actual stories, but that do possess the contours of the story form. Students need to be encouraged to engage in what I will call *aesthetic projects*. I will give some examples of what I mean.

In my vision of New American Schools the aesthetic impulse will be played out in ordinary classroom projects. These are individual and class projects that stand apart from the formless anesthetic experiences in the lives of schoolchildren. Aesthetic projects can be fashioned almost anywhere: in the science corner, in the library, in the nearby community, in the studio. They occur as students embark on the production of a class play, on an investigation of the political history of their town, on the creation of an essay about a facet of the natural world. But they all share the common shape of an unfolding story. Like a drama they begin with a sense of a dilemma, the discovery of a problem that the student seizes as her own. She may become curious about the ethics of training circus animals, or entranced by a film about insects, or be moved to compose a poem about the birth of a baby sister, or pulled into the world of a character in a story about the battle of Gettysburg. Her engagement springs not from an extrinsic source such as a desire for praise or a fear of not doing well on a test, but from within the activity itself. The commitment involves the exploration of an unfamiliar path. The student is intrigued by the uncharted nature of the territory, fascinated by what she will uncover about the world to incorporate into her own life story.

The pedagogue plays an important role in making these engagements more likely to occur. It is true that sometimes the student, unguided, may stumble upon aesthetic and educational activities that transgress against the familiar by casting it in a new light. But I believe (with Dewey) that it is the role of the educator consciously to select and arrange features of the classroom environment so as to increase the likelihood of such encounters. She can suggest stories for students to read or promote ideas for group projects like those mentioned above. But she must never coerce students into particular activities, or attempt to force upon them "correct" descriptions of their selves and their world. She will not move to write her own chapter in (let alone prescribe an ending for) what must be her students' *auto*biographies. She must contribute to the elegance and the strength of each self-narrative indirectly, without insisting upon her own style.

But in order to succeed at this pedagogical move of bringing to the classroom environment that which is likely to engage the student in stories and projects, the teacher must make a prior move. She must first come to know (in common parlance) "where the student is coming from." And this requires that she engage in the aesthetic project of empathic understanding.

Empathy as an Aesthetic Project

Empathic understanding is the ability to participate vicariously in a form of life as manifested in a particular pattern of actions. Its practice rests on certain ordinary if implicit assumptions, namely, that the "object" of attention is a fellow human being; that there is a shared reality in which all of us participate because we are persons; that we can and do in fact imagine ourselves in other situations. Empathic understanding is more than mere intuition or feeling because what is striven for is not purely emotional identification but rather an *idea* of a piece of subjective life.

The process of acquiring this idea is, like the process of writing and understanding one's own life text, a process of interpreting *meaning*. And what is meaning? I like the definition of the German philosopher Wilhelm Dilthey. Meaning, Dilthey said, is "the vital unity maintained in the structural relations and processes in an individual life." And empathic understanding is "apprehending a portion of [that] mental life or history . . . seeing all its parts and aspects in relation to the vital movement of the whole" (Hodges, 1944, p. 159).

Coming to know the self of a student, therefore, is as much an interpretive process as is coming to know one's own self. Knowing a student requires interpretation of the relationship between particular actions and the structured life-process of that child. In practical terms this involves reading those actions against the backdrop of what is already known about that student's perspective, and the cultural milieu in which the actions occur. In turn, encountering a new "life expression" can deepen the teacher's appreciation of the student's *funded biography* (Dewey, 1963), the integral mass of her accumulated life experiences. A dialectic is evident in this process of reconstructing the life story of the child: a particular action gains sensibility through its participation in a larger pattern, and the teacher's awareness of the student's life story is enriched as it accommodates this new piece of evidence. Empathic understanding grows as each new component contributes to and derives meaning from an emerging whole.

Success in leading students out from where they are requires that the teacher offer stories or suggest other aesthetic projects that first speak to students in their present locations. Teachers must be ever mindful of the experiential and developmental readiness of students for an activity. Awareness of a story or project's capacity for engaging a student is acquired through acquaintance with the student's life-story-thus-far. The projects described above can indeed speak directly to some students, pulling them into the problems that are posed. Working toward a resolution of these dilemmas can be empowering. The learning event may become the kind of aesthetic experience that Dewey (1963) called *educational*: a growth-inducing experience that grants the capacity for having even richer experiences in the future. By the culmination of a story or storylike project a student may have discovered new options for interpreting the world and new possibilities for living. She may have gained greater control over her destiny. She may have redescribed her *self*. With the guidance of a wise and empathetic teacher, she may have written some mighty strong poetry.

Closure: Knowing Our Students as Poets and Storytellers

So the educator comes to understand empathically the lives of her students in order to arrange the environment intelligently toward the promotion of aesthetic experiences. But I can think of a second reason for the hermeneutical effort expended by the teacher in reading the text of the student's self. Empathic understanding performs another crucial function in the New American Education: it is the first step toward resolving the nagging issue of *student assessment.*

In the traditional American school, student progress is generally measured in accordance with the factory model's emphasis on external standards. In the (Truly) New American School evaluation methods based on conformity and sameness give way to strategies that honor the complexity and uniqueness of each student's life text. Assessment will entail the publication of chapters within student life-stories. The forms that this publication may take still have not been fully imagined. But I can foresee teachers weaving into biographical sketches evidence of their students' aesthetic experiences derived from sources that include anecdotal records of important classroom events, sample artifacts from student projects, and excerpts from student journals.

Whatever forms emerge, wise assessment of educational activity is critical for designing good new schools. For our evaluation strategies inevitably influence the shape of educational encounters and suggest to students the character of our educational values. If we desire New American Schools that truly break the mold then we must abandon our compulsion for prototypes, for having students converge toward predetermined, standardized end results, "world class" or otherwise. Instead, we must see education as a fundamentally aesthetic enterprise in which each New American Student is challenged to see her life as an ongoing project with no final end in view, a project comparable to the creation of a work of art. And we must indicate to the New American Pedagogue that we value her guidance of each student toward the continual revision of the poem of who that student, specifically, can be.

Note

1   In this essay the terms *story* and *narrative* are used synonymously.

References

Berliner, D. (1991). If the metaphor fits, why not wear it? The teacher as executive. *Theory into Practice, 32* (2), 85–93.

Bloom, H. (1973). *The anxiety of influence*. Oxford: Oxford University Press.

Dewey, J. (1958). *Art as experience*. New York: Capricorn Books. Original work published 1934.

Dewey, J. (1963). *Experience and education*. New York: Collier Books.

Dewey, J. (1966). *Democracy and education: An introduction to the philosophy of education*. New York: The Free Press.

Foucault, M. (1977). *Discipline and punish*. New York: Pantheon.

Hodges, H. A. (1944). *Wilhelm Dilthey: An introduction*. New York: Oxford University Press.

Kermode, F. (1967). *The sense of an ending: Studies in the theory of fiction*. London: Oxford University Press.

Mead, G. H. (1934). *Mind, self, and society*. Chicago: University of Chicago Press.

Mecklenburger, J. A. (1992). The braking of the "break-the-mold" express. *Phi Delta Kappan, 74* (4), 280–289.

New American Schools Development Corporation. (1991). *Designs for a new generation of American schools: Request for proposals.* New American Schools Development Corporation. Arlington, Virginia.

Polkinghorne, D. E. (1988). *Narrative knowing and the human sciences*. Albany, NY: State University of New York Press.

Ricoeur, P. (1981). *Hermeneutics and the human sciences: Essays on language, action, and interpretation*. (John B. Thompson, Trans.). Cambridge, U. K.: Cambridge University Press.

Rorty, R. (1989). *Contingency, irony, and solidarity*. Cambridge: Cambridge University Press.

Sizer, T. (1988). Editorial: Dailiness. *Educational Researcher, 17* (3), 5.

Taylor, C. (1991). *Sources of the self.* Cambridge: Harvard University Press.

United States Department of Education. (1991). *America 2000: An education strategy.* Washington, DC.

THE NEOPRAGMATISM OF RICHARD RORTY

In the late 1980s, as I was becoming better acquainted with the thinking of the neopragmatists, I was invited to a conference at Stanford on Qualitative Inquiry in Education. The paper presented at that conference is included here as Chapter 8. Although his work is cited only twice in the paper, the thinking of Richard Rorty greatly influenced its organization and theme. The contrasts between narrative and paradigmatic texts reflect Rorty's distinctions between two primary purposes of human inquiry, and the paper's theme honors his neopragmatist insistence that inquiry texts should be ethically, as well as practically, useful.

Neopragmatist epistemology dominates Chapter 9, published in 1992. It contains a critique of the valorization of subjectivity by some qualitative researchers who have, I argue, failed to understand the debilitating ramifications of maintaining a subjective/objective dualism when thinking about research texts, especially those that are fictional in character.

Chapter 8

Using the Narrative Text as an Occasion for Conspiracy (1990)

A Sunday morning should be the occasion for a sabbatical.[1] On most Sunday mornings, the closure of a cycle has been, once again, achieved, and preparations for the next one can be momentarily deferred. A Sunday morning, therefore, should never be needlessly disturbed. It is a time for congenial gatherings of family and friends, not a time for contentious challenges to comfortable beliefs. Or maybe you try, as I often do when I am home next to my stereo, to reserve your Sunday mornings for engaging in a musical kind of concelebration, for listening to the contrapuntal harmonies of a fugue. Alas, how I would have enjoyed leading you into one today!

Now, my assigned topic may seem, at first glance, suited for a Sunday, fit for the back of the book. A text of qualitative inquiry ready for use implies a previous resolution of nettlesome questions, including questions of epistemology and ethics, that might have arisen during its preparation. We might, therefore, be expected merely to imagine appropriate contexts for their application or consumption. We would thus confine our attention to the most obvious sense of *use*, the one in which the verb rubs elbows with the name of an implement. I use a handkerchief. You use a computer. The educational policy maker uses research findings. Subject uses object. This sense of *use* denotes the employment of the research text as a tool. It implies a text designed in accordance with one of two modes of thought (discussed in Bruner, 1987) that guide projects of social inquiry. This mode is the *paradigmatic* or *logico-scientific* (Bruner, 1987).

But I wonder about the appropriateness of this metaphor, educational-inquiry-text-as-tool. Fortunately, as a participant in other predicates, *use* acquires a second sense, one only marginally related to the first. How, for example, does one use an occasion? What does it mean to use time? In what sense is an opportunity used? Occasion, time, and opportunity are abstract nouns, not concrete persons, places, or things. Despite our impulse to reify, to think of occasion as if it were a physical object, the verb *to use* is now only nominally transitive. In the sentence "I use this occasion," the subject precedes a kind of objectless verbal unit. I, the subject, employ no thing. I, the subject, engage in an experience.

When used for *educational purposes,* a text of qualitative inquiry is, I propose, better viewed as an occasion than as a tool. It is, more precisely, an occasion for the reader to engage in the activities of textual re-creation and dismantling. These activities require a mode of thinking fundamentally different from the paradigmatic. Bruner (1987) calls it the *narrative* mode. The primary form of written narrative discourse—and therefore of qualitative texts about human experience—is literature.

This, in barest outline, is my thesis. It suggests a reordering of the totem pole of qualitative inquiry genres, a challenging of important premises of the educational research establishment. In my defense of it I must occasionally return across the borders to earlier topics in this conference and disturb the finality of Friday's and Saturday's agreements to disagree. It may appear rude to offer, on a Sunday morning, Bartok instead of Bach. So I devote the remainder of this paper to an earnest explanation of why it had to be done.

Using the Literary Text

How does a reader use a literary text? Two dimensions of the reading act demand our attention. In the first the reader constructs the reality of the text, a reality that resides neither in the literary work as object-in-the-world nor in a subjective "mind" of the reader, but within a continuous field of experience between the two. The text, that is, is given a place among the contents of consciousness. What occurs there is not, strictly speaking, a reader's response to the text. Although *reader response* names a school of theorists who have shifted the focus onto the literary experience and away from the "text itself," the term connotes to me a reader passively reacting to cues that emanate from the text. Instead, it is the reader who moves toward the text, exploring, while traversing, the landscape of meaning that Ricoeur (1976) calls the *sense* of the text.

When the text is perceived as literary, this sense is a formal reconstruction. Dewey (1934/1958) explains:

> For to perceive a beholder [of a work of art] must create his own experience. And his creation must include relations comparable to those which the original producer underwent. They are not the same in any literal sense. But with the perceiver, as with the artist, there must be an ordering of the elements of the whole that is in form, although not in details, the same as the process of organization the creator of the work consciously experienced. Without an act of recreation the object is not perceived as a work of art. (p. 54)

In this reordering, elements of experience are recast into a form that is analogous to but does not replicate an actual experience. A work of art, said Langer (1957), is a semblance, a composed apparition. In experiencing this semblance the reader lives vicariously in a virtual world, only temporarily bracketed off from the mundane, the nearby. What he experiences there is an idea of a piece of subjective life. In this reconstructive process, I mean, the self of the reader discovers an *otherness* (Poulet, 1986). Awareness arises of an alternate consciousness, a self behind the effect, a fellow being responsible for the virtual event now formally recreated. The reader hears the voice of another subject offering the fruits of her inquiry into the qualities of lived experience.

But there are two dimensions to this offering, dialectically intertwined within an aesthetic whole. These are the co-equal, mutually supportive constituents of the literary text: aesthetic form, which embodies a personal vision, and aesthetic content, or evidence of the seriousness of that vision. Danger arises when either establishes dominance over the other, disallowing the aesthetic tension that characterizes the dialectic in good art. In some texts the bully is form.

Pure form is pure fancy. It is imagination roaming untethered in a nether realm, a world where the self can reside in solipsistic harmony, undisturbed by thoughts of the other. The thoroughly formal text is self-contained, rigid, closed. It can merely be overheard by the worldly reader, for its elements speak only to one another within the beautiful universe they comprise. Some, like the formalist critics, see all literature thusly, fallaciously equating the entire event of using fiction with the construction of illusion. And illusion, as the formalist Northrop Frye (1967) puts it, is "fixed and definable, and reality is best understood as its negation" (p. 169). If the formalists were correct, then the exclusion of all fictional literature from the club of qualitative inquiry would be justified. Who, after all, seeks the advice of the schizophrenic, the lonely madman whose texts are so long on visions but so short on evidence? Of course, not only schizophrenics imagine impossible worlds. Some works of fiction (I refuse to call them literature) also offer escape into fantasy. For evidence, visit the Gothic novel section of your local bookstore. Or watch *Dallas* on a Friday evening, followed immediately by *Falcon Crest*. Bereft of credible evidence, such fiction is ill-equipped to inform the reader about "reality." It remains harmlessly self-contained, lounging forever within that fantastic realm we sometimes call the *aesthetic remove*. Using this kind of fictional text, the reader engages in a process of *psychical distancing* (Bullough, 1957). This is the occasion for romance, for contemplation free of impulses to action or thoughts of the practical.

Romantic visions are, interestingly, also the stuff of classical utopias. Hansot (1974) has noted the obsession with transcendent, atemporal form evident in most pre-Kantian utopian texts. The *Utopia* of Thomas More, the *Christianopolis* of Johann Valentin Andraea, and the *Republic* of Plato are self-contained entities, each static and nondevelopmental in its perfection. The notion of social change, of a more fully realized political arrangement, is rendered absurd in these ethereal worlds. Their imagery represents the desirable-but-*impossible*: it aims to show us ideology alienated from history.

To frustrate the totalitarian tendencies of sublime illusion, and otherworldly romance, and unalloyed subjectivity, and transcendent ideology, the reader must turn to truly literary texts. Since I want to highlight their qualifications as texts of social inquiry, I introduce the antithesis to aesthetic form. This is the historically undervalued dimension in art, aesthetic substance.

Not even poets, certainly not good ones, spin their imaginary webs from within a realm of pure fantasy. But novels and plays are often more obviously drenched in social realism. At least since Fielding, novelists have attended to specific characters in particular sociohistorical milieus, acutely observing the minutiae of human activity. "The basic talent of the novelist," Cook (1960) notes, "is to observe social behavior—the way a person furnishes his house or makes love or reacts to death or folds an envelope or constructs his sentences or plans his career" (p. 84). The writer of fiction fishes for this empirical evidence to be shaped into aesthetic content in the ongoing stream of everyday life. Although the autobiographical novel, which aims to transmute the essence of a lifestream into words, may best illustrate this point, all fiction is bathed in, or at least splashed by, personal experience. Roiphe (1988), for example, reminds us that Bernard Malamud's father owned a store, Chekhov was a doctor, Hemingway ran bulls, and Erica Jong was married to a psychoanalyst. Sometimes, however, the writer purposely diverts that lifestream into unfamiliar territory. She moves "into the field," intending to position herself effectively for a bestowal of meaning on a strange and distant land-scape. This was Dickens's strategy as, in preparation for writing *The Life and Adventures of Nicholas Nickleby* (1839/1950), he gained admittance to several notorious Yorkshire boarding schools by assuming the false identity of someone seeking a school for the son of a widowed friend (Wolfe, 1973). Occasionally, an author's fascination with the particulars in the research setting causes the line between reportage and literary fiction to become blurred. For example, which of the following literary works, each crafted upon intense investigative research, shall we label "novelistic"? Hersey's *Hiroshima* (1946)? Capote's *In Cold Blood* (1965)? Twain's *Innocents Abroad* (1869/1899)? Michener's *Texas* (1985)? Haley's *Roots* (1976)? Orwell's *Down and Out in Paris and London* (1933/1961)?

The history of literature is replete with examples of elaborate, if non-systematic, investigative efforts aimed at increasing the array of perceptions available to the author for arrangement into a plausible story. Upon that arrangement, however, the individual knowledge claims are transformed into what Ingarden (1968) has called *intentional sentence correlatives* (p. 32). These are component parts of the text, but as contributors to a fashioned totality their specific content is immediately qualified. Similarly, Pepper (1945) labels these pieces of aesthetically fashioned evidence *danda*, to distinguish them from nonfictional *data*. Both Ingarden and Pepper understand that to construe narrative meaning the reader must focus away from individual statements as claims of factuality and toward the insinuations in their interactions as correlatives. The particulars are arranged to foreshadow that which is to come: the central insights acquired within the whole experience of using the text.

Of course, in a good marriage of aesthetic form and substance, the whole of the story is, in turn, conditioned by the particulars that comprise it. For the reader of literature who demands edification and not merely good feelings, aesthetic content will provide the ballast that grounds the lofty formal text. Aesthetic content opens up the text to the multiplicities of experience, conditions it, plants it specifically in virtual space and time, and provides (in Ricoeur's term) a *reference* for the sense of the text.

This view of the function of aesthetic content offers an answer to Miller's (1976) rhetorical question, why is there criticism instead of silent admiration of the text? The reader uses aesthetic content to avoid entrapment in her own re-creation. In the literary text ambiguity displaces both propaganda and literalness, for multiple interpretations, even conflicting ones, become possible. The once seamless illusion is interrupted and disturbed, and associations alien to the sealed-off world of the text can be imagined. It is at that moment, with the text off its pedestal and in hand, that the reader finds his own voice as observer/critic. The dimension of textual usage antithetical to reconstruction is entered. The text can now be *dismantled*.

I might have said "deconstructed," but I shrink from the intimations of finality in that term now identified with the likes of deMan and Derrida. It is difficult to return to a text that has been mocked, derided, trashed. Some texts may indeed invite such a fate, but others offer a hope undeserving of such cynicism, and so return to them we must. Still, even these worthy texts must be opened to the continuous processes of reconstruction and dismantling (and reconstruction and dismantling . . .) that constitute their very existence. These two dimensions in the use of literary texts are at once antagonistic and mutually nurturing. Only in the tension emanating from the pull toward a closed meaning and the countervailing enticements of indeterminate significance is the relationship not merely sustained but enhanced, as described here by Iser (1980):

> The text provokes certain expectations which in turn we project onto the text in such a way that we reduce the polysemantic possibilities to a single interpretation in keeping with the expectations aroused, thus extracting an individual, configurative meaning. The polysemantic nature of the text and the illusion-making of the reader are opposed factors. If the illusion were complete, the polysemantic nature would vanish; if the polysemantic nature were all-powerful, the illusion would be totally destroyed. Both extremes are conceivable, but in the individual literary text we always find some form of balance between the two conflicting tendencies. The formation of illusion, therefore, can never be total, but it is this very incompleteness that in fact gives it its productive value. (pp. 59–60)

Iser sees a balancing operation as the reader oscillates between these poles. Ironically, the dynamism and buoyancy of the literary experience can be maintained only if this balance is never quite achieved. Instead, the balance is elusive, remaining always tantalizingly ahead but out of reach. The text engages the reader by continuously offering surprising, even shocking, revelations that confound literary clichés and formulae but that also avoid arbitrariness and implausibility.

This, then, is the readable text, inviting literature, the useful piece of social inquiry in narrative form. Its allure derives not merely from the elemental (or eidetic) nature of its dynamic form, which (as Langer, 1957, has noted) mimics the rhythms of human physiology, the ebb and flow of life itself. Nor does its attractiveness stem solely from a desire to experience vicariously a cycle completed. Of course each of us is, as Kermode

(1967) has suggested, "in the middest" (p. 7), in the middle of history, in the middle of life—in the process, that is, of authoring our own autobiographical text. And while we seek a meaningful orientation in the world, from our finite perspective the full meaning of events eludes us. We do hanker for release from the tension between the actual and the potential that pervades our lives. But it is not simply to feel an ersatz resolution to this tension that we commit the act of reading literature. The most useful literary texts offer more: They suggest, through their verbal imagery, plausible options for the future; that is, the configuration of images in a good story comprises a vision of what might be called a *concrete utopia* (Hansot, 1974).

Concrete utopic imagery differs in kind from the idealized imagery that haunts transcendent, classical utopias. The ethereal beauty of the latter, we recall, is privately contemplated from a psychic location safely distanced from the potentially corrupting presence of empirical phenomena. The aesthetic remains aloof from the everyday world. Concrete utopias, on the other hand, are located in that imaginary space where a seriously deficient here-and-now meets a desirable, but possible, future. Concrete utopias thrive on the tension between the goodness of their formal aspirations and the viscous contingencies of the formless mundane world. This kind of imagery serves, that is, as a social critique. Like the classical utopia, the concrete utopia defies the moral imperialism of the present by offering a sharp contrast for its inadequacies. But unlike the former, which "often locates the ideal future at too great a distance to be functional" (Goodwin and Taylor, 1982, p. 26), a concrete utopia proposes an accessible replacement. These utopian images are therefore provisional, for the critique itself is necessarily open to criticism and reconstruction.

Of course, a good story is sometimes cautionary. The reader may be distressed by the plight of the characters in the virtual world he has recreated. Then the imagery is anti-utopian, functioning much like negative space in a painting. In dismantling the textual illusion, the reader attempts to imagine its preferable reverse. That is how I use a pair of texts, a historical drama entitled *Another Country* (Mitchell, 1982) and a short story by John Updike (1959).

The play by Julian Mitchell is about dropping out of school and society. The protagonist, Guy Bennett, is based on Guy Burgess, an infamous British spy who defected to the Soviet Union in 1955. The script recounts certain key incidents in Bennett's youth in an upper-crust public school. Despite his awareness of his homosexual tendencies, Bennett is initially devoted to the acquisition of status within the rigidly hierarchical school system. He craves membership in the ruling student elite, called the "demigods." Bennett's ultimate aspirations are even grander, for "life is ladders. That's all. Prepper to here. First form to sixth. Second assistant junior Undersecretary to Ambassador in Paris" (p. 45). But Bennett's aspirations crumble when his liaison with a schoolmate for whom he cares deeply is revealed. Disillusioned and embittered, he ponders the apparent futility of further participation in a hypocritical way of life. Suddenly Bennett resembles what we nowadays awkwardly refer to as an "at-risk" student, a potential dropout. Ultimately he does indeed leave the school and the sociopolitical system that feeds and is fed by it. The last lines of the script suggest Bennett's embrace of a drastic alternative to that system. He finally succumbs to the Marxist ideology of his hetero-sexual friend, Tom Judd, and sets about living a life of revenge through total indiscretion.

Through re-creating the illusion of this text, I understand the alienation of one student trapped in an institution that demands loyalty to repressive features of the larger culture. I directly apprehend Bennett's desire to honor, instead, loyalty to his own authenticity as a human being. I feel his despair and anger that he would later assuage through a flight to another country and a vengeful act of treason. Now I carry this configuration of meanings I have re-created to my professional life outside of the text. I search out the undergrounds to which adolescents with stifled aspirations might nowadays retreat—places where they engage in risky business, whether seething in silence, or plotting strategies of resistance, or simply melting away. The adolescents in the Cincinnati area schools that I visit seem quite unprepared for conducting international espionage. But evidence of Bennett-like resentment abounds, from the flagrant vandalism of school property to the subtleties within a surly and insolent demeanor. When weariness overtakes defiance, the vanquished may simply regress to form, relinquishing all hopes of authoring their own life texts for the privacy of romantic daydreams, or the blank stare of the tube, or the abyss of chemical dependency, or even abandonment of life itself. My exploration of the geographies of these "other countries" helps to heighten my sensitivity to schooling conditions that may serve as breeding grounds for these acts of vengeance or resignation.

Using the second text requires less travel. I am not William Young, the protagonist in Updike's short story "A Sense of Shelter" (1959), but I admit to occasional jolts of self-recognition as I confront this character. Young is an academically capable but socially awkward adolescent who will *never* leave school. Fearful of life in the unfamiliar and uncertain realm outside, he resembles only the early Guy Bennett in his vow to remain sealed in and secure forever,

> high school merging into college, college into graduate school, graduate school into teaching as a college-section man, assistant, associate, full professor, professor of a dozen languages and a thousand books, a man brilliant in his forties, wise in his fifties, renowned in his sixties, revered in his seventies, and then retired, sitting in the study lined with acoustical books until the time came for the last transition from silence to silence, and would die, like Tennyson, with a copy of *Cymbeline* beside him on a moon-drenched bed. (pp. 73–74)

The use of Updike's text can sensitize the reader to the presence of the school shut-in, the student for whom school offers easy passage through safe if narrow corridors that emancipate by providing direction but that simultaneously limit possibilities. Who among us, and our students, are the William Youngs, the human hothouse plants who thrive only in the rarefied atmosphere of the classroom? "A Sense of Shelter" points out qualities of school life that tend to reinforce the isolation of at least a certain type of student from the larger world.

Like *Another Country,* this text reorganizes my experiences of familiar commonplaces by challenging a tired, habitual response to them, offering a strange new way of perceiving and interpreting their significance. Now more "wide-awake" (Greene, 1977), I attempt to imagine a landscape of learning that offers the reverse of the dismal landscapes recreated in this pair of texts: a concrete utopia where personal growth is affirmed rather than stifled or narrowly channeled. And then, having listened (as Barthes, 1975, would say) to this "something else" (p. 24), I reenter, in each case, the world of the text to find that its configuration of meanings, now set against the backdrop of these newfound references, is itself enhanced. Upon my return, the voice of the other in the text grows more articulate, its insinuations about the shortcomings of the world-at-hand more obvious and persuasive. Suddenly my act of reading is achieving its end: I am using the text as an occasion for conspiracy.

I propose that the will to interpret a narrative text can arise from a desire for conspiracy. I do not mean conspiracy in the obvious, shallow, political sense. Nor do I acknowledge connotations of evil or treachery as inherent in an act of conspiracy. Quite the contrary, conspiracy can be a profoundly ethical and moral undertaking. "Conspiracy: combination or union of persons for a single purpose or end" (*Webster's New Collegiate Dictionary*). From the Latin, "*con* plus *spirare*, to breathe together," or better, from the Old French, "*conspirer*, a learned borrowing" (*World*

Book Dictionary). A conspiracy, thus, is a conversation about the relationship between present and future worlds. The reader, a historically situated self, learns from the re-created Others in the text to see features of a social reality that may have gone previously unnoticed. And if the reader, although cautious and wary, ultimately resonates with the interior vision of the text and is persuaded of its usefulness, he borrows it for his own. There is a "breathing together," a sharing of ideas and ideals for the purposes of an improved reality. This conspiracy is a plot against inadequate present conditions in favor of an emancipatory social arrangement in the future.

In a useful act of narrative reading, the conspiratorial discourse is pregnant with images of a proximate future. These are utopian visions, but never hapless ones immaculately conceived through mere wishful thinking. The visions are substantial, concrete in their attentiveness to current conditions. The most useful accurately diagnose social maladies and suggest potential cures. They are offsprings of a potent union of the virtuous and the feasible.

I suggest that such images can contribute to an educator's professional platform, the web of personally held beliefs and values that, like a good novel, recognize these established realities of the common order even while calling them into question.[2] This platform is provisional in that it must undergo continuous critical reexamination. Educators, as professionals, engage in an ongoing process of reconstructing what they hold to be the educationally good, true, and beautiful. Still, educational decision-making is contingent upon this professional platform, no matter how fragile and tentative its nature. We carry it with us as we enter into political deliberations with others in our professional communities. A professional platform provides the space from which we launch the educational projects that aim to change what is into what ought to be.

Using the Paradigmatic Text

Good narrative texts, therefore, offer an occasion to conspire about, and so make visible, new worlds that are both desirable and possible. A paradigmatic text, on the other hand, possesses the characteristics of what Illich (1973) would call an *industrial tool* (p. 33). Flowing out of the familiar creation-diffusion-dissemination pipeline, these texts are commodities designed upon utilization to produce systematically "knowledge" and "decisions." As social devices these texts are deliberately shaped to achieve this end. Their elements of design are selected to fulfill paradigmatic purposes. Polanyi (1962, 1964, 1966) has been especially helpful in illuminating the subjective elements of the scientific research process. Choice points pervade that process—in the selection and conceptualization of the research question, in the preference for particular methods and strategies for securing information, in the opting for a propositional form of language to represent that information, in the selection of a linear format for disclosure (Allender, 1986).

The text-as-tool, it seems, is "something fashioned," which is coincidentally, as Geertz (1973) reminds us, the original meaning of the word *fiction.* In a basic sense, therefore, *all* texts, including paradigmatic ones, are fictional. Of course, the manner of fashioning, or *modes of fiction,* favored by the author will vary greatly in accordance with purpose. A novelist with a narrative purpose will select different modes of fiction from, say, the emic-oriented anthropologist who aims to fashion a "correct" actor-oriented interpretation. As Geertz (1973) notes:

> In the former case, the actors are represented as not having existed and the events as not having happened, while in the latter they are represented as actual, or having been so. This is a difference of no mean importance . . . but the importance does not lie in the fact that [one] story was created while [the other] was only noted. The conditions of their creation, and the point of it (to say nothing of the manner and the quality) differ. But the one is as much a fiction—a "making"— as the other. (pp. 15–16)

The modes of fiction closest to the paradigmatic ideal disallow the aesthetic structuring of details that promotes the re-creation of an illusory world. They also bar (as do the antithetical modes of fashioning preferred by romantic novelists) the presence of aesthetic substance and the attendant ambiguity of meaning. Banished are what Iser (1980) calls "gaps . . . the unwritten part [of the text] . . . elements of indeterminacy [without which] we should not be able to use our imagination" (p. 58). The text-as-tool is not meant to be dismantled and reconstructed. Its modes of fiction call for a seamless, denotative, linear discourse that rearranges the relationship among complex phenomena into propositional form. This promotes the logical deduction of suitable contexts for the application of the tool.

The text-as-tool does not prize metaphorical aptness; it offers technical precision. It is not designed to surprise the reader-as-user. Its modes of fashioning are not selected to challenge the common order. As an object of craft rather than art, a tool is fashioned for use within that order, tacitly bestowing legitimacy upon it. Illich (1973) notes that industrial tools do not give the user much "opportunity to enrich the [social] environment with the fruits of his or her [personal] vision" (p. 21). As I use a tool, my images of the desirable should conform to the technical possibilities offered by its design. I become implicated in a taken-for-granted notion of the ideal. The text-as-tool is designed to mask any sense of values beyond the apparent value inherent in its utilization. No human agent, the text implies, guided its production; no utopian visions attend its utilization. This text offers one verbal version of reality, meant to be taken literally, taken for the only world that can be represented, the real one.

So the modes of fiction used to fashion the text-as-tool ironically deny its fictional status. They are selected for their effectiveness in misrepresenting a fashioned reality as objective, impersonal, and formless. Take the design element of language. We have all heard the detached, passionless textual voice that strives toward the impossible language "which the universe uses to explain itself to itself" (Rorty, 1982, p. 130). A closer monitoring reveals not the homogeneous hum of universal language but a bewildering cacophony of idioms. These are the various tongues of the research communities or (borrowing Toulmin's, 1953, term) the *participant languages* (p. 13) of those who work in specialized fields. Each has been developed to further a paradigmatic purpose. One may even stand in contradistinction to another. The grammar and vocabulary of the Freudian text may, for example, compete with that of the Skinnerian text to channel the vision of the reader in accordance with the preferred interpretive framework. Each tool, moreover, is infatuated with the possibility of its own use. Or as Buchmann (1985) has written:

> Using one's resources is taken so readily to be a good thing because value and utility are equated. One's tools should not lie idle: Where knowledge is valued for its instrumental qualities the charge to use it is almost implied. (p. 156)

Accompanying these imperious demands for attention and use is advertisement for a kind of safety in a correct, if theoretically framed, interpretation of how things really are. The use of a text-as-a-tool implies deliverance from a dread first sensed by Heidegger as pervading Western philosophical tradition: the awful anxiety that "the manifold possibilities offered by discursive thought will play us false, will make us 'lose contact' with the real" (Rorty, 1982, p. 130). Feeling anxious about the responsibilities inherent in personal judgment, the user of the paradigmatic text may succumb to this false offer of security in the technically correct, the conventionally valid. Thus anesthetized, he avoids the difficult assessment of the relative worth of visions that lie beyond the mere utility of the text.

Texts fashioned to provide knowledge within a particular theoretical framework may, therefore, be readily welcomed and eagerly consumed by a researcher already initiated into that paradigm. His purpose and vision are, after all, in accord with the paradigmatic mandate: to accumulate "objective" knowledge and to use it for prediction and control. He is "a truth-seeker . . . who deems himself to be faced with a problem which has one right answer. His business is . . . to converge upon . . . the truth-to-be-found" (Shackle, 1966, p. 767). But how to explain the widespread research aliteracy, the reluctance of educational practitioners to use the paradigmatic text? Perhaps these tools are too narrow, too specialized for the educational lay reader whose purposes and visions and decision-making process must transcend paradigmatic boundaries. If only education were not a profession. If only educating were synonymous with instructing or training, then educators might find the apparently nonproblematic technologies of paradigmatic texts more useful. But the languages of these texts conceal too much. The visions they offer are too restricted for engaging in an enterprise such as education, whose value-saturated subject matter must inevitably roam the broad expanses of life. The educator is more like the "poet-architect-adventurer [who] sees before him a landscape inexhaustibly rich in suggestions and materials for making things, for making works of literature or art or technology, for making policies and history itself" (Shackle, 1966, p. 767). Educators, in this sense, are not truth-seekers. They are *truth-makers* who engage in originative acts, creating the social worlds in which they will live (Noblit, 1984).

Truth-makers, I suggest, relate more readily to texts composed in forms of language that eschew the parochial dialects of paradigmatic texts, for example, the vernacular language of characters in the modern drama or the robustly evocative language of the novel. Barthes (1975) reminds us of the seductive quality of narrative texts so fashioned. The hopeful reader will, in Barthes's playful phrase, "cruise" the literary text seeking a pleasurable occasion. He desires, I believe, the opportunity to re-create a virtual world that stands against, and comments upon, the qualities of life-at-hand. Anticipation of a climax in the interplay between the actual and the potential, between aesthetic form and content, impels the reader to remain engaged in the textual act. This anticipation, not a compulsion to know and utilize a literal version of the truth, explains the allure of a good story.

Because the narrative will be riddled with gaps in meaning, fraught with ambiguity, the educator-reader must expect to face the anxieties inherent in the use of personal judgment. But because she understands the nature of the educational enterprise, she will not choose to work at it with implements fashioned for narrow utilitarian purposes. She will not surrender a rigorous consideration of goals and visions for the anarchy of values implied in the facile application of any tool at hand. Instead, the educator will seek out texts that are occasions for a critical re-examination, for a dismantling and reconstruction, of her professional platform. She will then stand ready to take responsibility for the educational decisions that platform inspires and supports.

Conspiratorial Texts and the Education of Educators

I am optimistic about the future of educational inquiry, for its recent history reveals a steady recovery of the human voice. Only decades ago virtually all educational researchers were quantitatively oriented social scientists praying in silence to what Langer (1957) has called the "idols of the laboratory." The high priests Campbell and Stanley offered holy communion in strict accordance with paradigmatic canons, and *every day was Sunday*. Who could have imagined the heresies about to be uttered?

Educational ethnographers, members of one of the earliest sects of qualitative educational inquirers, would never stray too far from the fold. Most have remained afflicted by what Finn (1988) recently called *status envy* (p. 5), strongly desiring for their own work the respect accorded the confident knowledge claims of the so-called hard sciences. Oblivious to the inevitably ideological nature of all methodology, they still seek to fix their texts under a halo of literal truth. But even qualitative research classics, such as *Life in Classrooms* (Jackson, 1968) and *The Complexities of an Urban Classroom* (Smith and Geoffrey, 1968), exhibit a curious mixture of narrative and paradigmatic design features. And in more recent works, such as *Schooling as a Ritual Performance* (McLaren, 1986), the language of disclosure swings back and forth from dense theoretical analysis to storytelling that approaches the grace and evocative force of literature. Listen to the voice of Peter McLaren in the final paragraph of that text, an excerpt from one of his remarkably eloquent and illuminating field notes. It captures the texture of life outside of a Portuguese middle school in Toronto:

> Wednesday, 28 June
> The school stands empty. The doors are bolted and the grounds are bare. Yet nearby the sidewalks are alive with people. With brisk strides, they make their way from the subway exits and disappear down the narrow streets. Several girls from the Hairdressing School, resplendent in their stained white smocks and

overly rouged faces, order coffees and cigarettes at the donut shop. Rust-splotched cars with metallic impressions of Senhor Santo Cristo dangling from the mirrors wind their way through the growing traffic. In the distance the procession of Mary, Queen of Angels, solemnly wends its way to the Iglesa Santa Cruz, led by an out-of-tune brass band. The statue of Our Lady is reverently held aloft on the shoulders of stocky men in oversized gray suits. At the far end of the procession the madman begins to howl, then stumbles and falls to the ground. And all around the pilgrims, children cry and tires screech and sirens wail. And church bells sound the mass. (p. 256)

Ethnography remains the dominant form of qualitative educational inquiry, but during the last decade we have been introduced to a new generation of approaches to storytelling about lived experiences, including phenomenological writing, biography and autobiography, and educational criticism. In the best examples of these genres the reader is greeted by a voice that conveys, more strongly and consistently than in most other qualitative research, a sense of personal authorship. Still, some of the compunctions of a literal mode of rhetoric linger. For example, in my own efforts at educational criticism, I have felt a tension between my pledge to refer adequately to qualities located within the research setting and the enticements of novelistic modes of fiction. Genre-related constraints against composite characters and invented dialogue have unduly restricted the process of truth-making. They have prevented the fashioning of phenomena-at-hand into a story of even greater power and usefulness.[3] The text would be no less empirical (based, that is, upon experience) and, at least in Geertz's sense, no more fictional, but who (I admit to fretting about this) would bless it?

So this present paper temporarily serves as testimony to my resolve for making truths about educational research, and I suggest that future truths include these: that editors of prominent journals of educational inquiry will publish the most accomplished pieces of literary fiction with educational themes; that reading a doctoral dissertation will mean entering a virtual world that offers a fresh perspective on the reader's own *Lebenswelt*; that, therefore, graduate research classes . . . well, you imagine the desirabilities!

What kind of utopian vision is this? It is dismissable as idle daydream only by ignoring the history of the last quarter-century. More and more, qualitative educational inquirers are finding their own voices, and soon the most resolute among us may follow the lead of anthropologists such as Bowen (1964) and Bandelier (1898) who chose to novelize their texts. Meanwhile, educators and educators of educators need not sit idly by waiting for the millennium, the time when the literary works of a reformed research establishment pour out of the pipeline. A pool of useful novels and short stories about life in schools already exists.[4] Moreover, literary texts that speak to broader concerns can also contribute to the education of professional educators. Literature has only one theme, Eudora Welty notes: human life. The reading list for Professor James March's "Issues in Leadership" course at Stanford has included Cervantes's *Don Quixote*, Shakespeare's *Othello*, Shaw's *Saint Joan*, Tolstoy's *War and Peace*, Ibsen's *The Wild Duck,* and Stoppard's *The Real Thing* (Kurovsky, 1986). Robert Jennings of the State University of New York at Buffalo has used Wouk's *Caine Mutiny* to examine the problem of the organizational man and radical change, and Ibsen's *A Doll's House* on the clash between societal and personal values (Williams and Willower, 1983).

Students in my own curriculum courses read not only texts by Mitchell and Updike but ethnographic works by, among others, Rist (1970) and Anyon (1980), as well as educational criticisms I have written (1983, 1987). 1 encourage the use of these texts, not as tools, but as occasions for conspiracy. Together we attempt to lift the veils of objectivity to see the face of an author making choices about method, language, plot. We seek evidence of visions of educational significance that have inspired and guided the fashioning process. We strain to hear the personal voice that research conventions may have tended to muffle. "What is the author's story?" we ask. "Who are the characters? What is the nature of their plight? How is the central dilemma (as our dilemma) to be resolved?" Since we will not be making decisions affecting the lives of these characters, we re-create them as illusory inhabitants of virtual worlds. We attempt to use even the non-novelistic texts as if they were pieces of novelistic fiction.

Of course, this attempt increases in difficulty as paradigmatic modes dominate the fashioning of the text. Thin description and systematic methods are features that are generally debilitating to the process of sharing useful stories. But while the narrative character of the autobiography, or the critique, or the novel may recommend these genres in principle, each text, regardless of genre, must be judged according to its individual merits. A text fashioned ethnographically may offer a less than ideal mixture of paradigmatic and narrative features but may be preferable to a novelistic short story that is poorly researched, unimaginatively plotted, and uninspiringly written. Indeed, I do not disagree with Williams and Willower's (1983) observation that, with the possible exception of Siegel's *The Principal* (1963), no existing novel provides a more insightful characterization of the work of the modern school principal than does the ethnographic *The Man in the Principal's Office* (Wolcott, 1973). But, I wonder, would this still be so, had Sinclair Lewis put a school administrator into his portrait gallery of professional figures that includes the physician Arrowsmith, the real estate salesman Babbitt, and the preacher Elmer Gantry?

Still, we do not take the words of any author, once heard, as final. Not Wolcott's or McLaren's or Anyon's. Not even Dickens's or Updike's or Lewis's. Even the most radical of artists cannot completely escape the prejudgments inherent within the cultural traditions upon which they comment. No understanding, Gadamer (1975) reminds us, is free of all prejudices, and so the literary text must be greeted with a spirit of skepticism. One voice does not a conspiracy make. The reader is obliged to speak. Lest he become enraptured in a "close reading," unable to move beyond the private universe of textual meaning, the reader must cast a suspicious eye on all texts. This may be especially difficult with a curriculum of literary masterworks, the intricacies of their formal beauty so dazzling and intimidating. But the reader must inquire about historical limitations; the voice in the text, no matter how mellifluous and seductive, must be questioned, perhaps even, as the post-structuralists would have it, interrogated.

Educational practitioners may need encouragement and guidance in overcoming habits of passive response to the literary text. But this gives the teacher educator something to do: She will work to facilitate the conditions for an act of conspiracy. Part of her task is, indeed, to aid in a reconstruction of the formal illusion, to help make more audible the nuances of meaning in the textual voice. But she must not treat the text like a cognizable object, a tool that is privately owned. She is not the final judge of interpretive rectitude. Instead, the teacher-educator should act as *critical co-investigator* (Freire, 1970, p. 68), serving as leader of a discursive community of professionals in which each member shares responsibility for critical reflection and discussion. The "student" is encouraged to intervene in the reconstructed imaginary world of the text to tell about his particular approach to its dismantling, to speak of perceived strengths and limitations in the vision it proffers, to describe its place within his own personal/professional landscape.

Perhaps in this and other kinds of discursive gatherings we can begin to redress the sense of alienation pervading Western culture that Walker Percy (1986) suggests is partially traceable "to the surrender, albeit unconscious, of valid forms of human activity to scientists, technologists, and specialists" (p. 43). Language and meaning, he says, have largely disappeared, leaving a "great gap in our knowing" (p. 43). Modern man is like Robinson Crusoe on his island, a castaway. "He does not know who he is, where he came from, what to do, and the signs on his island are ambiguous. If he does encounter another human, a man Friday, he has trouble communicating with him" (p. 44). Many of the encounters portrayed in modern literature, Percy notes, "in novels and plays from Sartre to Beckett to Pinter to Joseph McElroy" (p. 45), consist of quasi-conversations or non-conversations between two who are suffering from the common complaint of our age: the loss of meaning, of purpose, of identity, of values, of vision, of voice. They are like "prisoners who find themselves in adjoining cells as a consequence of some vague, Kafkaesque offense. Communication is possible only by tapping against the intervening wall" (p. 45).

I am personally acquainted with schoolpeople who have been reduced to tapping messages on the walls between their classrooms. Many teachers and administrators who are also my students and friends speak bitterly of limited opportunities for substantive conversations with colleagues and supervisors. Extra-institutional mandates for skills curricula and standardized tests even reduce possibilities for critical co-investigations with their students. Add to the list of debilitating conditions a heavy workload that squeezes out time for personal reflection, for meaningful dialogue with oneself. And as we include professional norms such as institutional loyalty, dependence on authority, and harmonious pseudo-collegiality—norms that dampen hopes of sparks generated from ideas rubbing together—it begins to appear that the modern technocratic institution of the school abhors conspiracy.

Denied the possibilities of formulating and progressing toward concrete utopian visions, educational practitioners may, like their students, become "at risk." They may exhibit the extremist tendencies of the moral dropout, their personal notions of the educationally desirable torn asunder. One part is chained to the conventional, forced to work toward technically virtuous, institutionally sanctioned ends-in-view, using any tool available. The other part flies off in frustration or outrage to search for "another country" on a magic carpet of utopian daydreams. There is nostalgic pining for impossibly perfect worlds that never really were. Or like the co-conspirators in *Another Country,* one imagines alien ideologies that can never be. Bennett and Judd, the homosexual and the communist, occupants of adjoining cells, are appalled at the distance between their ideals and the oppressive realities of life-at-hand. Tapping against the intervening wall, they finally learn each other's language. But their conversation is merely self-defeating pseudo-conspiracy. Bereft of all hopes for making concrete, incremental improvements in the educational and political status quo, they can only plot its annihilation. So texts of inquiry into the quality of educational life must offer more than the documentation and cataloguing of its impoverishment, on the one hand, or abstract theorizing about it, on the other. Instead, they must participate in the larger project of serious fiction in our age, the aim of which, Percy (1986) insists, is nothing less than "an exploration of the options of postmodern man" (p. 44).

I have been arguing that the aesthetic episodes wherein we use serious literature—or even use essays, such as this one, that discuss serious literature—are occasions for tense negotiations between the self of the reader and the contents of the experienced world. Of course, in a good story the resulting growth of meaning gradually culminates in a harmonious resolution that, placed against the ongoing drama of life, appears as merely provisional. Such conspiratorial episodes are like acts in that drama, their resolutions temporary at best. Still, like Bennett and Judd, we all need what has been achieved upon the conclusion of a successful story: a sense of progression toward a concrete utopian vision and ideas about desirable possibilities for approaching the next chapter of our autobiographies. We also need to feel the special mixture of fatigue and fulfillment associated with the closure of an aesthetic experience, the kind of wearied elation that lingers after, say, a round with Dickens or with Bartok. It is the feeling that accompanies the true sabbatical, the intermission between the phases in our explorations of options. It is how we should feel on a Sunday morning.

Now, having offered this exploration of our options as educators and inquirers into the qualities of educational experiences, I at last find myself at such an intermission—and to the degree that we have achieved conspiracy, perhaps you do, too. So maybe it is time for us to lower our voices, put on some Bach, and, before the next cycle of exploration commences, together call it a week.

Notes

1   This paper was presented on a Sunday morning, at the final session of the Stanford Conference on Qualitative Research. In composing this paper I used its assigned position in the conference schedule as a central metaphor in critiquing the usual view of the implementation of research findings as the culmination of the inquiry process. In order to maintain the integrity of the text and to provide the reader with a fuller sense of the occasion for which it was prepared, I have chosen not to delete references to the context in which its original presentation took place.

2   This concept of an *educational platform* is borrowed from Walker's (1971) discussion of a curriculum platform. For Walker, "the word [platform] is meant to suggest both a political platform and something to stand on. The platform includes an idea of what is and a vision of what ought to be, and these guide the curriculum developer in determining what he should do to realize his vision" (p. 52)

3   There are, of course, different kinds of constraints inherent in the use of novelistic modes of fiction. Working successfully within these constraints requires a qualitative problem-solving process that is as rigorous, in its own way, as science-based research processes. See Ecker (1966) for a discussion of the artistic, qualitative problem-solving process.

4   Authors who have identified and discussed examples of fictional school characters include Bass (1970), Kramer (1981), and Williams & Willower (1983). An updated anthology of good stories with educational themes is sorely needed. [Author's update: See Blanchard and Casanova, 1996]

References

Allender, J. S. (1986). Educational research: A personal and social process. *Review of Educational Research, 56*(2), 173–193.

Anyon, J. (1980). Social class and the hidden curriculum of work. *Journal of Education, 162*(1), 67–92.

Bandelier, A. (1898). *The delight makers.* New York: Dodd, Mead.

Barone, T. (1983). Things of use and things of beauty: The Swain County High School Arts Program. *Daedalus, 112*(3), 1–28.

Barone, T. (1987). On equality, visibility, and the fine arts program in a black elementary school: An example of educational criticism. *Curriculum Inquiry, 17*(4), 421–446.

Barthes, R. (1975). *The pleasure of the text* (R. Miller, Trans.). New York: Hill and Wang.

Bass, A. T. (1970). The teacher as portrayed in fiction. *Contemporary Education, 42*(1), 14–20.

Blanchard, J. & Casanova, U. (Eds.). (1996). *Modern fiction about schoolteaching: An anthology.* Allyn & Bacon, 1996.

Bowen, E. S. (1964). *Return to laughter: An anthropological novel.* Garden City, NY: Doubleday.

Bruner, J. (1987). *Actual lives, possible worlds.* Cambridge: Harvard University Press.

Buchmann, M. (1985). What is irrational about knowledge utilization. *Curriculum Inquiry, 15*(2), 153–168.

Bullough, E.(1957). *Aesthetics: Lectures and essays.* Stanford, CA: Stanford University Press.

Capote, T. (1965). *In cold blood.* New York: Random House.

Cook, A. (1960). *The meaning of fiction.* Detroit: Wayne State University Press.

Dewey, J. (1958). *Art as experience.* New York: Capricorn Books. (Original work published 1934)

Dickens, C. (1950). *The life and adventures of Nicholas Nickleby.* Oxford: Oxford University Press. (Original work published 1839)

Ecker, D. (1966). The artistic process as qualitative problem-solving. In E. Eisner & D. Ecker (Eds.), *Readings in art education* (pp. 57–68). Waltham, MA: Blaisdell.

Finn, C. (1988). What ails education research. *Educational Researcher, 17,* 5–8.

Freire, P. (1970). *Pedagogy of the oppressed.* New York: Seabury Press.

Frye, N. (1967). *Anatomy of criticism.* Princeton, NJ: Princeton University Press.

Gadamer, H. (1975). *Truth and method* (G. Barden & J. Cumming, Trans. & Eds.). New York: Seabury Press.

Geertz, C. (1973). *The interpretation of cultures.* New York: Basic Books.

Goodwin, B., & Taylor, K. (1982). *The politics of utopia: A study in theory and practice.* London: Hutchinson.

Greene, M. (1977). Toward wide-awakeness: An argument for the arts and humanities in education. *Teachers College Record, 19*(l), 119–125.

Haley, A. (1976). *Roots.* Garden City, NY: Doubleday/Anchor Press.

Hansot, E. (1974). *Perfection and utopia: Two modes of utopian thought.* Cambridge, MA: MIT Press.

Hersey, J. (1946). *Hiroshima.* New York: Modern Library.

Illich, 1. (1973). *Tools for conviviality.* New York: Harper & Row.

Ingarden, R. (1968). *The cognition of the literary work of art.* Evanston, IL: Northwestern University Press.

Iser, W. (1980). The reading process: A phenomenological approach. In J. P. Tompkins (Ed.), *Reader-response criticism: From formalism to post-structuralism.* Baltimore: Johns Hopkins University Press.

Jackson, P. W. (1968). *Life in classrooms.* New York: Holt, Rinehart and Winston.

Kermode, F. (1967). *The sense of an ending: Studies in the theory of fiction.* New York: Oxford University Press.

Kramer, J. (1981). College and university presidents in fiction. *Journal of Higher Education, 52*(l), 81–95.

Kurovsky, R. (1986). Novels, plays, poetry help aid leadership development. Stanford Observer.

Langer, S. (1957). *Problems of art.* New York: Scribner's.

McLaren, P. (1986). *Schooling as a ritual performance.* London: Routledge & Kegan Paul.

Michener, J. A. (1985). *Texas.* New York: Random House.

Miller, J. H. (1976). Stevens' Rock and criticism as cure, II. *Georgia Review,* 30, 330–348.

Mitchell, J. (1982). *Another country.* Ambergate, UK: Amber Lane Press.

Noblit, G. W. (1984). The prospects of an applied ethnography for education: A sociology of knowledge interpretation. *Educational Evaluation and Policy Analysis, 6*(l), 95–101.

Orwell, G. (1961). *Down and out in Paris and London.* New York: Harcourt Brace Jovanovich. (Original work published 1933)

Pepper, S. C. (1945). *The basis of criticism in the arts.* Cambridge: Harvard University Press.

Percy, W. (1986). The diagnostic novel: On the use of modern fiction. *Harper's Magazine, 272*(1633), 39–45.

Polanyi, M. (1962). *Personal knowledge: Toward a post-critical philosophy.* Chicago: University of Chicago Press.

Polanyi, M. (1964). *Science, faith and society.* Chicago: University of Chicago Press.

Polanyi, M. (1966). *The tacit dimension.* Garden City, NY: Doubleday.

Poulet, G. (1986). Phenomenology of reading. In R. C. Davis (Ed.), *Contemporary literary criticism: Modernism through post-structuralism* (pp. 350–362). New York: Longman.

Ricoeur, P. (1976). *Interpretational theory: Discourse and the surplus of meaning.* Fort Worth: Texas Christian University Press.

Rist, R. (1970). Student social class and teacher expectations: The self-fulfilling prophecy in ghetto education. *Harvard Educational Review, 40*(3), 411–451.

Roiphe, A. (1988, February 14). This butcher, imagination: Beware of your life when a writer's at work. *New York Times Book Review,* pp. 3, 30.

Rorty, R. (1982). *Consequences of pragmatism.* Minneapolis: University of Minnesota Press.

Shackle, G. L. S. (1966, December). Policy, poetry and success. *The Economic Journal,* pp. 755–767.

Siegel, B. (1963). *The principal.* New York: Harcourt, Brace and World.

Smith, L. M., & Geoffrey, W. (1968). *The complexities of an urban classroom: An analysis toward a general theory of teaching.* New York: Holt, Rinehart and Winston.

Toulmin, S. (1953). *Philosophy of science.* London: Hutchinson University Library.

Twain, M. (1899). *The innocents abroad.* New York: Harper. (Original work published 1869)

Updike, J. (1959). A sense of shelter. In J. Updike, *Pigeon feathers and other stories* (pp. 63–74). New York: Fawcett Books.

Walker, D. (1971). A naturalistic model for curriculum development. *School Review, 80*(1), 51–65.

Williams, R. H., & Willower, D. J. (1983). The school administrator in fiction. *The Educational Forum, 47*(3), 353–363.

Wolcott, H. F. (1973). *The man in the principal's office: An ethnography.* New York: Holt, Rinehart and Winston.

Wolfe, T. (1973). *The new journalism.* New York: Harper & Row.

Chapter 9

On the Demise of Subjectivity in Educational Inquiry (1992)

The death of the notion that objective truth is attainable in projects of social inquiry has been generally recognized and widely accepted by scholars who spend time thinking about such matters. In this article I will take this recognition as a starting point and call attention to a second corpse in our midst, an entity to which many refer as if it were still alive. Instead of exploring the meaning of subjectivity in qualitative educational research, I want to advance the notion that following the failure of the objectivists to maintain the viability of their epistemology, the concept of subjectivity has been likewise drained of its usefulness and therefore no longer has any meaning. Subjectivity, I feel obliged to report, is also dead.

Why should one be startled by this news? No signifier, historians of language tell us, is guaranteed immortality. Each enters into a language as a foot soldier in what Nietzsche has called a "mobile army of metaphors." Each is born as a participant in a new vocabulary that allows for things to be described in a way they could never have been described before. But after their initial attack on our common sense the foot soldiers' capacity for surprise is blunted, and they take to the trenches. Their meanings become conventionalized, taken for granted in everyday usage. No longer mobile and metaphorical, they become static and literal. And then when, inevitably, paradigms or world views shift, entire regiments are decimated.

Because individual words depend upon each other for their survival, isolated casualties are rare. After reading Saussure (1966), we understand the ecological character of language systems—how words depend upon each other for their existence, entangled as they are in a kind of linguistic web. After reading the later Wittgenstein (1968) we see that the meanings conveyed by words are social constructions, players in a language game with rules agreed upon by members of a culture. Upon the invention of a new game with different rules, teams of signifiers become dysfunctional and meaningless. Their collective demise becomes imminent.

Within the structure of any language there is the special case of dyadic relationships. Dyads are pairs of words with opposite meanings, each logically dependent upon the other for its existence. I think of these binary opposites as conceptual Siamese twins severely conjoined at birth, each incapable of living independently of the other. When a shifting culture no longer finds either of these signifiers useful, its opposite number dies with it. But while we have come to understand that it is no longer helpful for purposes of doing educational (or any other kind of) inquiry to think in terms of either an ontological objectivity or a *procedural objectivity* (Eisner, 1990), with its privileged criteria meant for approaching an external reality, we still often fail to notice what this must mean for its conceptual twin.

It means, of course, its corresponding demise. In this article I want to pay my respects to both members of a binary dualism that has had enormous influence over the way we have construed reality and to explore some of the ramifications of this passing from history for our work as educational inquirers. I also want to suggest terms within a new vocabulary that might better serve the purposes formerly served by the old dyad. I will recommend that as educational inquirers we no longer talk about research texts as being objective or subjective but about texts that are more or less useful or, in varying degrees and ways, persuasive.

An Obituary for a Dyad

Although eulogies fittingly accompany the death of good friends, a detailed recounting of the biography of this dyad is beyond the scope of this article. But allow me, in a highly abbreviated obituary, to note a few historically significant moments in the objectivity/subjectivity life story.

As far as we know the dyad was fathered by the Greek philosopher Parmenides. Parmenides supposed that we could come to know a "real world" with certainty. This would be genuine objective knowledge, requiring "complete permanence and simplicity, or absolute unity" (Diefenbeck, 1984, p. 10). Confounding progress along this ideal Way of Truth are our impermanent, shifting perceptions of the world that lead us astray and take us along the Way of Belief. Thus was the dyad conceived in a form of anxiety and fear, one that has been identified by Heidegger as pervading Western philosophical tradition. This was the awful anxiety that the "manifold possibilities offered by discursive thought will play us false, will make us lose contact with the real" (Rorty, 1982, p. 130).

But if our dyad was nervously conceived in Greece, the neoclassical discourse of Descartes perhaps represents the point at which the qualities of subjective knower and objective known, of mind and matter, of consciousness and body, achieved conceptual adulthood. Each human being, said Descartes, is both substance and spirit. The latter is the "ghost" of the mind that lives in the "machine" of the body. Ideas, however, are viewed not as spiritual but as corporeal entities. Knowledge of ideas thus implies a kind of material possession, the ownership of pieces of "mental furniture" (Ryle, 1949).

Descartes was also a victim of the Anxiety of Parmenides. Charged by Williams (1972) with harboring a "preoccupation with the indubitable" (p. 346), Descartes aimed to discover that which is beyond all doubt. But the complexity of Descartes' epistemological project has led to disagreement among philosophers as to which member of the dyad Descartes ultimately trusted. Williams, for example, sees as one result of the Cartesian project a positioning of subject over object, a temporary inversion of the hierarchy that has largely dominated Western thinking. Descartes, notes Williams, believed that the knower has privileged access only to the subjective Self, and that introspection is the only way of knowing that can guarantee immunity from illusion. Hence, for Williams "the Cartesian system . . . was the true ancestor of many later . . . subjectivist and idealistic developments" (p. 349). This reading of Descartes finds him giving encouragement to those who would later insist that knowledge of the contents of an external physical world is grounded in a subjective structure that exists prior to, and transcends all experience with, those contents.

But others, such as Thomas Kuhn, see the work of Descartes, developed in conjunction with Newtonian dynamics, as the real origination of the "traditional epistemological paradigm" (Kuhn, 1962, p. 121). Bleich (1978, p. 13) similarly emphasizes Descartes' distinction between qualities of things such as size and shape that are primary, and material and qualities such as color and smell that are *secondary* and mental. Descartes, argues Bleich, delineated the very objectivist paradigm that undergirds modern-day scientism.

Later the dyad reached maturity during the era of positivism. Although long discredited as a philosophical movement, certain premises of positivism still suffuse the research culture into which we were professionally socialized. Lest there be doubts about positivism's lingering influence, even in its epistemological afterlife, consider this passage from the *Encyclopedia of Philosophy* (Abbagnano, 1972):

> [One] characteristic [thesis] of positivism [is] that science is the only valid source of knowledge and facts the only possible objects of knowledge . . . Positivism . . . denies the existence or intelligibility of forces . . . that go beyond facts and the laws ascertained by science. It opposes . . . in general, any procedure or investigation that is not reducible to scientific method. (p. 14)

Current educational research texts continue to pay homage to these scientistic premises. These texts presume to identify those "forces or substances" that "go beyond" the "facts and laws of science." Often with more than a hint of Parmenidesian anxiety, they warn against the contamination of objective findings about the "real world" (Sowell and Casey, 1982, p. 12) with "personal experience" (McMillan and Schumacher, 1984, p. 6) or "value decisions" (Ary, Jacobs, and Razavich, 1985, p. 14).

Moreover, despite the disappearance of positivism as a body of theory, objectivity can still be found, well past its prime, living in the philosophy of the postpositivists. For example, the philosopher of inquiry Denis Phillips (1987) rejects a realistic epistemology but nevertheless speaks of objectivity as a "regulative ideal" toward which educational researchers should strive. Thus, writes Phillips, the "worry about warrant will not wane."[1] Smith (1984), moreover, has demonstrated how a realist epistemological orientation has shaped the criteria formulated by various theorists of qualitative educational inquiry for discriminating between trustworthy and untrustworthy research texts.[2] These thinkers would prolong this final moment in the life of the dyad by administering a certain brand of hermeneutics as a kind of artificial respiration. This is an approach to the interpretation of texts (i.e., as Derrida would have it, all cultural phenomena) that recommends converging on an "independent reality out there that can be read [with certainty] for what it is" (Smith, 1984, p. 386).

But, again, I leave it to others (e.g., Smith, 1989) to detail the deficiencies of this objectivist world view and focus on those of us who, although having abandoned an objectivist epistemology, still speak in the quaint vocabulary of Parmenides, Descartes, the positivists, and the postpositivists.

Sustaining a Non-Objectivist Version of the Dyad

There are at least three kinds of non-objectivist theorists who, denying the news of the dyad's passing, long for at least one of its members to

have another productive life phase. The first includes the extreme epistemological idealists who, in the spirit of the German idealist Husserl, see
reality or Truth as residing deep within a human Self that has an intrinsic
nature waiting to be discovered. These theorists would see material reality
relegated to the subordinate position in the dyadic relationship, while the
"mind" or "spirit" partakes of some higher, transcendental reality, aloof
from, and more trustworthy than, empirical (experienced) phenomena.
These are absolutists of a subjectivist ilk.

But nowadays there are few subjectivists who romantically posit an
unconditioned, private reality to be "expressed" from the inside. There
are, however, those who speak of an emerging "subjective paradigm"
(Bleich, 1978, p. 19) to replace the prevailing objective one. Either ignoring or deliberately working against the telling etymology of the term (*sub*
= under + *jacere* = to throw or place [*Webster's New World Dictionary*]),
they would prefer to celebrate the notion of subjectivity rather than seeing it as a pejorative term or a hopelessly outdated concept. Writes Bleich
(1978), for example:

> The role of the observer is paramount. An observer is a subject, and his means of
> perception define the essence of the object and even its existence to begin with.
> An object is circumscribed and delimited by a subject's motives, his curiosities,
> and above all, his language. (p. 18)

Bleich represents, I believe, a group of non-absolutists who, in the tradition of the idealist Descartes, seek to reverse the positions of the members of the dyad rather than simply ignoring the concepts.

Finally, there are those who similarly employ this outdated vocabulary
but who would deny hegemony to either member of the dyad. Included
among them are theorists attracted to the constructivist or naturalistic
"paradigm" of qualitative research. Peshkin (1985, 1988), for example,
seems to have been convinced by Hanson that all observation is theory-
based and by Kuhn (1962) that not even the so-called hard sciences operate outside the consensually validated world view of a culture-bound community of researchers, but an outdated vocabulary causes him (more than
Bleich) to wonder about the responsibilities of the knowing "subject."

But while Peshkin has embraced the term more often in prominent
places, I myself have in the past (Barone 1990b) used the word *subjective*
to describe the inevitably personal, judgment-based nature of educational
inquiry. Mobilizing one's army of metaphors by imagining new foot soldiers and ridding one's language of shell-shocked veterans are challenging
tasks indeed. And so if I may be allowed my own metaphorical shift, we
should not be judged too harshly for unimaginatively transporting some

familiar pieces of verbal furniture into our newly incorporated constructivist community of discourse. But now I want to help us notice how, given their new postmodern surroundings, these pieces simply do not fit in.

Systematically Monitoring Subjectivity

Subjectivity, I repeat, is a goner. The term is no longer needed to serve as a foil for its discredited dominant twin. Moreover, unless we view "pure" subjectivity as a kind of regulative ideal toward which all researchers should strive, then the term is useless for discriminating among research texts. Indeed, if *all* knowledge is mind dependent and/or culturally contextual, then *no* text is *not* subjective. And so, save burying it, what are we to do with a term so indiscriminate that it purports to describe a characteristic common to the discourses of the critical playwright *and* the romantic novelist, the astrologist *and* the astronomer, the ethicist *and* the physicist, the "sane" rationalist *and* the schizophrenic?

One ploy is to attempt to distinguish between good and bad forms of subjectivity. Peshkin (1985, 1988), for example, has opposed *virtuous* subjectivity to *unvirtuous* subjectivity, *examined* or *monitored* subjectivity to the *untamed* or *unexamined* or *unmonitored* kind. Subjectivity in qualitative research, argues Peshkin (1988, 20), is unavoidable, but when the researcher systematically monitors it through introspection she avoids the trap of doing "blatant autobiography," rife with distortion and projection.

How does a qualitative inquirer tame her "unbridled subjectivity"? Peshkin (1988, p. 18) recommends a kind of "subjectivity audit procedure," the result of which is a list of discretely characterized but functionally complementary "I's," or "aspects of the whole that constitutes me." This list is not meant for publication, but instead as

> a workout, a tuning up of my subjectivity to get it into shape. . . . And it is a warning to myself so that I may avoid the trap of perceiving just that which my own untamed sentiments have sought out and served up as data. (Peshkin, 1988, p. 18).

A good qualitative inquirer (whatever her preferred genre, including autobiography and ethnography) is, I agree, a constant monitor of experienced phenomena. But unless one is interested in securing a static, conventional interpretation of cultural phenomena, then "elevating" to the status of a formal method what is essentially a dynamic, fluid process of constructing meaning, is not, I suggest, a wise move. I see it as an inverted version of the ploy used by procedural objectivists (Eisner, 1990) to gain some sort of ontological privilege for their insights by appealing to a supposedly value-neutral procedure that purports to transcend self-interest or ideology. Does this formalized introspective maneuver differ in purpose from more common systematic auditing procedures, from triangulation to audit trails?[3] A virtuous subjectivist may claim that the purpose of his auditing procedure is to keep his account "subjectively respectable" (Peshkin, 1988), but I see it, with Geertz (1988), as a procedure undergirded by

> the simple assumption that although [anthropological phenomena] are, of course, inevitably seen through an author-darkened glass, the darkening can be minimized by authorial self-inspection for "bias" or "subjectivity," and [the phenomena] can then be seen face to face. (p. 145)

It is a method that seems fueled by more excessive worry about warrant.

Peshkin is too epistemologically sophisticated for any form of absolutism. But, like the critical theorists, who appeal to self-reflectivity as a means of preventing research from being undermined by self-serving interests, he ultimately seeks a methodological solution to the problem of avoiding the pitfalls of moral and epistemological relativism. Fearful of an abyss inhabited by the dangerous demons of passion and bias, he seems drawn to the kind of futile exorcismic methodological rituals at which the objectivists have traditionally excelled.

I am not denying that there exists in the authoring of an ethnographic text that which Geertz (1988) calls the *signature problem*, the question of how to establish an authorial presence. This problem of "finding somewhere to stand in a text that is supposed to be at [once] an intimate view and a cool assessment" (p. 10) has been so deeply buried "beneath . . . rather exaggerated . . . anxieties about subjectivity" (p. 9) that it has been insufficiently addressed. But this issue will remain ignored unless qualitative inquirers learn directly to confront that anxiety. This would entail abandoning a vocabulary that offers the illusory hope of making meaningful distinctions between the characteristics of textual objectivity and subjectivity. How we should speak instead is the question that demands to be addressed next.

Pragmatism, Neopragmatism, and the Criterion of Usefulness

The terms *subjectivity* and *objectivity* have become what neopragmatist Richard Rorty (1989) would call "nuisances": they attempt to take to the field in an already abandoned language game. The phenomena they purport to describe have already been satisfactorily redescribed. What is the source and shape of this redescription? Others (e.g., Bernstein, 1983) point to Heidegger as the first to question "the whole mode of thinking whereby we take the 'subjective' and the 'objective' as signifying a basic epistemological or metaphysical distinction" (p. 12). But I see the texts of the American pragmatists Dewey, James, and Mead as the primary origins of a post-dyadic mentality. Dewey, in particular, was deeply influenced by a Darwinian view of a human being as an organism engaging in transactions with features of her environment. Reality resides neither within an objective external world nor within the subjective mind of the knower, but within dynamic transactions between the two. To inquire about reality, therefore, is always to inquire about the construction of meaning within a particular situation that is being existentially transformed. Fixed boundaries, or dichotomous divisions between subject and object, are, within this schema, simply not useful devices for engaging in such inquiry.

The field of literary criticism has recently taken a pragmatist (or neopragmatist) turn that honors this Deweyan view of reality. For textualists in the reader-response and poststructuralist schools the literary work is not perceived as an object-in-the-world, as was the case with the formalists, for example. Gone is the "text itself" from which emanated cues to guide the reader toward a single, correct textual reading. Instead the reader is viewed by these theorists as actively constructing the reality of the text, giving it a place among the contents of her consciousness.

This construal occurs within an integral mass of previous experiences that facilitates sense-making in the interpretive act. But the act is dialectical in nature, for the reader-organism can in turn be conditioned by the text, and new meaning thereby incorporated into his or her being. He or she is transformed, occasionally radically, in the process, so that future interpretations will be made in light of this refined or expanded awareness.

And in the work of George Herbert Mead the Cartesian view of the individual as an existential isolate, the forlorn guardian of privately held thoughts that are her own sacred property, gives way to the notion of the human organism as an inherently social being. The genesis of the self occurs, he wrote, within a social setting, even if "each individual stratifies the common life in a different manner, and the life of the community is the sum of all these stratifications" (Mead, 1960, p. 266). The experience of any individual necessarily will be colored by the prejudgments inherent in a shared tradition and culture, and therefore, as Wittgenstein noted, a shared language.

Indeed, within a radically subjective paradigm, language makes no sense as a communicative tool, for it ignores the fact that every speaker implies immediately a receiver—real, fictive, or ideal—to whom the speech act is directed. And, as Gadamer (1975) has argued, interpreting a text can also never be a totally arbitrary exercise of purely independent will. The reader's belief and value system can never fully escape the prejudices embedded in an inherited tradition, "however much the will of our knowledge is directed toward escaping their thrall."

Gadamer and others who have elaborated upon the transactional, communal nature of thought first suggested by the pragmatists are persuasive. But the discovery of an omnipresent dialectical process between self and text does not, ipso facto, yield a new set of goodness criteria to replace those (e.g., rationality, objectivity, and methodological rigor) that operated within the old, dyadic world view. Again, if all discourse is culturally contextual, how do we decide which deserves our attention and respect?

The pragmatists offer the criterion of usefulness for this purpose. For William James, a belief is to be considered true, and therefore valuable, insofar as it yields a "completed function in experience" (James, 1960, p. 48). An idea, like a tool, has no intrinsic value and is "true" only in its capacity to perform a desired service for its handler within a given situation. When this criterion of usefulness is applied to context-bound, historically situated transactions between a self and a text, it helps us to judge which textual experiences are to be valued.

Neopragmatism and the Criterion of Critical Persuasiveness

Now, the pragmatists have been misunderstood by many as necessarily promoting a narrow kind of utilitarianism that admires the expediency of "whatever works," or the "cash value" of an idea. But Cherryholmes has identified this as the less interesting of two pragmatic orientations. This *vulgar pragmatism* (Cherryholmes 1988, 151)—or as I would prefer to call it, *conventional pragmatism*—is "premised on unreflective acceptance of explicit and implicit standards, conventions . . . meanings, rules, and discourses-practices that we find around us" (Cherryholmes 1988, 151). Cherryholmes contrasts vulgar pragmatism with critical pragmatism, the kind of neopragmatism favored by writers such as Richard Rorty and Hilary Putnam. Critical pragmatism results when a sense of crisis is brought to our choices, when it is accepted that our standards, beliefs, values, and guiding texts themselves require evaluation and reappraisal.

Critical pragmatism is "unbounded, radical, visionary, and utopian, based upon visions of what is beautiful, good, and true" (Cherryholmes 1988, 151). This distinction between pragmatic orientations is, I believe, itself critically useful as we strive radically to reconstruct our visions of what is a true, beautiful, and good textual experience. It helps us qualitative educational inquirers to reconsider, for example, the matter of *research genre legitimacy*. I will explain.

Critically Persuasive Encounters with Literary Texts

Craving the respect accorded the confident knowledge claims of the so-called hard sciences, qualitative educational researchers have been generally unable and/or unwilling to imagine useful alternatives to the premises, principles, and procedures of social science. Inquirers who do not partake of these premises and procedures (such as arts-based inquirers who work in an unbounded, nonsystematic fashion) have been forced to live outside of the research citadel and to endure the epithets hurled at them from within. For example, the texts of poets, novelists, storytellers, essayists, autobiographers, dramatists, and even literary ethnographers and journalists have been derided as being "merely subjective." But as the legitimate cause for disbarment from the citadel is shifted from subjectivity to uselessness, the epithet loses its sting. The gates are opened for textual encounters, in any inquiry genre or tradition, that serve to fulfill an important human purpose.

In the past, writers in certain schools of literary criticism did not view literature as useful. Indeed, one finds the dyad at its prime in the thinking of the formalists such as Northrop Frye. Frye (1957) distinguished between two basic types of language use. Centrifugal, or cognitive-scientific discourse, moves outward from words to "real world" objects. But centripetal, or poetic-literary, discourse collapses inward into the internal imaginative realm of human meaning, rendering it objectively false but subjectively true. Frye and other critics in the formalist and structuralist schools thus relegated fictional works to a category of texts that are admirable but useless (read "subjective") rather than instructive and useful (read "objective").

But poststructuralist literary critics reject the notion that narrative forms participate in a static, logical "deep structure," a grammar that transcends temporarily and cultural context. Ricoeur (1984–86), for example, following Dewey, understands how literary narrators operate *within* the world, their observations quite dependent upon their stock of previous transactions with experienced phenomena. Hence the truism that a novelist, to be an interesting writer, must first have lived an interesting life. Some fiction writers, acting like good ethnographers but without any pretense of a formalized method, even move "into the field," purposely transporting themselves to exotic locations—Mark Twain, Thomas Wolfe, and Joseph Conrad come to mind—to observe meticulously and to comment powerfully upon the lives and cultures of strangers, and thereby upon their own.

Like other artists, qualitative educational inquirers engage in a kind of qualitative problem-solving process (Ecker, 1966). In this process they carefully but non-systematically reflect upon—or "monitor," if you will—not (as Peshkin might have it) their subjectivity, but the content of their historically contingent transactions with the world. Then, with a particular purpose in mind, they transmute these qualities of experience into a narrative form. Dewey (1958) might describe the purpose of this artistic publicizing of experience as the re-education of those who confront the text. Rorty couched his description in more sociopolitical terms. You must, writes Rorty, "redescribe lots and lots of things in new ways," until, as in the endeavors of utopian politics or revolutionary science, "you have created a pattern of linguistic behavior which will tempt the rising generation to adopt it" (1989, p. 9).

What are these "lots and lots of things" to be redescribed? For qualitative educational inquirers the domain of interest is, of course, the sociopolitical phenomena of education and schooling. Among those who have undertaken redescriptions in this domain, one of the most successful was Charles Dickens (see Barone, 1990b). Upon reading *Hard Times* (Dickens, 1854/1955) and *The Life and Times of Nicholas Nickleby* (Dickens, 1839/1950), Dickens's countrymen were persuaded to adopt his redescriptions of life in the north Yorkshire boarding schools. The persuasiveness of Dickens's text is not the kind fueled by a rhetoric of "objective" scientific findings[4] or by appeals to comfortable consensus, to moral absolutes, or to dispassionate logic. His text is critically useful because it successfully appeals (1) to experience, and (2) to a desire to lessen the humiliation of other human beings. Dickens's achievement was to enable his readers vicariously to experience life as Yorkshire schoolchildren, so that they might attain a sense of solidarity with those schoolchildren, seeing them no longer as strangers but as "fellow sufferers" (Rorty, 1989).

This is not, therefore, a kind of textual usefulness that hides behind a pretense of moral or political neutrality. Indeed, Rorty (1989) would characterize Dickens's works, along with novels like *Sister Carrie, Uncle Tom's Cabin*, and *Black Boy,* as books that "help us to see how social practices which we have taken for granted have made us cruel" (p. 141). Such books offer experience-based critiques that challenge conventional, politically comfortable descriptions of social phenomena. The authors are, therefore, in Cherryholmes's (1988) terms, successful *critical pragmatists* in their reappraisals of prevailing "standards, beliefs, values . . . and discourse-practices" (p. 151). Charles Dickens, Theodore Dreiser, Harriet Beecher Stowe, and Richard Wright offered readers occasions for reconstructing their tired, safe views of social conditions into more radical and utopian ones. My hope is for educational inquirers soon to do the same.

On Critically Persuading Utilitarians

In the past, of course, a masterpiece of educational inquiry such as *Hard Times* would not have sufficed as, say, a doctoral dissertation. But within the new world view we see how dismissing persuasive literary works as "merely subjective" wildly misses the point. As I have noted, that particular pejorative has been rendered harmless and replaced by a more critically useful criterion of textual quality. In succeeding in their critical purposes, novelists such as Dickens have, in my judgment, earned entrance into the hallowed citadel of educational inquiry. Now the issue becomes whether to continue to accommodate inquirers working within genres whose texts are composed for more conventional purposes. Those texts of qualitative inquirers that are less purely literary, exhibiting features of the quantitative tradition, or those qualitative texts that describe, analyze, and categorize within a taken-for-granted *Weltanschauung*—do they still deserve respect? Or should the critical literary textualists, those "last who have become first," in turn take to hurling invectives such as "vulgar" at the "narrow-minded" utilitarianism of their former antagonists?

Does reform of the educational research establishment demand reverse discrimination based on genre? My view is that of a liberal democrat who prefers that all sorts of voices be accorded the respect of a hearing. Representatives of all discursive subcommunities (and pioneers seeking to establish new subcommunities) should be accorded the freedom to persuade others of the usefulness of their claims for their genres. And effectiveness in practicing the art and psychology of persuasiveness surely rules out denigrating or insulting the purposes undergirding the lifework of those who need convincing.

I do not underestimate the task of persuading fellow academics already professionally socialized toward judging inquiry texts in dyadic terms to reconsider the usefulness of that portion of their vocabulary. Wide divergence in epistemological world views may indeed account for the blinks of disbelief among traditionalist readers who are no doubt finding my arguments for legitimizing fiction as a form of qualitative educational inquiry to be audacious and shocking. But I believe (with Geertz, 1988) that the concepts and values derived from one's cultural background are best examined critically by vicariously experiencing the lives of those from other backgrounds, and (with Rorty, 1989) that this

> matter of detailed description of what unfamiliar people are like and of redescription of what we ourselves are like . . . is a task not for theory but for genres such as enthnography, the journalist's report, the comic book, the docu-drama, and especially the novel. (p. xvi)

This being so, I do not fail to appreciate the richness of the irony within this particular textual encounter: This is not a novel. Like Rorty, I am using instead the less critically persuasive tools of the essayist to plead a case for literature. So with my potential as an author perhaps diminished by choice of genre, I can approach closure only by way of a direct appeal to the already half-converted, to those readers, that is, who have not yet considered the full implications of their non-objectivist epistemology. To you I say this:

In our postmodern age we can no longer retreat from the awareness that human purposes and values undergird the production and consumption of our texts. Upon exploring the galaxy of axiology we find that, just as in the realm of epistemology, objectivity and therefore subjectivity are nowhere to be found. Moral certainty is of course as impossible a concept for us postmoderns to fathom as is objective empirical truth. So when we are out there on our textual expeditions with nothing ultimate to cling to, with our anxiety level rising until we are as fearful as Parmenides, let us hear the voices of others who have offered advice about living with the ambiguities of experience.

Some of us will no doubt resonate with the spirit of Oscar Wilde's comments about the heightened vitality of an aesthetic experience. In the midst of writing *The Importance of Being Earnest,* Wilde is reported to have remarked, "The anxiety is simply unbearable. I hope it never ends."[5] But in order to bear the anxiety the rest of us mere mortals may need to listen carefully to Nietzsche's response to his question, "*Was ist gut?*"

"*Tapfer sein ist gut,*" he answered. "To be brave is good."

A friend who has for centuries attempted to shelter us from those ambiguities has been found unable any longer to live a useful life. Some of us may persist in denying that her duty of denoting what is unacceptable about particular textual encounters is now better performed by the newly arrived foot soldier named "a lack of critical persuasiveness." But I have been suggesting that the concept of subjectivity is, like its dyadic twin, for all practical purposes, already dead. Rather than continuing to keep her breathing through the artificial means of outdated discourse, let us summon up the courage of Nietzsche and, together, bravely pull the plug.

Notes

The author would like to thank John K. Smith for his helpful comments on an earlier version of this paper.

1   I join in Lather's (1989, p. 28) rejection of the term *postpositivism* as defined by Phillips and others. I am taken with her alternative use of the term "to mark the era of possibilities that has opened up in the human sciences [I would prefer human studies] given the critique that has amassed over the last 20 years or so regarding the inadequacies of positivist assumptions in the face of human complexity."

2   And with what do critical theorists, following Habermas (1971), plan to replace "strict science" and "hermeneutical science"? Critical *science,* not revolutionary art. Hence, a "desire for methodological constraints" in their "openly ideological inquiry" (Smith 1988) betrays a faith in a procedural objectivity that lingers within a positivist heritage.

3   See Greene (1989, pp. 11–16) for a critique of so-called postpositivist views on how science progresses through triangulation and consensus within communities of inquirers.

4   Gusfield (1976) discusses the use of rhetoric in social science-based research reports. In Barone (1990b), I attempt to demonstrate how traditional educational research "texts-as-tools" attempt to persuade through a rhetoric of objectivity.

5   Wilde's remark parallels this comment of Gwendolen, a character in his play: "The suspense is terrible, I hope it will last" (Wilde, 1895/1985, p. 186).

References

Abbagnano, N. (1972). Positivism. In P. Edwards (Ed.), *The encyclopedia of philosophy,* (pp. 414–419). New York: Macmillan and The Free Press.

Ary, D., Jacobs, L. C., & Razavich, A. (1985.) *Introduction to research in education.* 3d ed. New York: Holt, Rinehart and Winston.

Barone, T. (1990a). Rethinking the meaning of rigor: Toward a literary tradition of educational inquiry. Paper presented at the annual meeting of the American Educational Research Association, Boston, April 1990.

Barone T. (1990b). Using the narrative text as an occasion for conspiracy. In E. Eisner and A. Peshkin (Eds.), *Qualitative research in education: The debate continues.* New York: Teachers College Press.

Bernstein, R. (1983). *Beyond objectivity and relativism: Science, hermeneutics, and praxis.* Philadelphia: University of Pennsylvania Press.

Bleich, D. (1978). *Subjective criticism.* Baltimore, MD: Johns Hopkins University Press.

Cherryholmes, C. (1988). *Power and criticism: Poststructural investigations in education.* New York: Teachers College Press.

Dewey, J. (1958). *Art as experience.* New York: Capricorn Books.

Dickens, C. (1854/1955). *Hard times for these times.* Oxford: Oxford University Press.

Dickens C. (1839/1950). *The life and adventures of Nicholas Nickleby.* Oxford: Oxford University Press.

Diefenbeck, J. A. (1984). *A celebration of subjective thought.* Carbondale, IL: Southern Illinois University Press.

Ecker, D. (1966). The artistic process as qualitative problem-solving. In E. Eisner and D. Ecker (Eds.), *Readings in art education,* (pp. 57–68). Waltham, MA: Blaisdell.

Eisner, E. (1990). Objectivity. Paper presented at the Annual Meeting of the American Educational Research Association, Boston, MA.

Frye, N. (1957). *Anatomy of criticism.* Princeton, NJ: Princeton University Press.

Gadamer, H. (1975). *Truth and method.* New York: Seabury Press.

Geertz, C. (1988). *Works and lives: The anthropologist as author.* Stanford, CA: Stanford University Press.

Greene, J. (1989). Three views on the nature and role of knowledge in social science. Paper presented at the International Conference on Alternative Paradigms for Inquiry, San Francisco, CA.

Gusfield, J. (1976). The literary rhetoric of science. *American Sociological Review, 41* (1), 11–33.

Habermas, J. (1971). *Knowledge and human interests.* Boston: Beacon Press.

James, W. 1960. *Pragmatism's conception of truth.* In M. R. Konovitz and G. Kennedy (Eds), *The American pragmatists.* New York: The New American Library.

Kuhn, T. 1962. *The structure of scientific revolutions.* Chicago: University of Chicago Press.

Lather, P. (1989). Reinscribing otherwise: The play of values in the practices of the human sciences. Paper presented at the International Conference on Alternative Paradigms for Inquiry, San Francisco, CA.

McMillan, J. H., & Schumacher, S. (1984). *Research in education: A conceptual introduction.* Boston: Little, Brown.

Mead, G. H. (1960). The genesis of self and social control. In M. R. Konvitz and G. Kennedy (Eds.), *The American pragmatists.* New York: The New American Library.

Peshkin, A. (1985). Virtuous subjectivity: In the participant-observer's I's. In D. Berg and K. Smith (Eds.), *Exploring clinical methods for social research,* pp. 267–282. Beverly Hills, CA: Sage.

Peshkin, A. (1988). In search of subjectivity—One's own. *Educational Researcher, 17* (7), 17–22.

Phillips, D. C. (1987). Validity in qualitative research. *Education and Urban Society, 20* (1), 9–24.

Ricoeur, P. (1984–86). *Time and narrative.* 2 vols. (K. McLaughlin and D. Pellauer, Trans.). Chicago: University of Chicago Press.

Rorty, R. (1982). *The consequences of pragmatism.* Minneapolis: University of Minnesota Press.

Rorty, R. (1989). *Contingency, irony, and solidarity.* Cambridge: Cambridge University Press.

Ryle, G. (1949). *The concept of mind.* New York: Barnes & Noble.

Saussure, F. de. (1966). *Course in general linguistics, 1907–1911.* Eds. C. Bally and A. Sechehaye. (W. Baskin, Trans.). New York: McGraw-Hill.

Smith, J. K. (1984). The problem of criteria for judging interpretive inquiry. *Educational Evaluation and Polity Analysis, 6* (4), 379–391.

Smith, J. K. (1988). Looking for the easy way out: The desire for methodological constraints in openly ideological inquiry. Paper presented at the annual meeting of the American Educational Research Association, New Orleans, LA.

Smith, J. K. (1989). Alternative research paradigms and the problem of criteria. Paper presented at the International Conference on Alternative Paradigms for Inquiry, San Francisco, CA.

Smith, J. K., and Heshusius, L. (1986). Closing down the conversation: The end of the quantitative-qualitative debate among educational inquirers. *Educational Researcher, 15* (1).

Sowell, E. J., and R. J. Casey. (1982). *Research methods in education.* Belmont, CA: Wadsworth.

Wilde, O. (1895/1985). *The importance of being earnest.* New York: Signet.

Williams, B. (1972). Rene Descartes. In P. Edwards (Ed.), *The encyclopedia of philosophy,* (pp. 344–354). New York: Macmillan and The Free Press.

Wittgenstein, L. (1968). *Philosophical investigations.* 3d ed. (G. E. M. Anscombe, Trans.). New York: Macmillan.

REDISCOVERING SARTRE: SOCIAL JUSTICE AND ISSUES OF AUDIENCE

A political turn in my thinking in the late 1980s is apparent in the four chapters of Section IV. The story of Billy Charles Barnett (Chapter 10), a troubled Appalachian youth, was written as the result of my involvement with a nationwide study of so-called "at risk students." Published in *Phi Delta Kappan* (1989), the case study was designed to raise important questions within an audience of practitioners (and others) about how, especially for youngsters from marginalized subcultures, the aims of schooling can conflict with worthwhile purposes of education.

Chapter 11 (1992) is a portrait of the process involved in researching and writing the biographical essay about Billy Charles. Labeled a piece of *critical storytelling*, the article is described as having been composed within a process of qualitative problem solving. In this process a theme gradually emerged to give shape to the endeavor. The theme enabled me to trace the effects of debilitating social conditions and a dysfunctional educational institution on a middle school student who may represent, metaphorically, alienated students from other American subcultures.

Chapters 10 and 11 reside, I believe, in the tradition of what Sartre called *litterature engagee*, but in them his ideas about the nature and purposes of social inquiry remain only tacit. In Chapter 12 (first published in 1992), however, I explicitly endorse a Sartrean brand of storytelling that is both popular and socially conscientious. Directly addressing issues of intended audience, I advance a scenario in which future educational researchers craft research texts that are broadly accessible, compellingly written, and morally persuasive.

The last selection in this section is a book review, published in 1992. It represents my reaction to *Savage Inequalities*, an important, widely

read book by Jonathan Kozol about the outrageous imbalances in educational funding in America. This essay offers an occasion for more fully
exploring Sartre's genre of socially committed literature as embodied in a
latter day exemplar.

Chapter 10

Ways of Being at Risk:
The Case of Billy Charles Barnett
(1989)

We are the representatives of two subcultures, meeting at a McDonald's along an interstate highway in northeastern Tennessee. Sitting across from me is Billy Charles Barnett, a tall lanky boy with dark hair, green eyes, a pug nose, and an infectious grin. He is a member of the rural "disadvantaged," a fifteen-year-old nominated by the vice-principal as the student least likely to remain in Dusty Hollow Middle School. I am a middle-aged urban academic who, secure in a tenured university position, will never leave school.

I am inclined to believe the warnings of others like me—teachers and administrators at Billy Charles' school—that this teenager from the hills will be "slow" and "hard to talk to." I am, therefore, surprised to discover almost immediately a keen intelligence and an eagerness to share his knowledge about his world. Even more jolting is a sudden realization of my vast ignorance about the ways of people who live within a two-hour drive of my home and about the fundamentals of a world no longer honored in the dominant culture.

Between slurps on a straw, Billy Charles speaks:

> You don't know what jugging is? When you go jugging, first you take a jug that bleach comes in. You rinse it out and tighten the lid and get some soft but strong nylon string. Then you need to get a two-inch turtle hook, real strong . . . and a three-or-four-foot line. The best bait is a bluegill, cut in half. You know, you really should use the head part. It's better than the tail, because turtles always go for the head of the fish first. But you can [also] catch catfish, bass, like this. I caught me a seven-and-a-half pound bass once, jugging. The jug just hangs in the water and nothing can get off the line unless they break it. I can catch a mess of turtles [this way], and then I make turtle soup. Do you know how to make turtle soup?

I find myself squirming in my seat. But why should I be the one feeling inadequate and defensive? No, I didn't know—until Billy Charles told me—that the market was bearish on coonskins this year, and that I could expect no more than $40 for a flawless one of average size. The topic had simply never come up in any graduate course on curriculum theory. Moreover, E. D. Hirsch and his co-authors had included no such items in their *Dictionary of Cultural Literacy: What Every American Needs to Know.* So I take comfort: not only am I the better educated, but also apparently the better *American* of the two strangers chomping on their cheeseburgers on this unseasonably balmy January afternoon.

Although I know nothing about the price of coonskins, I am better informed about Billy Charles than he is about me. For example, I know that Billy Charles is spending a second year in the seventh grade. I know that he has expressed on numerous occasions his intentions to drop out of school as soon as he can. And I know that, on occasion, he has entertained fantasies of dropping out of life, as well.

The last item is, of course, the most troublesome. *Specific suicidal ideations* is the phrase used by the school psychologist to characterize Billy Charles's morbid fantasies. Having ventured forth from my cozy, book-lined office to conduct a case study of what I thought would be a typical at-risk student, I would soon be forced to rethink my tired notions about such fundamentals as, oh, the meaning of life, the purposes of schooling, and the various ways in which an adolescent can be at risk of not being educated. To explain what I mean, let me tell you my own short version of Billy Charles's life story.

Billy Charles Barnett was born in the hills of northern Tennessee on 28 March 1974. When Billy Charles was two, his parents were divorced, and his mother received custody of him. His father moved to another part of the state, where he remarried and divorced several times, never receiving custody of any of the children from those marriages. When Billy Charles was eight, his father returned to live near Dusty Hollow. Billy Charles began to visit his father a few times a year. At age thirteen, in the seventh grade, he began to spend more and more time with a dad who passionately loved to hunt and fish and trap. Billy Charles decided to move into his father's house, located in (he still insists, even today) "paradise": a densely wooded area, thoroughly distanced from the world of convenience stores, gas stations, and book-lined classrooms.

What had begun to stir in Billy Charles is easily remembered by most former thirteen-year-olds. Billy Charles was beginning to think about who he was: the son, the grandson, the great-grandson, and maybe the great-great-grandson of frontiersmen in the upper South who remained in that region as the frontier moved on. Perhaps the sons of each succeeding generation felt what Billy Charles has hinted to me: violated and abandoned, as "civilization" barged in to distort the shape of their lives. But even today the allure of the woods remains intoxicating to many of the menfolk, who have traditionally been charged with providing their families with the necessities of life.

Some of these men (Billy Charles's stepfather among them) have managed to relegate outdoor activities to the margins of their lives, taking to their shotguns and fishing gear only on weekends. But not Billy Charles. At least not since he started to become a man. Billy Charles has always loved the outdoors, but what his mother calls his "obsession" with hunting, fishing, and trapping began a couple of years ago and accounts (she insists) for his initial desire to live with his father.

That was a glorious time, according to Billy Charles. He was ecstatic to finally have for his very own a father to connect him to the past that lived within him, a male parent versed in the ways of the wilderness to guide him into his own Appalachian manhood. Almost daily Billy Charles and his father went out in the wilds, the two of them together, teacher and apprentice. Billy Charles was joyously receiving an education in the *real* basics, eagerly learning the time-honored skills of survival (as opposed to such pale school-honored imitations as how to write a check or fill out a job application). He was absorbed in the fundamentals of the world around him. Almost daily for more than a year, rain or shine, this wilderness school was in session. Even after the master turned on his eager pupil. Even, at least for a while, after the beatings began.

The friction started early in the summer when Billy Charles's father introduced some female strangers into the household: a new wife and a nine-year-old stepdaughter. Billy Charles's version is that he was now burdened with cooking for four instead of for two. ("It was a lot more work and all she [the stepmother] ever did was eat ice cream and watch TV.") The resentment probably runs even deeper, rooted in the slight Billy Charles must have felt as his father's attention was divided and shared with others. Whatever the cause, tensions rose, and the beatings increased in frequency and in severity, reaching a peak when his father attacked him with a horsewhip.

So a father turns viciously on a son who, in a time of delicate adolescent need, is reluctant to leave—until the final incident of abuse when the new family decides to vacation in Florida.

While in Florida Billy Charles wrote a letter to his mother, describing his increasingly unhappy life. His father somehow managed to read the letter, and Billy Charles awoke, he says, to the pain of being pulled from the couch by his hair and slammed across the room. Not even the memory of the exciting encounter with a hammerhead shark on a previous day's deep-sea expedition could prevent a second change of custody. Not even the image of his father's face that, as Billy Charles poignantly admitted to me, now makes him depressed when it appears before him unbeckoned. So, on the verge of manhood, Billy Charles went back to Mama, back to a place strewn with so many obstacles to his escape.

Billy Charles has always resisted any encroachment of the school world on his freedom outside. Rarely, for example, has he deigned to do his homework. But he is frequently reminded of his sins of omission, as his mother and three sisters collaborate on school assignments in the crowded kitchen. So he retreats further inward, into a bedroom shared with two young men in their early twenties—his cousin, Carl, and Teddy, a friend of Carl's. (Only temporary boarders, says Billy Charles's stepdad, only until Carl's parents "work things out.") What does he do there all night? Billy Charles corroborated what one of his teachers told me: "I asked him and he said, 'I crawl into bed and I die.' That's what he said, 'I just die.'"

If Billy Charles feels cramped, is he ever tempted to create some artificial space for himself through the use of drugs? His mother once caught him using an amphetamine. He was promptly hauled off to the police station, and this experience, his mother believes, was sufficiently traumatic for him to swear off any further drug use. Maybe so. But an earlier, much more stunning incident seems to have produced a deeper fear, at least of harder drugs. Several years ago, as Billy Charles tells it, a good friend, while sitting right beside him, had injected himself with an overdose. Just a couple of nine-year-olds in northern Tennessee, one watching the other die, 1980s style. Recently the memory was revived when Teddy's girlfriend died in an identical manner. This, too, has depressed Billy Charles. I have wondered (but have lacked the courage to ask) about the possible relationship between these morbid memories and his own "specific suicidal ideations."

Billy Charles's imagination is his only source of escape during his self-described "imprisonment" by day. The school bus deposits him at Dusty Hollow Middle School at 8:15 every morning, and by second period—math, the period when the cage seems the smallest—Billy Charles is gone. He leaves through his mind—but always on foot. "I am walking in the hills," he says, recalling the leaves and the ground and the foxes and the possums. "I love to walk." Before meeting Billy Charles I had never known a fifteen-year-old without the slightest desire to drive a car. But driving is simply not of interest to him. Says Billy Charles, "I can walk to wherever I want to go."

Although Billy Charles is rarely present in spirit at school, he drifts less often out of his social studies and reading classes. The social studies class is taught by Billy Charles's favorite teacher, a bright, inventive young man who attempts to inject some liveliness into classroom activities with various simulation games, films, and student-centered projects.

Billy Charles's interest in reading class may be surprising, for Billy Charles has never been an avid reader. There is an encyclopedia in his house, and there are dictionaries. But there are few books and no daily newspaper. Billy Charles has not been raised in a home in which reading is seen as a delicious way to spend idle time. Perhaps his relative success in reading class is due to the special attention that is afforded him there. Billy Charles scores fairly well on most standardized tests, but he was placed in a "special education" reading class because he had been "disruptive" in other classes and was considered more "manageable" in smaller groups. He is reportedly less abusive and obnoxious to the reading teacher.

For the most part, though, school and the world of Billy Charles do not overlap. On weekdays, he is locked in his school's embrace, but he is often dreaming of another time, another place, imagining that he is free, his own man in a future when every day is Saturday. His is a vision awash in nostalgia, adamantly culling out for celebration only the pleasant features of the past—the thrill of the catch, the pan-fired trout, and the time spent under his father's benign tutelage—while screening out the unbearable: his father's scowl, his friend's limp body, or anything (like, say, a car or a classroom) invented since the Industrial Revolution. But the selectivity of Billy Charles's memory is understandable, and it represents, I believe, a hopeful sign. For it is only when his defenses break down and the grim ghosts of episodes past invade his psyche that Billy Charles seems most seriously at risk of abandoning more than just a formal education.

Does his vision of the future include earning a living? Billy Charles is utterly convinced that his own talents at tapping the bounty of nature will be sufficient to provide the necessities of life. As if to seal his argument, he points to his father, who works at odd jobs (currently selling bait out of a small store) to supplement his "natural" income. Others in the area are skeptical about the possibility of living only off the land these days, pointing to stringent enforcement of the legal limitations regarding season and size of catches.

And is Billy Charles foreseeing the possibility of a future family whose hungry mouths demand more than he can provide? Odds are that Billy Charles will once again find his hours divided into time lived and time served, as the time clock replaces the clock on the classroom wall. Still, his expectations are so robustly romantic, so close to those that even members of my branch of our frontier culture were so recently forced to abandon, that I have found myself hoping along with him: maybe there is a way. What if, for example, he changed his mind about the ethics of teaching for a living? Billy Charles recently forked over $100 for a weekend of instruction in a "trapping school." He found it rather useless (as would any advanced student in a remedial class). "But," I asked, "have you ever thought of opening a school of your own or becoming a guide to earn your own money?"

Grinning, Billy Charles answered, "Oh no, I don't believe that it's right to sell just words, to sell what you know, to make a living."

When I pointed out to him that words are precisely what his teachers sell, his reply was another grin. But Billy Charles is young, so we may hope for future compromises of his rigorous ethical standards. Getting paid for opening up his treasure chest of backwoods wisdom to weekend sportsmen still seems to me both pragmatic and honorable.

Of course, Billy Charles wouldn't need any more formal schooling for such an occupation. On the contrary, if this were his goal, school might then be precisely what he already believes it to be: an unwarranted roadblock on the path to the "good life." This is an unsettling notion to those of us who work devotedly toward fulfilling those goals of universal mandatory schooling. But what are those goals? By the time such academically disinclined students such as Billy Charles reach the middle grades, we think we see their future just ahead. To paraphrase the vice principal at his school, Billy Charles will, at best, become a common laborer like his stepfather, perhaps working nights operating within a forklift. And seldom, if ever, will he read a newspaper or a novel or a book of poetry.

So we abandon any lingering hopes for Billy Charles's conversion to a world of erudition and instead focus on *our* version of the basics. Teenagers unlikely ever to attend college must, we assume, be equipped with the mental skills appropriate to a working-class life: minimal competence in the basics; maybe an additional dash of content from the dominant culture (what *every* American needs to know); the basic skills of a trade, which we hope will be acquired in a high school vocational track; and, certainly, the employee's attitude, a demeanor tacitly encouraged by the organizational structure of the school and composed of a nexus of behavioral norms (such as perseverance, promptness, diligence, and intellectual docility) needed for the industrial workplace. If the non-college-bound acquire these learnings, we the taxpayers are placed at lower risk of having to fork over welfare money, and prospective employers are placed at lower risk of having to provide remedial education for candidates for employment.

But, I ask myself again, what of students such as Billy Charles who have equipped themselves to eke out a living (maybe even legally) within the cracks of the modern global economy? Billy Charles is not illiterate (and perhaps no more aliterate than the average citizen), and he possesses much more than the minimal knowledge needed for his own way of life. Could it be that Billy Charles's economic well-being is jeopardized only by our persistent attempts to inculcate values and behaviors that are, in fact, counterproductive to the successful conduct of his line of work? What use, after all, are passivity and punctuality to denizens of the forest?

Stated flatly, is Billy Charles at risk only if he stays in school? On those moments when I forget about the purposes of schooling that transcend the narrow focus on careers, my answer is yes. Then I am visited by Maria Montessori's vivid metaphor of students in rigid rows of desks as butterflies pinned to a display case. I confess to entertaining, at those moments, the impossible fantasy of pulling the pin and setting Billy Charles free.

How many other Billy Charleses are there—potential dropouts with the wits and wherewithal to survive financially in a world that worships the high school diploma? The conventional wisdom—the wisdom of my subculture, the legitimated wisdom—says "not many." There are other exceptions to the rule, of course, including the future stars of stage, screen, or playing field, the youthful heirs of family fortunes, or even the honest entrepreneurs-to-be. But I am incapable of imagining many stories like that of Billy Charles.

Nevertheless, I am reluctant to abandon the promises of schooling, even for such an exceptional case as Billy Charles. Indeed, his very exceptionality invites us to look beyond the narrowly pragmatic, utilitarian objectives of schooling to recollect a more substantial notion of the purposes of education. His case revives our fading dreams of a broader sort of empowerment that schools once hoped to provide for *all* American children, regardless of their economic or social backgrounds. This included the power to use the disciplines for penetrating more deeply into one's own past and present world, the power to imagine a wide range of alternative worlds in other times and places, and the power to express these understandings by employing many forms of literacy—verbal, visual, musical, kinesthetic, and so on.

This is where the exceptionality of Billy Charles ends and his commonality begins. For these are powers of thought and expression so often denied not only to the Billy Charleses among us, but also to the many respectable students for whom schooling is merely endured for the payoff of financial security and social standing. Them I have known much longer, those classroom drones who remain (like Billy Charles) seriously at risk of never becoming truly educated. They may pass their courses, but they are just as inevitably failed by their schools.

The institution of the school has also failed to facilitate mutual acquaintance among the people who inhabit it. I will not document the obstacles that have kept teachers and administrators from seeing Billy Charles as I have been privileged to see him. I leave it to other essays to explore the kind of restructuring that is needed before schoolpeople can pay closer attention to the life histories of other students like Billy Charles. His relatively benign experiences in a less crowded reading class and in a livelier social studies class only hint at the directions of that restructuring.

But even educators like Billy Charles's reading and social studies teachers will usually need help in acquiring the kind of knowledge that I lacked when I first met that scruffy stranger under McDonald's golden arches. Cocooned in the world of the middle-class educator, we are insulated from unfamiliar norms and ways of life. We have lost—indeed, we have been systematically encouraged to lose—the ability to reach out to honor the places (whether the barrio, the ghetto, the reservation, the Appalachian holler, or simply the peaks and pits of adolescence) where our students live.

Of course, a restructuring that gives teachers the time, the resources, and the motivation to learn about the individual worlds of their students will be only a beginning. Empathy alone is not enough. It is merely a necessary condition for a second element crucial to good teaching: the development of educational activities that can broaden students' horizons. Teachers in a school with a Billy Charles Barnett will not only need to understand the importance of making turtle soup, they will also need to entice students to study cuisines from other cultures. Math teachers will need the curricular finesse to lead students outward from field-and-stream economics to numeracy in other contexts. However, as John Dewey wisely noted long ago, one cannot effectively lead students outward without starting from the place where they currently reside.

Empowering teachers (and students) in this way may require more resources than our society is willing to provide. We will need to reeducate teachers, to reduce their workload, and to purchase material resources to link the local community with the larger one. Thus far, we have lacked the vision and the will to commit the resources necessary to this effort. Instead, we have sometimes resorted to gimmicks to lure our children back to school. In some Florida schools, pizza is offered as an incentive to attend classes. In one Kentucky district, a snazzy car is raffled off as a door prize for students with good attendance records. But should such bribery succeed in filling classrooms with warm bodies, will this no longer be a nation at risk of losing the hearts and wasting the minds of its young people? I think not.

I venture to suggest the heresy that we would not necessarily be better off were the dropout rate to decrease dramatically tomorrow. We conveniently forget the role of the traditional American school in perpetuating a seriously impoverished notion of what constitutes an education. Before we could say that a lower dropout rate is good news, we would need to know whether the reasons for not leaving school are valid ones. Are students remaining because we have become serious about introducing meaning into the life of the classroom? Are they staying because we have equipped our teachers with the means for knowing and respecting their students' pasts even as they attempt to open up their futures? And why would we need to know whether these things are occurring? Because Billy Charles Barnett has reminded us that doing anything less is still a very risky business.

Chapter 11

Beyond Theory and Method:
A Case of Critical Storytelling
(1992)

"In the absence of honest storytelling," the novelist/essayist Robert Stone (1988) has remarked, "people are abandoned to the beating of their own hearts" (p. 75). Once a secondary school teacher, I have lived what he describes. I still recall the shapes of the obstacles that prevented meaningful conversations with my colleagues about our daily struggles and the ultimate purposes of our work. Memories linger of a workplace, the features of which (including the content-centered and skills-driven curriculum) diminished my access to the life stories—the heartbeats—of my students, and theirs to mine.

Slowly I became aware of the extent of the problem. Over the last years the themes of isolation and silence have been prominent in the testimonials of my students who are themselves public school teachers. And recent professional literature has attended to the need for a greater sense of community in our professional lives (Flinders, 1989; Miller, 1990). Episodes of story sharing—honest or otherwise—remain hard to come by in the American public school.

It is, therefore, to the crafting of worthwhile stories that I, now as a teacher educator and especially as a qualitative researcher, devote a significant portion of my professional energies. Unlike most public school people, I possess the time and resources needed to gather the threads for weaving my tales. I envision a day when this privilege will be extended to empowered school people working in dramatically restructured educational settings. Meanwhile, however, I want to insist that, to be worthy of our privileges, we educational academics produce stories that promote two particular kinds of activities. The first is the introduction to each other of schoolpeople (especially teachers to their students) who are locked within the present system of schooling, enabling them to hear, if you will, each other's heartbeats. The second is inquiry into how schools may be transformed so that the people who live there no longer need to be introduced to each other by external intermediaries such as educationists.

Honest Stories, Critical Stories

The hallmark of the first of these two activities is, indeed, honesty. It is, more specifically, a kind of honesty achieved through a heightened empiricism, a determined scrutinizing of the world around us. Like all good art, honest stories are powerfully observed, carefully detailed. They must tend to generate in the reader awareness of the locations of (actual or fictitious) characters' thoughts, beliefs, desires, and habits, in the webs of contingencies that constitute their life-worlds.

Through descriptions of how people who appear as strangers are shaped by these particular contingencies, the reader can, paradoxically, achieve solidarity with them as fellow human beings (Rorty, 1989). Such empathy is the consequence of an ability to perceive and convey what is beneath the surface of behaviors, a clear-sightedness that avoids sentimental distortions, on the one hand, and cruel prejudices, on the other. It is the result of a writer who sees the truth and dares to use it at all costs (Burnett & Burnett, 1975). In other words, a courageously empirical storyteller is an honest storyteller, a soldier in the struggle against personal alienation.

But we qualitative inquirers should also strive to make ourselves redundant. We can do this by working for the transformation of schools into democratic communities in which honest storysharing is encouraged among its inhabitants. Accomplishment of this aim requires that educationists compose stories that promote inquiry into how schools, as currently constituted, discourage intimacy—stories that explore the connections between the pain of isolation, its attendant injustices, and the school as a sociopolitical institution.

For this purpose, the kind of honesty that might result from a gaze that is intensely empirical but politically disinterested is insufficient. The responsible story, I mean, must be what I will call critical, insofar as it adopts an openly political stance. Or, as Stone (1988) suggested about the process of writing moral fiction:

> I think the key is to establish the connection between political forces and individual lives. The questions to address are: How do social and political forces condition individual lives? How do the personal qualities of the players condition their political direction? (p. 76)

In other words, the critical educational storyteller is out to prick the consciences of readers by inviting a reexamination of the values and interests undergirding certain discourses, practices, and institutional arrangements found in today's schools. To what end? The ultimate aims of the critical storyteller should match those McLaren (1989) imputes to the members of that cadre of concerned educationists known as critical theorists: "to empower the powerless and transform existing social inequalities and injustices" (p. 160).

But these authorial comrades-in-arms, the critical storyteller and the critical theorist, differ in the modes of discourse employed to reach this common goal. The former eschews formal theory of either of Rorty's (1989) two general types—scientific and philosophical. Storytellers are, indeed, neither philosophers nor social scientists (critical or otherwise), but artists. As such, they do not engage in theorizing at any juncture in the process of researching and composing their stories. Nor do storytellers, strictly speaking, employ a systematic method, as might a social scientist. Therefore, no recipes or series of steps exist to guide the biographer, journalist, dramatist, poet, novelist, or essayist inevitably to success.

Talent at storytelling is not developed best through systematic instruction in the acquisition of standardized moves or proper research methods. Writers learn their craft by experimenting, reflecting on their experiments, studying the stories of others and criticisms of their own, and finally by confronting portraits of storytellers at work. The most helpful of these portraits not only tend to diminish the loneliness that may haunt the qualitative educational inquirer at the word processor; they are themselves stories, the kind that enable a writer to participate imaginatively in the creation of a text by another author and thereby to gain experience, albeit of a vicarious sort, at critical storytelling. What follows is one such account of the researching and crafting of a story that I, its author, strove to make both honest and critical.

The Making of a Critical Story

In the fall of 1987, 1 was approached by two colleagues who asked about my willingness to prepare a case study of a potential school dropout. The department of education at our university had been selected to participate in a nationwide Phi Delta Kappa project on "students-at-risk." Project tasks included the standardized and systematic collection of data about several elementary, middle, and secondary schools. But I consented to involvement in a more intimate phase of the study, the documentation of the life story of a student singled out as his middle school's "least likely to succeed."

The result was a manuscript entitled "Ways of Being at Risk: The Case of Billy Charles Barnett" (hereafter, "WBR") (Barone, 1989).[1] WBR is in fact, a story-within-a-story-within-an-essay. It is, first, a biographical sketch of a certified loser, a fifteen-year-old officially nominated as the student most at risk of leaving school. This portrait is enfolded within some auto-biographical musings that suggest the effect of coming to know Billy Charles Barnett on the life of the author. A final layer of wrapping addresses the broader implications that the story of Billy Charles may hold for educators, educationists, and the society at large.

Why did I agree to tell this story? My motives were mixed. First among them was curiosity. Of what tissue, I wondered, is the life of this officially designated "loser" made? What circumstances had laid him so low? What, if anything, would he, could he say for himself? I sensed an opportunity to fulfill that which, I recalled, Sartre somewhere had identified as the primary responsibility of the writer: to speak for those who cannot speak for themselves. A chance for honest storytelling had appeared.

Secondly, there was the less noble element of laziness. A potentially worthy protagonist had been identified without the initial struggle familiar to novelists and ethnographers alike. I was relieved of the hassles of seeking out (or inventing) a ripe setting. plotting a credible entree, negotiating from scratch a research bargain with wary school people. My nosiness was officially sanctioned. I came with a badge from Phi Delta Kappa.

Finally, my motives as I hopped on board this already moving research train included these: I hankered for certain feelings I had felt before and that, in all honesty, I am feeling now: the thrills of the storyteller composing and imagining readers as they comprehend, and are influenced by, what he has crafted. Take me to this distressed and distressing teenager. Let me tell his story. Through my efforts, I remember thinking, the world will hear the beating of his heart. And only later, as my honest efforts turned critical, would I implicate the world in the production of his heartache.

Critical Storytelling as Qualitative Problem Solving

A project of qualitative educational inquiry had thus begun. I would proceed, not in a methodical fashion, but through what in retrospect can be identified as a series of identifiable phases. These are the phases that, for Ecker (1966), constitute the pattern of inquiry that inhabits the creation of any work of art.

In the first of five phases in this process of *qualitative problem solving* (Ecker, 1966), the artist (or storyteller) confronts raw phenomena or qualities in the people and settings under scrutiny. These impressions are myriad and can appear to be random. For example, as I began my research, I took copious field notes that documented aspects of the personalities of my interviewees and the physical and social landscapes where Billy Charles lived his lives. A catalogue of informational snippets grew rapidly and without any apparent coherence.

My attention to particular phenomena and my ignorance of others was due not to the formulation of explicit theory but to a steering mechanism located somewhere beneath the surface of my psyche. Navigating without what Gadamer (1975) would call my "prejudices," that stock of beliefs, interests, and proclivities accrued within all my previous lived experiences, I would not have attended to *this* particular innuendo from an administrator at Billy Charles's school about my subject's "lack of intelligence," or to *that* attempt of Billy Charles to make the hole in his shirt disappear by rolling up its sleeve. But what could I make these things mean? At the outset of a storytelling excursion, the qualitative inquirer may feel anxious and adrift as phenomena flicker without discernible pattern, like phosphorescent jellyfish in the endless sea around him. I have learned to stay calm and paddle onward.

And doing so, I soon entered a second phase of inquiry. Now, as Ecker (1966) describes it, tentative relationships between qualities are apprehended. These patterns of qualities present themselves as structured fragments, but fall short of providing an ultimate theme or central set of insights around which the emerging story can be woven. As I pursued my investigation, most arresting were the clashes in the colors of the impressions I was receiving from various sources about the quality of Billy Charles's life—a dark existence, a bleak future, to hear some adults tell it, although Billy Charles seemed like sunshine personified when talking to me about the things he cherished. As an Appalachian teenager, he was an avid and extremely talented hunter, fisherman, and trapper. How could I reconcile the generally poor academic performance of this drop-out-to-be with his mastery over a wilderness environment in which I, the repeatedly credentialed academician, would be rendered virtually helpless? The qualities of safety and competence in the haven of the woods coalesced, as did, in an opposite corner, the menacing and destructive qualities in the institutional environment of the school.

Only as I entered the third stage of inquiry did the process climax, as a single pervasive quality emerged "from the qualitative components being introduced, manipulated, and related to other components" (Ecker, 1966, p. 67). This occurred as a single metaphor of *riskiness* emerged that placed the various dangers lurking in Billy Charles's life—the threats, for example, posed by an abusive father and by a dysfunctional school system—into a larger context. A relentlessly encroaching dominant culture of which school was a part was eliminating the only environment in which he could thrive, meting out a sentence of slow death to the backwoods Appalachian way of life that gave him his identity.

Billy Charles thus became a symbol for all those students endangered by educational institutions with deep structures that pay homage to the forces of that dominant culture and so render teachers and administrators who labor within it largely incapable of honoring their students' subcultures and life-worlds. With the appearance of this metaphor, the storytelling research turned *critical,* attending to the connections between an individual life and a debilitating sociopolitical milieu. And then came phase four, in which the actual composing commenced.

As I read (and reread) good literature, I marvel at the leanness of the writing. In a good story, all superfluous verbiage is eliminated, lest it acquire a characteristic that Aristotle (1961) deplored: it could become *episodic.* This occurs when the author includes descriptions or interpretations of events or actions that distract from the central thesis or point of the story. On what basis does an author determine what to include or exclude? Once a central metaphor or pervasive quality has emerged, it serves as what Ecker (1966, p. 67) calls a *qualitative control.* It facilitates, that is, selection among observed qualitative phenomena, while simultaneously serving as a kind of patterning principle for revealing relationships between these phenomena.

This is precisely what happened in phase four of my storytelling. Certain pieces of information about the landscape of Billy Charles's world were rendered less relevant for inclusion in this story, given the critical metaphor that had emerged. A vignette about an altercation on a school bus: omitted, insufficiently central to the theme. A description of the final revolting incident of physical abuse of Billy Charles by his father on a vacation trip to Florida: included, crucial to understanding Billy Charles's dangerous ambivalence toward the "significant other" who most closely personified his countercultural heritage, and therefore to understanding a significant dimension of the psychological and social turmoil that had placed him at risk of taking his own life.

The story gradually emerges, therefore, as each component part is tested for its "fit" in the overall schema so that in stage five, as Ecker states (1966), "the work is finally judged complete, the total achieved— the pervasive has adequately been the control" (p. 67).

Educational Inquiry and Critical Storytelling

I am not the only author who has fashioned an honest and critical story in a non-theoretical, nonmethodical manner. WBR, I suggest, falls within an established tradition of literature (most examples of which focus on dimensions of life other than formal education) that helps us "see the effects of social practices and institutions" on individuals (Rorty 1989, p. 41). Some of these, like WBR, are nonfictional, including works of investigative journalism such as Upton Sinclair's *The Jungle* (1906/1988), Mailer's *Armies of the Night* (1968), and Kotlowitz's *There Are No Children Here* (1991). Others are novels such as Sinclair Lewis's *Main Street* (1920), Victor Hugo's *Les Miserables* (1887/1893), and much of the writing of Charles Dickens.

These are critical stories *par excellence,* stories that are (much as critical theorists claim for their work) ideologically open, not hiding, that is, behind a pretense of moral and political neutrality. Consider another example, namely Steinbeck's *The Grapes of Wrath* (1939/1967). The author's disapproval of the kind of morally bankrupt sociopolitical and economic system that could result in a catacyclism like the Great Depression is apparent. But this novel's power to persuade emerges not from within a rhetoric of theory, whether scientific, philosophical, or critical. It emanates from a careful and committed empiricism that is made manifest through such features of writing as powerfully "thick" description and invented but convincing dialogue. The text thereby invites and enables the reader to locate the beating and, yes, the aching of other human hearts (here, those of Okies such as the Joad family) within a debilitating sociopolitical milieu.[2]

Authors of stories such as WBR similarly attempt to make palpable and comprehensible the pain and cruelty of isolation inflicted on people—more specifically, people who are the students, teachers, and administrators enmeshed in our institutions of education. It is my hope that ever more of today's qualitative educational inquirers will use their privileges to tell stories that enable readers to locate the sources of that pain. If we can make these stories sufficiently compelling, there may even be hope for the kind of meaningful educational reform that empowers schoolpeople to tell their own critical stories to themselves and to us all.

Notes

1 I suggest that readers, in order to gain a greater appreciation of my comments about the crafting of WBR, might become directly acquainted with the text (Barone, 1989). The name Billy Charles Barnett is a pseudonym.

2 Does it matter that this story and, therefore, these characters are fictional? Hardly. I would argue that the ultimate purpose of the critical storytelling I have described can be served equally well through journalistic or novelistic modes of storytelling. In that sense, critical storytelling moves qualitative researchers and readers not only beyond theory and method but beyond genre as well.

References

Aristotle. (1961). *Poetics.* (S.H. Butcher, Trans.). New York: Hill & Wang.

Barone, T. (1989). Ways of being at risk: The case of Billy Charles Barnett. *Phi Delta Kappan, 71,* 147–151.

Burnett, H., & Burnett, W. (1975). *Fiction writer's handbook.* New York: Harper & Row.

Ecker, D. (1966). The artistic process as qualitative problem-solving. In E. Eisner & D. Ecker (Eds.), *Readings in art education* (pp. 57–68). Waltham, MA: Blaisdell.

Flinders, D.J. (1989). Teacher isolation and the new reform. *Journal of Curriculum and Supervision, 4* (l), 17–29.

Gadamer, H. (1975). *Truth and method.* (G. Barden & J. Cumming, Eds. and Trans.). New York: Seabury Press.

Hugo, V. (1887/1893). *Les Miserables* (I.F. Hapgood, Trans.). Boston: Little, Brown.

Kotlowitz, A. (1991). *There are no children here: The story of two boys growing up in urban America.* New York: Doubleday.

Lewis, S. (1920). *Main street.* New York: Harcourt, Brace, & World.

Mailer, N. (1968). *Armies of the night: History as a novel, the novel as history.* New York: New American Library.

McLaren, P. (1989). *Life in schools: An introduction to critical pedagogy in the foundations of education.* New York: Longman.

Miller, J. (1990). *Creating spaces and finding Voices: Teachers collaborating for empowerment.* Albany, NY: State University of New York Press.

Rorty, R. (1989). *Contingency, irony, and solidarity.* Cambridge, UK.: Cambridge University Press.

Sinclair, U. (1906/1988). *The jungle.* Urbana, IL: University of Illinois Press. (Original work published 1906)

Steinbeck, J. (1939/1967). *The grapes of wrath.* New York: Viking Press.

Stone, R. (1988). The reason for stories: Toward a moral fiction. *Harper's, 276* (1657), 71–76.

Chapter 12

A Narrative of Enhanced Professionalism: Educational Researchers and Popular Storybooks about Schoolpeople (1992)

Could the prevailing sense of what it means to be a professional educational researcher actually work against the enhancement of a status that is less than fully professional? In this essay, I claim precisely that. I contend that our unfortunate allegiance to a certain view of professionalism has served to diminish the quality of discourse with layfolk in the larger civic culture whose images of schools and schoolpeople influence public policy on education. This view of professionalism is portrayed within a common story we tell about ourselves, a collective self-narrative about our genesis and current status as social scientists. This view, I contend, has limited our inclinations toward, and abilities for, persuading the polity to replace their generally negative conception of schools and schoolpeople with one that is more benign. As an ironic result, our opportunities to set a research agenda based upon this benign conception, and our professional autonomy, have been diminished. Ultimately, I suggest that we adopt an empowering view of ourselves as willing and able to educate the public through powerfully crafted, accessible stories about schoolpeople and the conditions under which they live and work.

Describing a Narrative of Professionalism

Haskell (1977) described the beginning of a prevailing collective self-narrative told by social science professionals about their origins and current status. The late ninteenth century, he noted, was a time of uncertainty and doubt among both intellectuals and the intelligent public. Confidence in unambiguous religious interpretations of human experience was being shaken by the tenets of Darwinism. Moreover, advances in communication and transportation increased the complexity of modern life while ensuring widespread participation in the attitude of skepticism. This broad-based collapse of confident belief, argued Haskell, gave rise to a "movement of cultural reform which intended to construct safe institutional havens for sound opinion" (p. 47). Both amateurs and generalist students of the human condition were replaced by scholars willing and able to devote years of study within discrete areas of specialization, the disciplines and subdisciplines of modern social science. Bothered and bewildered, the polity was receptive to the claims of expert knowledge resulting from this scholarly pursuit and conferred upon social scientists the same autonomy granted to other professional scholarly communities (Haskell, 1977).

What, according to this narrative, did the autonomy entail? It suggested authority broader than that usually associated with the three original *status professions*, the ministry, medicine, and law, or with more recent *occupational professions*, such as agricultural engineering and physical therapy (Friedson, 1986). Professionals in these fields are, as McGaghie (1991) noted, "individuals who use technical or specialized knowledge and skill in service of the public welfare" (p. 3). They apply esoteric knowledge and skills generated by others, especially natural and social scientists. On the other hand, professionals within universities are charged with generating the knowledge to be applied, and for them autonomy would come to be associated with notions of academic freedom. For academics who are social scientists, it would include the power of the professional community over its own research agenda and over quality control of its products.

Educationist narrators of this story about professionalism see their own research community as presently in possession of these two elements of autonomy and, therefore, as a community of professionals. First, the power of educational researchers over their own agenda is regarded as obvious. Researchers, this story goes, select an area of educational significance and then often locate available funding support. Second, in order to maintain its professional identity, the community of educational social scientists exercises its freedom to determine and uphold standards of research practice. These standards demand, for example, adequate methodological rigor and an acceptable format and language for presenting findings.

Of course, this narrative is not the relatively straightforward story that it used to be. Many premises, principles, and procedures once dismissed as nonscientific or as associated with the wrong *kind* of science (such as those engaged in by some qualitative researchers) are now an accepted part of the tale of social science professionalism in the field of educational research. Ethnographers in particular have, for a while now, been regarded as legitimate members of the professional community. This narrative has incorporated the seemingly incessant meta-talk that either heralds or bemoans the advent of a new social science research paradigm. It accommodates a splintered consensus on what precisely is social science. Nevertheless, the narrative continues to portray social science—whatever it is—as the only "institutional haven of sound opinion" sufficiently able to ensure the safety of its product.[1]

But identification with the social sciences does more than secure status for professionals who possess the expertise needed to generate trustworthy knowledge. This mutual identity (along with, of course, a common focus on educational phenomena) binds educational researchers together into a community of scholarly discourse. Of course, like others in complex fields of study, that community is departmentalized into many discursive subcommunities, each with a specialized vocabulary, or "galaxy of signifiers" (Barthes, 1974). But our common identity as social scientists locates these galaxies within the same professional universe. Our credentials therefore attest to an acquired ability to communicate not only with inhabitants of our local galaxy but also, to some degree, with others in that larger universe.

Indeed, an educational researcher's texts must, foremost, be informative and persuasive to professional colleagues, even if, in an applied field such as education, they may later be translated (in a kind of paraprofessional exercise) for the uninitiated, including educational practitioners, policymakers, and, to a lesser extent, the general public. An unabridged version of this tale of professionalism would describe how each of these constituencies becomes informed of the esoteric knowledge and skills generated by educational researchers. But I will focus on how educational research is translated for the public.

According to this story, the mass media, especially the press, possess the primary responsibility for informing the public of the substance of educational research reports. Unfortunately, educational researchers, policymakers, and journalists do not inhabit the same discursive community, and therefore, as McNergney (1990) noted, "do not communicate often or well with one another." As a result, he continued:

> The public loses. Good research does not find its way into practice . . . Education news that appears in print and on television becomes a blend of comments from sources deemed to be informed and descriptions of activities thought to be inno-

vative. Too often they are neither. Life in research centers remains seemingly
unconnected to life in schools. (p. 20)

The professionalism narrative finds its solution to this dilemma in the
design of a 1989 colloquium in Charlottesville, Virginia, at which researchers, policymakers, and members of the press talked to each other
about how to talk to each other better (McNergney, 1990). Recommenda-
tions for the researcher side of the table emphasized helping reporters to
be more accurate in their interpretations of research. Robert M. O'Neil
and George M. Kaufman (McNergney, 1990), for example, suggested
identifying the research stories likely to be attended to by the press and
placing them "in a context that explains the immediate story and the
larger educational setting to which the story contributes. Experts need to
be available to explain the details of complicated work [to the press]"
(p. 20).

And even if, as O'Neil and Kaufman (McNergney, 1990) put it, researchers are "prepared to follow up with . . . letters to the editor," the
narrative of professionalism continues to portray members of the media
as the appropriate communicators of the autonomously secured scientific
findings of educational researchers to layfolk.

Describing a Counternarrative of Deprofessionalization

Robbins (1991) has offered a counternarrative of deprofessionalization,
one that critiques the portrayal of the professional community as a collection of heroic figures successfully defending a nearly absolute autonomy
over its professional affairs. Robbins focused on the obvious role of bu-
reaucratic institutions in eroding this freedom, for example, the threat
posed by corporations to the privileges of doctors and lawyers. Because,
as C. Wright Mills (1953) noted, bureaucracies inevitably invade all professions, including the professoriat, academic scholars can never be true
professionals. Consider Robbins's (1991) example, one among many offered in this counternarrative, of university hiring of part-time staff against
the wishes of tenure-track faculty.

The counternarrative focuses on the two elements of autonomy (over
research agenda and textual quality) depicted by the narrative of professionalism as critical to the professional standing of social scientists and, in
particular, educational researchers. The counternarrative does not deny
that educational researchers currently possess the collective power to
determine their own community standards related to methodology and
format. Instead, this power is depicted as largely inconsequential, insofar

as educational researchers' autonomy in a more fundamental area is illusory. The professional community of educational researchers lacks real power to determine its own research agenda. This power is seen as resting largely in the hands of sources outside of the university, primarily government policymakers. House (1991), for example, provided an account of the pressures placed on educational researchers by recent policies of the national government.

Reagan economic policies, argued House, increased the disparity of income between the poor and the wealthy and diminished the economic status of the United States. Schoolpeople became the scapegoats for this faded policy. Public schools were identified as the institutions responsible for lower levels of job skills, a primary cause of the nation's economic decline; the inhabitants of those schools (students and teachers, in particular) were depicted as lazy and undisciplined. Many government policies in the 1980s, House noted, were based upon these images of the character of schoolpeople. These reform policies included mandates for additional course work and achievement testing, and for teacher accountability, policies that, House (1991) suggested, are not costly and "protect the interests of the middle and upper classes" (p. 25).

Under these circumstances, did most educational researchers act like the autonomous agents of the narrative of professionalism, conducting research based on a vision of schoolpeople as victims of complex, systemic cultural conditions rather than as perpetrators of crimes against the national well-being? House (1991) persuasively argued the negative:

> Educational research tended to be reactive rather than proactive, playing a subsidiary rather than a formative or challenging role. In other words, the content of the research was determined by the reforms rather than vice versa. Few reforms have been thoroughly researched in advance, and many are contrary to research evidence. *Research funding follows the reforms, and research seems to follow the funding* [emphasis mine]. (p. 25)

Of course, the counternarrative of deprofessionalization does not have all educational researchers docilely submitting to this extramural agenda. Some funding from nongovernmental sources could be found. Other (oppositional, or counter-hegemonic) educational scholars labored, usually without grant support, to craft alternative accounts of the role of schoolpeople in the decline of American culture. And there is recognition of the enormous potential for subversion of the explicit intentions of a grant once funding has been secured. Nevertheless, public blame of educators and schoolchildren has, according to the counternarrative, remained rife in the 1990s, and the dominant scenario of our socioeconomic woes goes largely unchallenged by the research community of educational scientists. Funding continues to honor this scenario; research continues to follow funding, and educational researchers with professional integrity oozing from their pores necessarily remain, as the deprofessionalization counternarrative would have it, mythical creatures.

For those who accept this counternarrative, it matters little if educational researchers do become more effective in communicating their research results to the general public, for these results are seen as based largely on unexamined and inappropriate conceptions of the nature and purposes of education and of the lives of schoolpeople. If educational research has failed to find its way into practice or into the public consciousness, well, this is no great loss. Its findings were not born within a "safe haven of sound opinion" and their accurate conveyance would only compound the bewilderment of the public. They are, after all, not the products of truly professional scholarship.

Describing a Narrative of Enhanced Professionalism

How could it be otherwise? In a third narrative about ourselves—my own—we educational researchers assert greater control over our scholarly endeavors. This is a narrative of enhanced professionalism. It forgoes the romance of the heroic narrative of professionalism and the despair of the deprofessionalization counter-critique. And unlike the other narratives, this one is overtly prescriptive. It aims not only to paint a plausible picture of our past and present as a community of educational researchers but also to present a modestly hopeful vision for our future.

In this narrative we educational researchers abandon any hopes of gaining absolute autonomy over our research, while nevertheless working to create support for conducting research based on our own professional ideologies. We strive to reverse the usual pattern of research-follows-funding by going over the heads of government policymakers to the primary source of power in a political democracy. We act to persuade the polity. We speak to them, not from a distance, not through texts that need translation by intermediaries, but directly and compellingly so that the public ceases to imagine teachers and schoolkids as essentially negligent and malevolent characters in need of externally imposed discipline, and begins to understand the nature of the unfortunate cultural and institutional forces that impinge upon their lives.

To do this, we make judgments about research methodology that expand the possibilities of professional scholarship in the field of educational studies. Indeed, my narrative begins after the stream of educational research has already flowed past the point at which educational research is identified *exclusively* with social science, whether it be what Habermas (1972) labeled *strict science*, or *interpretive science* or *even critical science*. The stream has been fed by observations such as those of Gordon, Miller, and Rollock (1990) concerning the cultural hegemony in social science knowledge production that has "enabled the development of phenomenal scientific, technological, and theoretical achievements, while remaining dysfunctional . . . because it favors too narrow a range of perspectives and investigative techniques" (p. 15). The stream has already carried us to a vast sea of research perspectives and approaches, some of which are not scientific (in any recognizable sense of that term). Indeed, the acts of mass persuasion suggested by my narrative are themselves most effectively accomplished through nonscientific sorts of texts. One kind is the nonfictional educational story. These stories are found in popular books about schoolpeople and are composed in the style and format of literary journalism.

The Promise of Popular Storytelling

Nonfictional educational storytelling is a form of narrative inquiry, the kind of research most prominently publicized by Clandinin and Connelly (1987,1988; see also Connelly and Clandinin, 1990).[2] For Connelly and Clandinin, nonfictional stories represent the structured quality of experience that is studied by narrative researchers: "Thus, we say that people by nature lead storied lives and tell stories of them, whereas narrative researchers describe such lives, collect and tell stories of them, and write narratives of experience" (1990, p. 2).[3]

Much nonfictional storytelling outside the field of education has been the product of modern literary journalists.[4] Their brand of literary nonfiction is rooted in the New Journalism of the 1960s and 1970s. One significant talent of accomplished literary journalists is an ability to tell compelling stories that enable readers vicariously to experience actual events in the lives of real people (Barone, 1980). A growing number of nonfictional storybooks, authored by journalists and others, have focused on the lives of schoolpeople[5] but I choose to illustrate the educational potential of this kind of writing by highlighting two recent examples. The first, Tracy Kidder's (1989) *Among Schoolchildren,* is a flawed piece of work, but does take readers on an interesting journey through one year in the life of a fifth-grade public school teacher. The second is Alex Kotlowitz's (1991) *There Are No Children Here,* a poignant, dramatic, and convincing account of the lives of two children growing up in an inner-city Chicago housing project.

Chris Zajak lives her life "among schoolchildren" as a teacher at Kelly School in Holyoke, Massachusetts. Early in Kidder's book the reader is introduced to those children as Zajak grades their social studies test papers. Here is bright, pretty, well-dressed Alice from an affluent family whose "father thought that at public school [she] would learn resiliency" (p. 91). Judith, from the public housing projects, is likewise highly intelligent, with concerned parents. There is short, deep-voiced Pedro, a diligent Puerto Rican boy who is prone to weeping at his desk and long absences from school. And Robert, wide-faced, big-bellied Robert, who had learned somewhere that "the best way to deal with failure is to embrace it" (p. 93).

But Chris Zajak, and therefore Tracy Kidder, focuses most intensely on her primary nemesis, a troubled African-American student named Clarence. Clarence acts belligerently toward Ms. Zajak, mocking and threatening her. In succeeding chapters the reader begins to sense the source and depth of Clarence's pain. Through descriptions of Clarence's mother's visits to the school as well as her failure to attend important meetings about his problems, the reader comes to comprehend her abusive neglect of her son. We learn, for example, about how Clarence is left unfed for an entire day after being accused of stealing from his mother's purse. Viewed against the backdrop of this dismal home environment, Clarence's classroom transgressions, from his neglect of homework assignments to his obscene utterances and violent outbursts, seem almost inevitable.

The depth of Zajak's concern for Clarence, and for all her charges, is especially well portrayed. Clarence becomes a near obsession with her, even invading her dreams at night. But she also worries that her attention is being unevenly distributed among her students. Indeed, the twin dilemmas of the first two-thirds of *Among Schoolchildren* are these: (a) How can Clarence be brought to succeed in school when the deck has been so unfairly stacked elsewhere and (b) what will his continued presence in the class cost the rest of Zajak's students? And as we apprehend the ease with which this single student disrupts the delicate social ecology of Zajak's traditionally organized classroom, the limits of this teacher's power and wisdom, if not her caring and compassion, also become visible. The momentous decision is made for her at the onset of spring in a "windowless, overheated conference room" by a "parade of five experts on troubled children" (p. 166): Clarence will be banished to an "Alpha Program" consisting of, in the words of the Alpha teacher, "a notorious group of troublemakers" (p. 167). His future looks grim indeed.

There Are No Children Here: The Story of Two Boys Growing Up in the Other America (Kotlowitz, 1991) is even more involving than *Among Schoolchildren*. It traces in excruciating and heartbreaking detail a couple of years in the lives of two out of the twelve million American children who live in poverty. The children are Lafayette and Pharaoh Rivers, an eleven- to fourteen-year-old and a nine- to eleven-year-old in south Chicago. The theme of the book is their struggle to maintain their innocence, their sanity, and, most basically, their lives, in one of the most dangerous and corrupting environments on the planet.

The arc of Kotlowitz's story carries us through the formation of the self-identities of these young brothers. Even though, as the book's title suggests, the boys, having seen too much, were *never* children, they grow inexorably toward the increasingly treacherous teen years and young manhood. The text is studded with descriptions of tragic incidents (the violent deaths of close friends and relatives, the imprisonment of their older brother, ugly episodes with their usually absent heroin-addicted father) and of the tolls these take on the psyche of Lafayette and his younger brother. For example, Pharaoh seeks refuge in the academic pursuit of spelling but also develops a nervous stutter. In one especially poignant vignette, Pharaoh loses the school spelling bee because, petrified, he is unable to speak the word *endurance*. But by the end of the book Pharaoh has indeed endured. He had begun to thrive in a private school west of his home in the Henry Homer Housing Project. (The author of the book arranged for this transfer.) On the other hand, Lafayette was academically unable to remain in the private school and was "wrestling again with the lures of the neighborhood" (p. 301).

There Are No Children Here takes place primarily outside of school, for the primary action for these two boys is on the streets and in their cramped apartment. But we do move occasionally into the classroom to view the impact of external forces on their school experiences. There we see the limitations faced by teachers struggling to educate damaged souls who merely visit them from the hell outside.

Although somewhat dissimilar in approach and substance, *Among Schoolchildren* and *There Are No Children Here* share at least three characteristics. First, both present, in an engaging, nonfunctional literary format, meticulously detailed observations about the conditions in which particular schoolpeople live their lives. They strongly challenge the cartoonish imagery of tired, uncaring schoolteachers and stupid, recalcitrant children that the counternarrative of deprofessionalization portrays as having undergirded our research agenda. Second, both were successfully mass-marketed. *Among Schoolchildren* spent twenty-six weeks on the hardcover and paperback bestsellers lists and may have been read by more noneducators than any other recent storybook about matters educational. Kotlowitz's book reached number two on the *New York Times* hardback list.[6] Finally, both books were written by journalists, or, to state it more directly, neither was written by a professional educator or a member of the educational research community. Nor have most works of literary journalism that tell stories of the "dailiness" of life in schools (Sizer, 1988). Why not? The prevailing narrative of professionalism has not honored—as scholarship—certain of the nontraditional textual characteristics suited for nonprofessional audiences that are common to books such as *Among Schoolchildren* and *There Are No Children Here.* Telling stories accessible to the masses has not been the kind of research activity most likely to advance the career of a scholar in the social sciences.

This recounting of my own narrative of enhanced professionalism will not rehash available arguments for legitimating—as scholarship—various nonscientific approaches to educational research. Instead, I will describe three dimensions of written nonfictional storytelling with the potential for educating members of the general public about life in schools. The first two dimensions, accessibility and compellingness, are achieved primarily through mastery of formal textual characteristics, including the form of language used and the compositional format of the text. Achievement of the third dimension, moral persuasiveness, depends on the substance of the stories told.

Accessibility: The Language of the Storyteller

Eisner (1976, 1985, 1991) has described differences between the language of social scientists and that of literary artists and critics. The former is generally linear, analytical, technical, denotative, while the latter is metaphorical, suggestive, figurative, evocative. The two languages serve different purposes. The first lends itself to explanation through propositional statements. The second, in its pristine form, can produce poetry, or what Langer (1957) called a *semblance*, a "shaped apparition of a new human experience." But even the nonfictional stories of literary journalists can grant readers vicarious access to the life-worlds of their characters. Consider these paragraphs from *There Are No Children Here.* The first describes the landscape of an inner-city ghetto; the second offers a glimpse into the life of a youngster living there:

> Sometimes at Henry Homer [housing project] you can almost smell the arrival of death. It is the odor of foot-deep pools of water that, formed from draining fire

hydrants, become fetid in the summer sun. It is the stink of urine puddles in the stairwell corners and of the soiled diapers dumped in the grass. It is the stench of a maggot-infested cat carcass lying in a vacant apartment and the rotting food in the overturned trash bins. It is, in short, the collected scents of summer. (p. 45)

When he got bored or had nothing better to do, he practiced his penmanship. His teachers noted that he had an unusually neat and delicate handwriting for someone so young. But Pharaoh worked at it, usually writing his name over and over on a piece of paper, so that by the time he had finished, his name appeared maybe two dozen times, leaping in all directions. The P's would stand out in their grace and dominance over the other letters; he would even loop the letter's stem to give it a more pronounced presence. Sometimes, if he got carried away, his name would angle upward, with curls adorning the other letters, too, as if his name were a fanciful spaceship about to rocket off the edge of the paper. (p. 62)

These passages exhibit a simple, prosaic eloquence. No social science academese in need of translation here. But how can we account for the reluctance of believers in the narrative of social science professionalism to grant such works legitimacy as educational research, and to write this way themselves? I do not believe that aesthetic qualities in the writing are primarily responsible for this reluctance. How far, after all, is this form of expressive language from, say, the now respectable realm of ethnographic "thick description"? One could cite equally artful passages from the works of ethnographers such as Peshkin (1986, 1991) and the sometimes quite literary McLaren (1986).[7] What seems most objectionable about this kind of research text is not the aesthetic but the vernacular nature of the storytelling prose, the fact that it partakes of a common idiom, with meanings too readily grasped and too broadly shared. I will return shortly to that point.

Accessibility may seem to be a hallmark of all storytelling language, but not all stories are equally accessible.[8] Those, for example, that approach the realm of "high art" can be as mystifying to readers unwilling or unprepared to labor in search of metaphorical associations as is the jargon of social science to layfolk. But not even the vernacular guarantees transparency of meaning. Indeed, as the poststructuralist literary critics have shown us, no text, however sincere and humble in appearance, can be taken at face value. Systems of power, Foucault (1977) explained, are founded on systems of language. Each text, therefore, must be carefully inspected to reveal the realities of power and authority that make them possible (Said, 1983). Even writing that is what Habermas (1979) calls "comprehensible" and "sincere" can be distorted by those realities.

Although never as innocent as they might seem, some forms of language are nevertheless more benign than others. Some texts are composed in language more *writerly* than *readerly* (Barthes, 1970). Writerly texts are more easily "rewritten" by the subversive reader, who must first participate in meanings assigned by a powerful culture before replacing them with his or her own. Readerly texts, on the other hand, are coated with lots of what William James called *privileged meaning*, meaning most accessible to those acculturated into a community of discourse. Their readerliness is one source of Jacoby's (1987) complaints about academic texts in general and Agger's (1990) criticism of texts of high theory.

Most social science research texts are similarly readerly, mystifying, off-putting, *disempowering* for nonresidents of the research universe, who are made dependent upon intermediaries for their translation. And it is precisely this kind of exclusive privilege (and the status and power implied by it) that is implicitly supported by the prevailing narrative of professionalism. For unless our texts *always* use language suited to conveying the esoteric knowledge discovered with specialized scientific skills, then our professional status seems in jeopardy. One fear that pervades the narrative of professionalism is this: that anyone who can speak the language of the masses will, credentialed or not, claim the right to homestead within our community of discourse. An even deeper fear is that social scientists who do not speak that language will face reverse discrimination and ultimate exclusion from the community.

Compellingness: The Story Format

My own narrative of enhanced professionalism seeks to allay these fears. First, mine is not a saga of ostracism, but a tale of inclusion. It honors the texts of social scientists that are judged by colleagues to be adequate for consumption by other social scientists. Second, the narrative demands that nonscientific research texts meant to persuade lay audiences be more than merely accessible. They must also be (among other things) inviting, even compelling, so that citizens who are fatigued from struggling to earn their daily bread will desire to read them. One element of design that can help supply this allure is the story format.

Aristotle (1961) first identified three essential phases of the story, namely, the beginning, the middle, and the end. For Dewey (1958) these phases were part of a dynamic form that provided structure for the aesthetic experience of the creator and consumer ("re-creator") of a work of art. At the outset there is the recognition of a dilemma, the discovery of a problem in whose solution one takes an interest. The second phase is characterized by movement toward a resolution of the dilemma, as new information contributes to and draws meaning from that which has gone before.

Finally, when the parts are nearly all in place, there is a tentative closure that is often accompanied by a state of wearied elation (Barone, 1983). Aestheticians have attributed the allure of art, including literature, to this dynamic form, which mimics the rhythms of human experience, the ebb and flow of life itself. Kidder and Kotlowitz have each provided an example of how the story format can invite the reader into a text and engage his or her imagination as the phases of its dynamic form are played out.

All former schoolchildren have felt the ebb and flow of the school year, and it must have seemed natural to Kidder to employ this familiar cycle for framing his story. In *Among Schoolchildren* Kidder uses his first chapter ("September") to introduce his protagonists and to pull the reader into the twin dilemmas of the book described above. As the school year and other chapters unfold, new characters appear and the plot is thickened. The book ends on the last day of school.[9] The framework for *There Are No Children Here* is less obvious. It begins with the involvement of Kotlowitz in the lives of Lafayette and Pharaoh and ends two years later. The plot is propelled by the theme of endangered innocence. The story builds as we become more intimately acquainted with the characters and their struggles, until we see the beginnings of the formation of their self-identities. As Kotlowitz admitted, his tale has no "neat and tidy ending" (p. xi). But in reading *There Are No Children Here,* even more than in reading Kidder's book, one experiences, in Dewey's words, "a sense of growing meaning, conserved and accumulating toward an end that is felt an accomplishment of a process" (1958, p. 39). The reader is seduced into the construction of an aesthetic experience.

Why have educational researchers typically not employed the story form? The logic of social science professionalism has demanded a different kind of textual plotting. The ordered format of more traditional research reports—chapters or sections, for example, on literature review, methodology and design, presentation and analysis of data, summary and conclusions—is sensitive to the purpose and intended audience for that kind of text. Form does indeed follow function, and traditional textual design compels the involvement of fellow empirical and analytical social scientists whose knowledge interests are prediction and control (Habermas, 1972). Accordingly, a linear format allows the researcher to demonstrate to professional colleagues the "objective" nature of the findings, the precise conditions under which they were ascertained, and therefore the context of their utility. Educational hermeneuticists and critical theorists, those other kinds of social scientists whose purposes are, respectively, "understanding" and "emancipation" (Habermas, 1972), use less standardized formats for their research reports. Typically, however, these researchers employ formats designed for persuading colleagues of the value of their particular brands of truth claims, and rarely employ the dynamic story form with its greater potential for engaging nonprofessionals.

Moral Persuasiveness

According to my narrative of enhanced professionalism, popular educational stories must possess a third attribute in order to be judged professionally worthy. They must be morally persuasive. A persuasive story is one with the capacity for promoting a kind of critical reflection that results in the reconstruction of a portion of the reader's value system. When a persuasive story is moral, the result is a reader who has grown to understand and deplore the cruel social forces that impinge on the lives of individual characters. I will elaborate.

Wolfgang Iser (1974) noted that the story is the form of discourse best suited to the task of *value negation*, of persuading the reader to doubt previously held outlooks, attitudes, meanings, and values. A good story does this by enticing the reader into an acceptance of a virtual world that is seen as credible. To attain credibility, the story must accurately portray the minutiae of daily life within a particular societal context and moment of history. As they stray from a lifelike portrait of human conditions, careless observations confound the reader's resonations with the interior vision of the text. But when a story successfully persuades a reader of the credibility of the world it recreates, he or she may be enticed to live vicariously within that world. This recreated vision then serves to stand against and comment upon analogous, taken-for-granted qualities of the familiar world nearby. Great stories enable readers to gaze in fresh astonishment upon a part of their world they thought they had already seen. They also allow readers to get better acquainted with people they thought they had already known.

A persuasive story tempts the reader to consider the usefulness of alternative meanings attributed to certain phenomena by the story's characters. The reader may thereby establish solidarity with these characters, and with real people outside of the text who are analogues of these characters. One particular sort of negation committed in the story-sharing process is against the belief that these people are not, as Rorty (1989) put it, "fellow sufferers," not "included in the range of 'us'" (p. 192). This kind of negation and this kind of solidarity, ironically fostered by honoring the contingencies of particular lives, are achieved in the stories told by Kidder and Kotlowitz as the reader vicariously experiences the worlds of Chris Zajak and Lafayette and Pharoah.

But these stories do something else as well. For the final goal of a morally persuasive nonfictional storyteller is more than hermeneutical understanding, empathy, *Verstehen,* looking at the world from the perspective of the story's protagonists. Readers must be persuaded not only to participate vicariously in what Fay (1975) called the "intentions and desires of dissatisfied actors," but also to accept the revelations of how certain "irrationalities of social life . . . are causing the dissatisfaction" (p. 98). Stories designed to challenge members of the polity to rethink their notions of schoolpeople as inherently lazy and undisciplined are, therefore, hardly morally and politically disinterested. To the contrary, they are examples of the kind of moral storytelling described by Stone (1988): They "establish the connection between social forces and individual lives." Indeed, the ultimate aims of the moral storyteller match those that McLaren (1989) imputes to critical theorists: "to empower the powerless and transform existing social inequalities and injustices" (p. 160). The interest served is the moral one of a Habermasian critical theorist—one of emancipation—albeit accomplished through literary journalism rather than critical social theory.

Among Schoolchildren and *There Are No Children Here* fall within the historical tradition of written moral storytelling identified by Rorty (1989) that has helped readers "to see how social practices we have taken for granted have made us cruel" (p. 141).[10] And the time is right for additional accessible, compelling, and morally persuasive storybooks about schools and schoolpeople. Like the books by Kidder and Kotlowitz, these stories would proffer redescriptions of the phenomena of schooling to those who matter most in a political democracy, the members of the polity. But my narrative foresees educational researchers themselves crafting this literature, rather than abandoning this task to talented noneducator journalists.[11] It describes educational researchers as determined to enhance their professionalism by using their own professional bootstraps.

Storytelling and Quality Control

This enhanced professionalism will require the educational research community to maintain quality control over its stories. Accessibility, compellingness, and moral persuasiveness will serve as criteria for judging the professional worth of educational stories. All three will be present in a good popular narrative. Accessible and compelling stories that fail to offer empirical, nonstereotypical portraits of schoolpeople will not be judged professionally worthy. On the other hand, neither will a carefully researched, morally sensitive story that is dull, malformed, and unattractive to a broad audience. In other words, these stories must exhibit both critical appeal, evidencing both craftsmanship and specialized knowledge that the researcher's colleagues would accept as "sound opinion" and popular appeal, or marketability.

My narrative does not downplay the challenge of meeting the demands of both lay and professional audiences simultaneously. It recognizes a pervasive *culture industry* (Horkheimer and Adorno, 1972) hawking popular literature as one more kind of commodity for sale to a general public that is less and less intellectually present. It sees this commodification of popular literature as one symptom of a decline of a literary political economy (Agger, 1990) within which popular writing of all sorts (journalism, film scripts, trade novels, etc.) is attributed worth only in terms of its exchange value (Best, 1989). The result is mediocre discourse: Politically imaginative, vibrant, challenging, critical, transgressive literature, no matter how accessible and compellingly crafted, is displaced commercially by mis-educational texts that feed into the comfortable, dominant, conventional beliefs of the culture, including the prevailing view of schoolpeople as primary initiators of our economic and social ailments.

In a world of literary products and an anesthetized reading public, uninspired writing flourishes. Writers become the victims of marketing experts and developmental editors or they become self-censors. Either way, authorial autonomy declines (Agger, 1990). So the notion of absolute control by the educational storyteller over the quality of his or her literary work is as problematic as the naive portrait of the researcher's total autonomy over his or her research agenda. But mine is not a fatalistic story, for it sees the field of literary production and consumption, like the larger culture, as a complex site of struggle and accommodation. It envisions strategies of resistance aimed at creating spaces within this field for authoring and disseminating texts that educate rather than patronize people-on-the-street about matters of schooling. These strategies include increasing the marketability of morally enlightened stories about schoolpeople by making them, yes, accessible and compelling.

Classic examples of superbly crafted, morally sensitive, oppositional, but still hugely popular, educational storytelling were provided by Charles Dickens (1839/1950; 1854/1955; see Barone, 1992). Installments of his compelling accounts of life in the north Yorkshire boarding schools, serialized in London periodicals, were eagerly devoured by the reading public of his day. The quality of Dickens's work suffered little from any pandering to a commercially driven literary market. Could a latter-day Dickens perform a similar feat? Perhaps, but today she or he would confront obstacles in addition to the deleterious effects of the modern culture industry on popular literacy. For example, more enlightened views of schooling logically imply increased taxes (see House, 1991). That uncomfortable political reality alone makes the kind of transformation of public perceptions and governmental policy that can provide maximum research autonomy seem, for the near future, unlikely indeed. So maybe the best that can be hoped for is not a full flowering of educational research professionalism, but the kind of integrity gained in struggling *toward* the utopian ideal of absolute academic freedom. Understanding this, I modestly describe my narrative as one of *enhanced* professionalism.

Storytelling and the Politics of Media

But am I too modest in my choice of media for reorienting public views about education? Why does my narrative envision researchers employing the medium of print when nowadays other media offer much wider audiences? Characterizations of teachers and children in stories on television and in film surely have greater impact on the public psyche—than do those in (even best-selling) storybooks. Do these mass media offer greater potential for changing the dominant view of schoolpeople as offenders to one of schoolpeople as victims? I do not rule out the use of any storytelling medium with educational potential, but there are at least two good reasons for my focus on literature generally and nonfictional educational storytelling in particular.

First, of all popular art forms, the printed story may be the one most free to exhibit the textual qualities needed for edifying rather than merely entertaining the general public. Scripts for television and film tend to be more fully absorbed into the maw of the culture industry (Agger, 1990, p. 37): Authorial integrity and literary quality are eroded as production costs rise and producers become increasingly concerned about what the trade market will bear. While blockbusters are always appreciated by publishers, literature can be produced for less money than high-tech art, and can therefore afford more creative risk.

Second, I recognize the mind-set of the intended audience for my story, namely, educational research professionals with a limited view of who they can be. In seeking to expand the boundaries of the research community, I am sensitive to the sources of intransigence within the prevailing orthodoxy. My narrative considers the conservative nature of the politics of educational research methods and gauges the stringency of its reform proposals accordingly.

The politics of method, I believe, are rooted partially in the ability or inability to exercise certain research skills. Skills required for the successful pursuit of literary and vernacular forms of educational writing have long been ignored or marginalized, and so remain underdeveloped. Jacoby's (1987) sad commentary about the recent history of American intellectualism seems pertinent here: "As intellectuals became academics, they had no need to write in a public prose; they did not, and finally they could not" (p. 7). Counternarratives that valorize talents for literary and vernacular writing are likely to be perceived as threatening by many educational researchers. As Eisner (1986) argued:

> Our methods and our power are intimately related to the games we are adept at playing. When the prospect for a new game arises, we quite naturally assess how good we are at playing it. The prospect of losing competence or sharing turf is not, for most of us, attractive; the familiar is much more comfortable. So we have a tendency to keep the game as it is, particularly if we have been winning. Power, control, and admiration are not easy to share. (p. 13)

So while a few of the educational research avant-garde have recently written and approved novels as doctoral dissertations,[12] I daresay that in many schools and colleges of education the accomplishment of this feat remains as politically improbable as the publication of compelling and morally persuasive short stories in most scholarly educational journals. Nevertheless, progress does occur. I have already noted that a revised narrative of professionalism now accepts certain kinds of qualitative inquiry with artistically based research procedures and textual design elements. Even "respectable" educational ethnographies now exhibit many features of the nonscientific, journalistic storytelling of Kotlowitz and Kidder. Of course, the prevailing narrative still insists upon calling such inquiry social science. That is a good reason to abandon it: Storytelling, even nonfictional storytelling, is not social science. Moreover, in my alternative narrative, widespread legitimacy as educational inquiry is eventually achieved even by works of fiction (not to mention plastic and performance art, and filmed and televised narrative). But it also sees the creation and dissemination of nonscientific, if still nonfictional, stories as a politically feasible alternative for now.

Closure: The Educational Researcher as Educator

My narrative of enhanced professionalism does not, therefore, underestimate the difficulty of creating professional space for ourselves by revising the public image of the people who inhabit our schools. It recognizes the obstacles to altering our collective view of ourselves as professionals who work apart from layfolk. It senses our difficulty in communicating directly with our fellow citizens. But is this a difficulty confined to those of us who have been taught to write in academese, or is it a common one that is simply exacerbated by a striving toward one unfortunate image of professionalism? The novelist Nadine Gordimer (1989) insisted, rather gloomily, that "writer potential" is limited for all authors, even storytellers. We will, she wrote,

> be understood only by readers who share terms of reference formed in us by our education—not merely academic but in the broadest sense of life experience: our political, economic, social, and emotional concepts, and our values derived from these: our cultural background. It remains true even of those who have put great distances between themselves and the inducted values of childhood: who have changed countries, convictions, ways of life, languages. (p. 59)

Such a distancing is, I believe, one of the primary consequences of our initiation into the professional subculture. We add a new galaxy to the plurality of worlds (home, the mass media, the public schools) which we educationists, as moderns, must learn to inhabit (Berger, 1973). But while my narrative conveys similar concern, it views Gordimer as overly pessimistic. It is possible, and can even be intellectually invigorating, to navigate between these galaxies. Indeed, such travel can sensitize us to the differences in values, languages, mythologies, and convictions between subcultures, including those of the academic and the layperson. It may even demand of us the practice we need to become better educators.

For ultimately, the optimism within my narrative emanates from the realization that many of us educational researchers were first and remain, foremost, educators. We are, therefore, in a Deweyan sense of that term, already competent dialecticians of world views, masters first of the empathic imagination and then of enticing others into redescribing their worlds. My story of who we will be envisions educational inquirers even more adept than noneducator journalists at coaxing our fellow citizens into accepting our closely observed, carefully imagined, invitingly framed redescriptions of people in the public schools. And as we move to educate the public in this fashion, we simultaneously enhance our own status as professionals, seizing greater control of our research destinies and thus becoming more of who we can be.

Notes

I express my appreciation to the faculty members and graduate students of the Arizona State University College of Education who discussed an earlier draft of this article at a colloquium in February 1992. Additional thanks go to John K. Smith and to several anonymous reviewers for their insightful comments.

1   Of course, not all educational researchers partake of this central tenet of the narrative of professionalism. But my description of this narrative is more than just a "straw story." The assumption that educational research is necessarily scientific is alive and well and inscribed in the thinking of many researchers, including qualitatively oriented ones. The literature is rife with examples, but my personal favorites include these: First, see an exchange between several prominent qualitative research theorists in *Review of Educational Research* (1989) over the notion of qualitative research traditions (Buchmann and Floden, 1989; Jacob, 1989). Only Lincoln (1989) refrained from assuming that all of those traditions arise from within the social sciences. (Elsewhere, Smith, 1987, included in her list of four qualitative approaches recognition of one that is arts-based.) Second, consult Rist's (1987) article in which he contended that Eisnerian-style educational critics are not fit to wear the "respectable cloak of educational research" because they are not anthropologists. Third, consider the fact that most of today's critical theorists in the field of education unhesitatingly accept the assumption of Habermas that ideology critique is necessarily a scientific endeavor (Keat and Urry, 1975) and never one of, say, revolutionary art.

Many of the methodologists cited in these examples (Rist, in particular) find it important to adhere to premises, principles, and practices associated with more traditional forms of social science. But others, still calling themselves social scientists, employ design elements (for example, a literary language, a story format) not previously associated with social science texts. The result has been a tendency toward "genre blurring, "a widespread phenomenon that has led to a "refiguration of social thought" (Geertz, 1983). But while the blurring of genres often makes it difficult to label authors or classify works, it hardly represents, even for Geertz, the demise of the social sciences. To the contrary, social scientists seem to assume a new form of preeminence as they "shape their work in terms of its necessities rather than according to received ideas as to what they ought or ought not to be doing. . . . Born omniform, the social sciences prosper as [genre blurring] becomes general" (Geertz, 1983, p. 21). One is left to imagine what, precisely, it is that is prospering. Nevertheless, to the chagrin of many inside the field of education and without, whatever it is has sometimes claimed the safe-text, professional social science seal of approval.

2   I thank an anonymous reviewer for quite rightly noting that my descriptions of the three narratives of research professionalism are, technically speaking, "arguments using a narrative style, though not narrative material." In describing and discussing the third of these narratives (enhanced professionalism), I argue for a

storytelling form of narrative inquiry that does indeed employ a narrative style and narrative substance.

3   Other kinds of narrative inquiry identified by Connelly and Clandinin (1990) include biography, autobiography, life histories, and oral history and folklore.

4   The antecedents of literary journalism can, in turn, be found in the travel literature of the eighteenth century, in some forms of autobiography, in British literary criticism from 1820 to 1840, and other diverse places (Wolfe, 1973).

5   A partial list: *Death at an Early Age* (Kozol, 1976); *Small Victories: The Real World of a Teacher, Her Students, and Their High School* (Friedman, 1990); *900 Shows a Year: A Look at Teaching From a Teacher's Side of the Desk* (Palonsky, 1986); *The Lives of Children: The Story of the First Street School* (Dennison, 1969); *Shut Up and Let the Lady Teach: A Teacher's Year in a Public School* (Sachar, 1991); *Our Last Term: A Teacher's Diary* (Natkins, 1986).

6   My thanks to Kyle Messner for this information.

7   Not to mention other educationists who write in a literary mode while not presenting research findings. They include Johan Aitken, Mark Johnson, Madeleine Grumet, Maxine Greene, and sometimes, in other places, the author of this article. My thanks to an anonymous reviewer for this point.

8   Accessibility is not, strictly speaking, a characteristic inherent within a text, but within the interactions between text and reader. Therefore, the use of certain forms of language and other rhetorical strategies may produce texts that are accessible to some readers but not to others. So, in this manuscript, even as I argue for layfolk-friendly research texts, I employ a scholarly mode of discourse meant to be accessible to academics who are familiar with certain features of conventional scholarship. For example, most educationists are more readily persuaded by discourse that mixes argument and narrative (see note 2) than by a literary-style story suited to a wider public. Moreover, nothing in my description of enhanced professionalism should be taken to suggest that we cease talking to each other in the manner to which we are accustomed.

9   In my view, Kidder's story would have been better served had he used the contours of the antagonistic student-teacher relationship as a framing device. Then the story would have ended with Clarence's departure in March. Having committed himself to a school-year-in-the-life of Ms. Zajak, however, Kidder needed to develop a new dynamic to hold the reader's attention until June arrived. Some reviewers have suggested that the book seems overly long. If so, it may be because Kidder only partly succeeds in replacing his most fascinating student-protagonist. Other students (Alejandro, Claude, Eduardo) take turns in the spotlight, but the drama never rises to its previous heights. The compellingness of the story suffers because the dynamic form is deflated.

10   Not all reviewers of *Among Schoolchildren* agree that it is a good example of a book that reveals a system of control and oppression. Ayers (1990), for example, argued that Kidder's story is an account of "what is, and what is fails all children

some of the time and most children all of the time" (p. 16). But the caring Zajak character is not portrayed as a successful teacher. Rather, she is a "semi-tragic figure," as Kohl (1989) put it, "a middle-class woman doing society's dirty work, with no support . . . facing problems that she cannot be expected to solve" (p. 538). Although, in my view, Kidder is less helpful than is, say, Kotlowitz in naming problematic, taken-for-granted social practices, lay readers should still gain a sense of how the cruel irrationalities of life outside of schools create victims inside as well.

11   The failure of my narrative to dwell on the storytelling of public school teachers is not meant to dismiss their accomplished narratives as something less than legitimate educational research. To the contrary, my narrative honors accomplished accounts of individual classrooms and schoolpeople written by teachers. Connelly and Clandinin (1990) list the following as illustrations: Coles (1989), Barzun (1944), Rieff (1972), Booth (1988), Natkins (1986), Paley (1981, 1986), Calkins (1983), Steedman (1982), Armstrong (1980), Dennison (1969), Rowland (1984), and Meek, Armstrong, Austerfield, Graham, and Placeter (1983). But why have more teachers not become authors of compelling and morally persuasive stories that could change negative public perceptions of them? Why have they waited for noneducator journalists like Tracy Kidder to tell their stories for them? The problems, I believe, are structural. Outlets for publicizing their stories are few. More importantly, teachers lack the time and resources to devote to this kind of communicative endeavor. My narrative, however, envisions a day in which the privileges presently extended to academics and journalists are possessed by schoolpeople working in dramatically restructured educational settings. In *that* utopia, those who are presently forced to live silent lives in the relative isolation of their classroom compartments will have acquired the powers of observation and the skills of composition needed for shaping and sharing their own stories about life in schools. Paradoxically, that day is more likely to arrive after the public perceives that teachers are the kind of people who deserve professional status. Until then teachers will remain largely dependent upon others to tell their stories.

12   Examples of educational novels as dissertations include Sellito (1991) and Ross (1986).

References

Agger, B. (1990). *The decline of discourse: Reading, writing, and resistance in postmodern capitalism.* New York: Falmer.

Aristotle. (1961). *Poetics.* (S. H. Bucher, Trans.). New York: Hill & Wang.

Armstrong, M. (1980). *Closely observed children: Diary of a primary classroom.* London: Writers and Readers in association with Chameleon.

Ayers, W. (1990). Classroom spaces, teacher choices. *Rethinking Schools, 5*(19), 3–16.

Barone, T. (1980). Effectively critiquing the experienced curriculum: Clues from the "new journalism." *Curriculum Inquiry, 10* (l), 29–53.

Barone, T. (1983). Education as aesthetic experience: "Art in germ." *Educational Leadership, 40* (4), 21–26.

Barone, T. (1992, April). Critical storytelling and the deep persuasion of the polity. Paper presented at the annual meeting of the American Educational Research Association, San Francisco.

Barthes, R. (1970). *Writing degree zero.* Boston: Beacon Press.

Barthes, R. (1970/1974). *S / Z.* (R. Miller, Trans.). New York: Hill & Wang.

Barzun, J. (1944). *Teacher in America.* New York: University Press of America.

Berger, P. (1973). *The homeless mind: Modernization and consciousness.* New York: Random House.

Best, S. (1989). The commodification of reality and the reality of commodification: Jean Baudrillard and post-modernism. *Current Perspectives in Social Theory, 9,* 23–51.

Booth, W. C. (1988). *The vocation of a teacher: Rhetorical occasions 1967–1988.* Chicago: University of Chicago Press.

Buchmann, M., & Hoden, R. E. (1989). Research traditions, diversity, and progress. *Review of Educational Research, 59*(2), 241–248.

Calkins, L. M. (1983). *Lessons from a child: On the teaching and learning of writing.* Melbourne: Heinemann.

Capote, T. (1965). *In cold blood: A true account of a multiple murder and its consequences.* New York: Random House.

Clandinin, D. J., & Connelly, F. M. (1987). *Narrative, experience, and the study of curriculum.* Washington, DC: The American Association of Colleges for Teacher Education.

Clandinin, D. J., & Connelly, F. M. (1988). Studying teachers' knowledge of classrooms: Collaborative research, ethics and the negotiation of narrative. *The Journal of Educational Thought, 22*(2A), 269–282.

Coles, R. (1989). *The call of stories: Teaching and the moral imagination.* Boston: Houghton Mifflin.

Connelly, F. M., & Clandinin, D. J. (1990). Stories of experience and narrative inquiry. *Educational Researcher, 19*(5), 2–14.

Dennison, G. (1969). *The lives of children: The story of the First Street School.* New York: Vantage Books.

Dewey, J. (1958). *Art as experience.* New York: Capricorn Books.

Dickens, C. (1839/1950). *The life and adventures of Nicholas Nickleby.* Oxford: Oxford University Press.

Dickens, C. (1854/1955). *Hard times for these times.* Oxford: Oxford University Press.

Eisner, E. W. (1976). Educational connoisseurship and educational criticism: Their forms and functions in educational evaluation. *Journal of Aesthetic Education* (Bicentennial Issue), *10*(3–4), 135–150.

Eisner, E. W. (1985). *The educational imagination* (2nd ed.). New York: Macmillan.

Eisner, E. W. (1986, September). *The primacy of experience and the politics of method.* Lecture presented at the University of Oslo, Norway.

Eisner, E. W. (1991). *The enlightened eye: Qualitative inquiry and the enhancement of educational practice.* New York: Macmillan.

Fay, B. (1975). *Social theory and political practice.* London: G. Allen.

Foucault, M. (1977). *Discipline and punish*. New York: Pantheon.

Friedman, S. G. (1990). *Small victories: The real world of a teacher, her students, and their high school*. New York: Harper & Row.

Friedson, E. (1986). *Professional powers*. Chicago: University of Chicago Press.

Geertz, C. (1983). *Local knowledge: Further essays in interpretive anthropology*. New York: Basic Books.

Gordimer, N. (1989). The gap between the writer and the reader. *New York Review of Books, 36*(14), 59–61.

Gordon, E. W., Miller, F., & Rollock, D. (1990). Coping with communicentric bias in knowledge production in the social sciences. *Educational Researcher, 19*(3), 14–19.

Habermas, J. (1972). *Knowledge and human interest*. Boston: Beacon Press.

Habermas, J. (1979). *Communication and the evolution of society*. Boston: Beacon Press.

Haskell, T. L. (1977). *The emergence of professional social science: The American Social Science Association and the nineteenth-century crisis of authority*. Urbana, IL: University of Illinois Press.

Horkheimer, M., & Adorno, T. W. (1972). *Dialectic of enlightenment*. New York: Herder & Herder.

House, E. R. (1991). Big policy, little policy. *Educational Researcher, 20*(5), 21–26.

Hugo, V. (1887/1893). *Les Miserables*. Boston: Little, Brown.

Iser, W. (1974). *The implied reader*. Baltimore: Johns Hopkins University Press.

Jacob, E. (1989). Qualitative research: A defense of traditions. *Review of Educational Research, 59*(2), 21-9-235.

Jacoby, R. (1987). *The last intellectuals: American culture in the age of academe*. New York: Basic Books.

Keat, R., & Urry, J. (1975). *Social theory as science.* London: Routledge & Kegan Paul.

Kidder, T. (1989). *Among schoolchildren*. Boston: Houghton Mifflin.

Kohl, H. (1989, November 6). Teach-by-number schools. *The Nation,* pp. 537–538.

Kotlowitz, A. (1991). *There are no children here: The story of two boys growing up in the other America.* New York: Doubleday.

Kozol, J. (1967). *Death at an early age.* New York: Houghton Mifflin.

Langer, S. K. (1957). *Problems of art.* New York: Scribner's.

Lincoln, Y. S. (1989). Qualitative research: A response to Atkinson, Delamont, and Hammersley. *Review of Educational Research, 59*(2), 237–239.

Mailer, N. (1968). *Armies of the night: History as a novel, the novel as history.* New York: New American Library.

Mailer, N. (1979). *The executioner's song.* New York: Warner Books.

McGaghie, W. C. (1991). Professional competence evaluation. *Educational Researcher, 20*(l), 3–9.

McLaren, P. (1986). *Schooling as a ritual performance.* London: Routledge & Kegan Paul.

McLaren, P. (1989). *Life in schools: An introduction to critical pedagogy in the foundations of education.* New York: Longman.

McNergney, R. F. (1990). Improving communication among educational researchers, policymakers, and the press. *Educational Researcher, 19*(3), 20–21.

Meek, M., Armstrong, S., Austerfield, V., Graham, J., & Placeter, E. (1983). *Achieving literacy: Longitudinal studies of adolescents learning to read.* London: Routledge & Kegan Paul.

Mills, C. W. (1953). *White collar.* New York: Oxford University Press.

Natkins, L. G. (1986). *Our last term: A teacher's diary.* Lanham, MD: University Press of America.

Norris, F. (1870/1958). *The octopus.* Boston: Houghton Mifflin,

Orwell, G. (1903/1986). *Down and out in Paris and London.* London: Secker & Warburg.

Paley, V. G. (1981). *Wally's stories: Conversations in the kindergarten.* Cambridge: Harvard University Press.

Paley, V. G. (1986). *Molly is three: Growing up in school.* Chicago: University of Chicago Press.

Palonsky, S. B. (1986). *900 shows a year: A look at teaching from a teacher's side of the desk.* New York: Random House.

Peshkin, A. (1986). *God's choice: The total world of a fundamentalist Christian school.* Chicago: University of Chicago Press.

Peshkin, A. (1991). *The color of strangers, the color of friends: The play of ethnicity in school and community.* Chicago: University of Chicago Press.

Rieff, P. (1972). *Fellow teachers: Of culture and its second death.* Chicago: University of Chicago Press.

Rist, R. C. (1987). Research in the shadows: A critique of "On equality, visibility, and the fine arts program in a Black elementary school." *Curriculum Inquiry, 17*(4), 447–452.

Robbins, B. (1991). Oppositional professionals: Theory and the narrative of professionalization. In J. Arac & B. Johnson (Eds.), *Consequences of theory* (pp. 1–21). Baltimore: Johns Hopkins University Press.

Rorty, R. (1989). *Contingency, irony, and solidarity.* Cambridge, UK: Cambridge University Press.

Ross, V. J. (1986). *Bite the wall!* Palm Springs, CA: ETC Publications.

Rowland, S. (1984). *The enquiring classroom.* London: Falmer.

Sachar, E. (1991). *Shut up and let the lady teach: A teacher's year in a public school.* New York: Poseidon Press.

Said, E. (1983). *The world, the text, and the critic.* Cambridge: Harvard University Press.

Sellito, P. (1991). *Balancing acts: A novel.* (Doctoral dissertation, Hofstra University). *Dissertation Abstracts International, 52,* 1166A.

Sizer, T. (1988). Editorial: Dailiness. *Educational Researcher, 17*(3), 5.

Smith, M. L. (1987). Publishing qualitative research. *American Educational Research Journal, 24,* 173–183.

Steedman, C. (1982). *The tidy house.* London: Virago.

Steinbeck, J. (1939/1946). *The grapes of wrath.* New York: Bantam Books.

Stone, R. (1988). The reason for stories: Toward a moral fiction. *Harper's, 276*(1657), 71–78.

Wolfe, T. (1973). *The new journalism.* New York: Harper & Row.

Wolfe, T. (1979). *The right stuff.* New York: Farrar, Straus & Giroux.

Wright, R. (1966). *Black boy: A record of childhood and youth.* New York: HarperCollins.

Chapter 13

On Kozol and Sartre
and Educational Research as
Socially Committed Literature
(1994)

*The writer is neither a Vestal nor an Ariel. Do what he may, he's in the thick
of it, marked and compromised down to his deepest refuge.*
—Jean-Paul Sartre

One early morning in January, unable to sleep, I turned to my favorite
late night channel, C-SPAN. On the screen were members of the Labor
and Human Resources Committee of the United States Senate questioning the Secretary of Education Designate, Governor Richard Riley of South
Carolina. Senator Wellstone of Minnesota spoke with a degree of passion
about what he described as a long ignored educational issue, equity in
educational funding. The senator then cited a recently read book that
detailed the enormous disparities in school funding in the United States.
The book was *Savage Inequalities* by Jonathan Kozol (1992).

Governor Riley's vague and rambling response seemed to ignore Senator
Wellstone's suggestion about federal incentives for states to attend to the
issue of fairness in school funding. And it is certainly possible (a pessimist
would say "likely") that, despite a fresh, semi-liberal Democratic administration, the stark contrasts between rich and poor school districts that
Kozol describes will remain with us. But I was thinking about the infre-
quency with which this work of educational research that derives much of
its power from passionate descriptions of the experiences of schoolpeople
is cited in prominent public forums. Indeed, not only has *Savage Inequalities* been cited in congressional hearings; Kozol's book is a best-
seller that (whatever its ultimate impact on educational policy) has el-
bowed its way into a corner of the national consciousness. This includes

the consciousness of the educational research establishment: one of two recipients of the 1993 American Educational Research Association Outstanding Book Award, it was also the subject of an entire issue of *Educational Theory* (1993). So why, I wondered that night as I do today, was such an important and honored book about the sad state of American schooling not written by any of my academic colleagues, by a credentialed educational researcher?

This question frames my discussion here of the ultimate purposes of those of us who toil as educational researchers, and of how we design our research endeavors to further those purposes. Focused on a single text, I do not intend to catalogue all the conceivable worthwhile motives for doing educational research. I point, instead, to a particular tradition of research and writing about social (including educational) affairs in which, I suggest, Kozol's book participates—a venerable tradition, but one rarely engaged in by members of the educational research community. *Savage Inequalities*, like Kozol's earlier works, *Rachel and Her Children* (1988) and *Death at an Early Age* (1967), exemplifies the kind of writing I call *socially committed literature*. It is, I suggest, a latter-day example of the sort of literary endeavor favored by Jean-Paul Sartre. In the essay *What Is Literature?*, Sartre (1988) began to develop the concept of *litterature engagee*, or *engaged literature*.

Over the course of a lifetime he returned to the concept, modifying and refining it in works such as *Introducing Les Temps Modernes* (Sartre, 1988) and *Black Orpheus* (Sartre, 1963). Sartre believed strongly in the irreducible historicity of the writer, and his own writing represents an involvement in a moral project fashioned specifically for the world war and postwar eras. Of course, as an inhabitant of a later era, a participant in a postmodern intellectual culture, I cannot endorse every Sartrean assertion about the nature and purpose of committed writing. But I find at least three intriguing dimensions of Sartre's notion of engaged literature, each reflected in the work of Kozol, that prompt me to commend it to the attention of educational researchers, especially qualitative researchers. These relevant dimensions concern the attitudes of the researcher/author toward issues of social justice, her/his intended audiences, and her/his choice of rhetorical modalities for addressing those audiences about those issues.

Writing to Make History

The work of Sartre was one of several sources of some news about the nature of human discourse that today is commonplace, if still useful. This was news of the moral weight of language. Sartre was a precursor to those speech act theorists (Austin, Searle) who understood that words are not merely mirrors that reflect the essences of objects in the world, but that all speech is a form of action. For speech act theorists, when the author of a text chooses her words s/he chooses how to act. Action, moreover, necessarily implies a choice of values, which are, in turn, supported by the particular interests of the actor/author. Ethical questions, therefore, cannot be avoided in the human endeavor of authoring a literary text.

And what were Sartre's interests in writing? Not to merely describe the world (description is "pure contemplative enjoyment" [Sartre, 1988, p. 234]), nor to explain it ("explanation is acceptance, it excuses everything" [1988, p. 234]). Sartre wrote to transform the world. He chose a kind of writing that rejected the purity of knowledge allegedly found in abstract, speculative philosophy in favor of a synthesis that included interpretation and critique aimed toward an intervention in history. This was a literature, not of consumption, but of production. Sartre (1988) put it this way: "The world and man reveal themselves by *undertakings*. And all the undertakings we might speak of, reduce themselves to a single one, *making history*" (p. 104).

Although Foucault and others were later to explore more fully the relationships between power and language, Sartre seemed to understand that words are inevitably tools, "the instruments of a possible action" (Sartre, 1988, p. 54). Both written texts and tools are, he said, "the congealed outline of an operation" (1988, p. 55). But Sartre was insistent that the text was also unlike a tool inasmuch as the text was not "a means for any end whatever" (1988, p. 55). In *What Is Literature?* Sartre clarified what he considered to be a desirable end for a work of literature: "Whether he speaks only of individual passions or whether he attacks the social order, the writer, a free man addressing free men, has only one subject—freedom" (1988, p. 68). Sartre elaborated on his general assertions about freedom as the primary goal of literature in a discussion of a particular text of a contemporary American writer.

Perhaps because Jonathan Kozol had yet to write *Savage Inequalities*, Sartre focused on the work of Richard Wright, author of *Black Boy* (1966). In writing about the situation of a Black man transported to the North to experience oppression anew, Wright was not aiming to inspire "contemplation of the True, Good, and Beautiful when ninety percent of the Negroes . . . are practically deprived of the right to vote" (Sartre, 1988, p. 78). Sartre saw that, as a novelist, Wright cast his concerns in terms of specific contingencies, as the lived experiences of a particular man at a particular moment of history. And most importantly, Wright wrote about a particular kind of social injustice. Wright's commitment to his story, averred Sartre, was to transforming that part of the world in which those freedoms were, at that moment in time, curtailed.

Black Boy, wrote Sartre, was a tool that appealed to freedom, and its appeal was aimed at both segments of a divided audience. The first segment was comprised of Wright's black American contemporaries. As read by that audience, Wright's work resembled what bell hooks (1991) would later refer to as a *narrative of struggle*, a narrative in which the subjectivity of a member of an oppressed group asserts itself. Sartre's speculations about the effects of Wright's writings on black Americans preceded those of latter-day commentators on the usefulness of this kind of narrative: "[A] mere hint is enough for them; they understand with their hearts. . . . [Wright] mediates, names, and shows them the life they lead from day to day in its immediacy, the life they suffer without finding words to formulate their sufferings. He is their conscience. . ." (Sartre, 1988, p. 79).

Unlike Wright, however, Kozol is a white liberal describing the travails of poor children who are mostly black. And the sensibilities of some postmodernists are offended by the notion of privileged authors attempting to enlighten the oppressed about themselves. Writing from my own privileged perch, I wonder less about that particular ethical conundrum than about the ability of even an extremely talented investigative journalist to promote in (white or black) poverty-plagued readers the sort of "decolonization of the imagination" that hooks (1991) attributed to works of "critical fiction." But Sartre argued that a book such as Black Boy also spoke to an additional audience, one of whites who were unfamiliar with, even antagonistic toward, African Americans, and I suggest that the usefulness of Kozol's book may lie in its power to edify and disturb comfortable middle-class readers who are reticent to face certain realities of American society.

Concerning white readers of Black Boy, Sartre (1988) wrote that "Wright does not completely know them. It is only from without that he conceives their proud security and that tranquil certainty . . . that the world is white and that they own it . . . . [I]t is a matter of implicating them and making them take stock of their responsibilities" (p. 80). Sartre was adamant about the need for literature to work toward freedom through that kind of political transgressiveness. Engaged literature was an activity challenging to the established interests within society:

If the society sees itself and . . . sees itself as seen, there is . . . a contesting of the established values of the regime. The writer presents it with its image; he calls upon it to assume it or to change itself. At any rate, it changes; it loses the equilibrium which its ignorance had given it; it wavers between shame and cynicism; it practices dishonesty; thus the writer gives society a guilty conscience; he is thereby in a state of perpetual antagonism towards the conservative forces which are maintaining the balance he tends to upset (Sartre, 1988, p. 81).

Indignation? Shame? Feelings of guilt? These terms seem appropriate for describing the attitudes induced in some privileged readers by *Savage Inequalities* as well as *Black Boy*. As a storyteller who has not lived the stories he recasts, a powerful journalist/researcher who presumes to speak on behalf of the downtrodden, Kozol might be accused of exhibiting the souls of the disenfranchised out of a peculiar need to move history closer to his own liberal vision. Reacting against the arrogance of modernist anthropologists, some poststructuralists hold that, just as privileged authors should not presume to tell tales of oppression to the oppressed, so should they, regardless of motive, refrain from offering tours of the personal landscapes of the disempowered to privileged voyeurs. Many might have preferred that the marginalized characters in Kozol's book tell their own stories to others of their social class, naming the sources of particular injustices, cultivating a sense of community and "strategies that . . . ensure survival in the face of abuse and open up the possibility of a transformed future . . ." (hooks, 1991, p. 54). Although neither Kozol nor Sartre deny the necessity of the reclamation of voices, Kozol's book, like some other socially committed literature, defies the Foucauldian insistence that it matters less what is said than who is speaking. For Kozol and Sartre it is more important that what is said (whether by the formerly silenced who are still living in pain or by skilled, well-intentioned strangers) be effectively designed to disturb the sociopolitical and economic status quo.

Of course we know that such products of righteous passion and outrage usually fail to move the elite whom Sartre cited as important targets of the socially committed writer. History is replete with successful ploys for marginalizing and even muzzling authors whose writings are perceived as blasphemous in their attempts to lay bare the ways in which relations of domination are maintained. One example of a silencing strategy (familiar to, among others, the researcher/evaluator) is the pensioning of the writer, buying his/her technical expertise on terms set by the commissioner. And a marginalizing ploy is the cordoning off of literary texts (which are portrayed as collapsing inward into an imaginary realm, and therefore, subjectively felt but practically useless) from those supposedly trustworthy, dispassionate, "truthful," scientific texts-as-tools that honor real-world objects. The masterminds of this particular approach to diminishing the aesthetic have included various sorts of positivist and postpositivist theorists, as well as formalist aestheticians who have served as allies of those who would turn artists into political eunuchs.

Often critical writers themselves serve as dupes for their ideological opponents, unknowingly abetting those who would dismiss their work. These self-defeating tendencies have been subject of recent criticism from within the field of education and without. Complaints have been lodged about the zealous self-righteousness of oppositional theorists, about their presumption of knowledge secured within a realm that lies beyond time and space, about their intimidation of audiences with works of (not art but) propaganda suffused with a kind of moral positivism. Critics, including feminists such as Ellsworth (1989), would prefer, instead, a recognition that all knowledge is "contradictory, partial, and irreducible" (p. 321).

There is, moreover, the issue of accessibility. The authors of much oppositional writing in education stand accused of poor pedagogy in advocating social and economic democracy in arcane language that is incomprehensible both to the disempowered on whose behalf they claim to speak and to privileged lay audiences who reside outside of the discursive subcommunity of the critical theorist (Jacoby, 1987; Agger, 1990; Barone, 1992a; Gore, 1990; Liston, 1988; see Giroux, 1992, for a defense).

It is, I suggest, a tribute to Sartre and to Kozol that they (ultimately, largely) managed to sidestep these mines that lie in wait for those who move to reconcile their hopes for social justice with their role as writers. Despite leftist commitments, each avoids conformance to a political agenda that might override literary considerations. Indeed, Sartre championed a kind of writing that is transgressive but not hegemonic, a (shall we say) Kozolian brand of authorship that partakes of neither the academic obscurantism nor the meretricious totalizing that often characterizes radical writing. Sartre's call was instead for what, I will argue, Kozol delivers: oppositional texts that offer readers certain benefits of works of literature.

Writing to Make Literature

Sartre saw the fundamental purpose for writing a piece of literature as coaxing the reader toward a novel view of certain social phenomena. Literary texts are, therefore, essentially rhetorical devices. (All texts are, of course, even, as theorists such as Latour [1988] and Vattimo [1988] have insisted, scientific ones.) The art of writing, however, must not be turned into the creation of propaganda (Sartre, 1988, p. 214), a tendency more easily resisted when a writer does not presume that s/he is in possession of a final, correct interpretation of those phenomena. The socially committed writer must attempt to make history through a discourse that is subtler than logical/linear/propositional/theoretical discourse, by gently enticing the reader indirectly to reconsider the political and historical realities of a particular situation.

How does a writer accomplish this? Sounding much like latter-day phenomenological aestheticians such as Susanne Langer, Sartre spoke of literature as a medium of intersubjective communication. The task of the literary author not than simply to designate objective realities, but rather to evoke in the reader an image that could be directly *sensed*, an experience that could be relived. Sartre came to see literary language as a medium that not only conveyed but embodied that which is non-conceptual, as a means of access to the *vecu* of another person" (Howells, 1979, p. 218). Part of Sartre's prescription was to put the reader in touch with "a manner of being" (Suhl, 1970), to artfully locate specific characters within the alienating and oppressing contingencies of their lives, thereby suggesting a means of escape from that oppression. In this manner, "we recall . . . that in committed literature, *commitment* must in no way lead to a forgetting of *literature*" (Sartre, 1988).

Sartre used the term *literature* broadly. To be literary a work did not require all of the formal qualities demanded by, say, the structuralist critics. Likewise, *Savage Inequalities* is hardly art in any rigorous sense of that term. It does not, for example, embody the kind of eidetic form that characterizes most works of fiction. Moreover, in describing the conditions in the schools of the poor in six American cities, Kozol does not heavily invest in metaphorical allusions. He performs less like a novelist than as an investigative journalist who is as infatuated with numbers as with portraits of singular characters. But *Savage Inequalities* is indeed rife with images that enable the reader to directly sense the "manner of being" of poor students in under-funded city schools. It is primarily the compellingness of those mini-portraits that, to my mind, serves to qualify Kozol's work as Sartrean-style *litterature engagee*. For example, in a passage of which Sartre would certainly approve, Kozol (1992) describes the oppressive life conditions of an eight-year-old Chicago orphan:

> He talks to himself and mumbles during class, but he is never offered psychiatric care or counseling. When he annoys his teacher, he is taken to the basement to be whipped. He isn't the only child in the class who seems to understand that he is being ruined, but he is the child who has first captured my attention. His life is so hard and he is so small; and he is shy and still quite gentle. He has one gift: He

draws delightful childish pictures, but the art instructor says he "muddles his paints." She shreds his work in front of the class. Watching this, he stabs a pencil point into his hand.

Seven years later he is in the streets. He doesn't use drugs. He is an adolescent alcoholic. Two years later he has a child that he can't support and he does not pretend to try. In front of Lord & Taylor he is seen in a long leather coat and leather hat. To affluent white shoppers he is the embodiment of evil. He laughs at people as they come out of the store; his laugh is like a pornographic sneer. Three years later I visit him in jail. His face is scarred and ugly. His skull is mapped with jagged lines where it was stitched together poorly after being shattered with a baseball bat. He does not at all resemble the shy child that I knew ten years before. He is regarded as a kind of monster now. He was jailed for murdering a white man in a wheelchair. I find him a lawyer. He is given 20 years. (pp. 194–195)

What is (blessedly, I say) missing from such a passage is the penchant of many of today's oppositional writers for hovering above the ground upon which real injustices are dealt out. Rather, Kozol's—and Sartre's—devotion is/was to particular historical contingencies at the expense of academic abstractions. An author cannot put the reader in touch with "a manner of being" through high theory: Iris Murdoch (1953, p. 78) pointed out Sartre's awareness that "we can no longer formulate a general truth about ourselves which shall cover us like a house." This is not to deny the usefulness (or "generalizability") of such writings. Indeed, Sartre identified two dimensions of works of literature. Howells (1979) described the first as "*relative* . . . [that dimension] which makes the work of art this particular work and none other, created by a particular artist belonging to a particular society and epoch" (p. 55). The second dimension is *universal* insofar as the work calls to mind similar qualities in other experiences and rescues the work from a fate of narrow relevance. But most importantly, in good art "*the second element can only be known through the first*" (Howells, 1979, p. 55 [emphasis mine]).

Sartre's demand for the presence of both elements in a text meant that mere establishment of empathic identification with a character was insufficient for good socially committed literature. The text must do more: it must also reveal the webs of injustices in which characters are entangled, show how debilitating social and institutional forces intrude upon and distort the lives of those characters. And Kozol's work does indeed honor this dialectic of the general and the specific. His text oscillates between two poles, moving back and forth between a broad thesis about the nature and causes of the gross inequalities within the American school system and the gruesome details of lived experiences that feed that thesis.

Perhaps most importantly, Kozol's choice of rhetorical modality is suited for at least one kind of audience Sartre had in mind for his *litterature engagee*, namely, readers who require persuasion of the reality and depth of the injustices portrayed. Sartre hoped that, instead of aiming primarily at fellow intellectuals, socially committed writers would reach out to the broad masses of people and their leaders who might, in the kind of socialist democracy Sartre favored, be moved to enact regressive public policy.[1] And while Kozol's achievement would have been even more impressive had I heard it quoted by Senators Thurmond and Helms in addition to Wellstone, it seems safe to say that Kozol has at least been heard by some of the leaders (and other privileged citizens) in our own political democracy.

Sartre was, in fact, so convinced of the need for wide dissemination of socially committed works that he recommended employment of the popular media: "The book is the noblest, the most ancient of forms; to be sure, we will always have to return to it. But there is a literary art of radio, film, editorial, and reporting. . . . We must learn to speak in images, to transpose the ideas of our books into these new languages" (Sartre, 1988, pp. 216–217). As Ungar (1988, p. 15) noted, Sartre honored his own advice by engaging in radio broadcasts, and producing plays *(The Dirty Hands)*, screenplays *(The Chips Are Down)*, novels *(Iron in the Soul)*, and essays *(Saint Genet)*.

Qualitative Research as Literature That Makes History

But perhaps it was the failure of any of his works to produce the radical kinds of social changes for which he yearned that led to the elderly Sartre's disillusionment with his notion of *litterature engagee*. Late in life Sartre (1964, p. 212) could be heard lamenting that "for a long time I took my pen for a sword; now I know our impotence." *Too* late in his life, in my judgment. For while the jaded Sartre of the 1960s is unable to reclaim the spirit of hopefulness unleashed through his earlier works, he cannot erase the definition his youthful writings gave to a whole tradition of literary endeavors that do precisely what he once so rightfully insisted they must, namely, transform the world though writing that is simultaneously insistent and graceful.

Writing years after Sartre's death, the neopragmatist philosopher Richard Rorty (1989) is among the latest authors to identify an *oeuvre* of literature that does indeed succeed in Sartrean terms. This literature, wrote Rorty, is of the kind that is dedicated to the quest for human solidarity, granting its readers "the ability to see more and more traditional differences (of tribe, religion, race, customs, and the like) as unimportant when compared with similarities with respect to pain and humiliation—the ability to think of people wildly different from ourselves as included in the range of 'us'" (p. 141). For Rorty, as for the youthful Sartre, these works are:

> detailed descriptions of particular varieties of pain and humiliation (in, for example, novels or ethnographies) rather than philosophical or religious treatises . . . the modern intellectual's principal contributions to moral progress . . . . [They include] . . . books about slavery, poverty, and prejudice . . . [such as] *The Condition of the Working Class in England* and the reports of muckraking journalists and government commissions, [as well as] novels like *Uncle Tom's Cabin, Les Miserables, Sister Carrie, The Well of Loneliness,* and [yes, Richard Wright's] *Black Boy.* Such books help us to see how social practices we have taken for granted have made us cruel. (p. 141, 192)

But these books, more like strategically placed levers than mirrors of nature, these books with "redescriptions that change our minds on political situations" are, said Rorty (1989, 174) "the sort of thing which only writers with very special talents, writing at just the right moment in just the right way, are able to bring off." Ironically, Sartre's nemesis, Orwell (1946), was able to write such a book (*Animal Farm,* his persuasive redescription of the realities of Stalinist communism that changed the minds of American liberals), while Sartre, by his own admission, was not. I believe that Jonathan Kozol has certainly demonstrated the ability to write books with the potential for transforming public perceptions of what ails American schools. But more to the point, I believe that many of today's educational researchers (especially qualitative researchers) also possess, to a much greater extent than they can imagine, the "very special talents" needed for making history.

What has prevented us from trying? It is beyond the scope of this paper to trace the historical roots of the educational research community's dominant attitudes about the relationships between politics and scholarship, of our beliefs concerning to whom we should address our writing, of our prevailing notions about which forms of rhetoric are acceptable for composing a research text.[2] But I believe that Sartre would recommend rethinking those attitudes and beliefs. He would, more specifically, propose shifts that are embodied in the work of Jonathan Kozol: away from a posture of scholarly detachment toward one of passionate commitment to a redistribution of social resources; away from texts aimed exclusively at our academic colleagues toward direct communications with additional constituencies (such as educational practitioners, policymakers, and the public-at-large) who must join in the enactment of such a redistribution; away from the detached, arcane, technical languages of philosophical and scientific theory, toward modes of discourse feared by powermongers throughout history, the vernacular languages of literature.

Let me repeat that I am not claiming that making history in the Sartrean sense through writing Kozol-style socially committed literature is the only purpose for embarking on our research outings. But I do suggest that it is a noble purpose, and one to which more of us might dedicate ourselves. For in doing so, I believe that we can transform, not only the field of educational research, but also the landscape of American schooling.

Notes

1   If there is any doubt about Kozol's political motives, consider that the paperback
     version of his book included a detachable postcard addressed to "President George
     Bush" from "A Voter (Signature)."

2   The history of these attitudes is the subject of Barone, 1992b.

References

Agger, B. (1990). *The decline of discourse.* Bristol, PA: Falmer Press.

Barone, T. (1992a). Acquiring a public voice: Critical storytelling, curriculum specialists, and school reform. *JCT: An Interdisciplinary Journal of Curriculum Studies, 10*(1), 139–152.

Barone, T. (1992b). A narrative of enhanced professionalism: Educational researchers and popular storybooks about schoolpeople. *Educational Researcher, 21*(8), 15–24.

Educational Theory. (1993). *43* (1).

Ellsworth, E. (1989). Why doesn't this feel empowering? Working through the repressive myths of critical pedagogy. *Harvard Educational Review, 59,* 297–324.

Giroux, H. (1992) Language, difference, and curriculum theory: Beyond the politics of clarity, *Theory into Practice, 31*(3), 219–226.

Gore, J. (1990). What can we do for you! What can "we" do for "you"? Struggling over empowerment in critical and feminist pedagogy. *Educational Foundations, 4*(3), 5–26.

hooks, b. (1991). Narratives of struggle. In P. Mariani (Ed.), *Critical fictions: The politics of imaginative writing,* pp. 53–61. Seattle, WA: Bay Press.

Howells, C. (1979). *Sartre's theory of literature.* London: The Modern Humanities Research Association.

Jacoby, R. (1987). *The last intellectuals: American culture in an age of academe.* New York: Basic Books.

Kozol, J. (1967). *Death at an early age: The destruction of the hearts and minds of Negro children in the Boston public schools.* Boston: Houghton, Mifflin.

Kozol, J. (1988). *Rachel and her children: Homeless families in America.* New York: Crown.

Kozol, J. (1992). *Savage inequalities: Children in America's schools,* New York: HarperCollins.

Latour, B. (1988). *The Pasteurization of France.* Cambridge: Harvard University Press.

Liston, D. (1988). *Capitalist schools.* New York: Routledge.

Murdoch, I. (1953). *Sartre.* Cambridge: Harvard University Press.

Rorty, R. (1989). *Contingency, irony, and solidarity.* Cambridge: Cambridge University Press.

Sartre, J-P. (1963). *Black Orpheus.* (Arthur Gilette, Trans.). New York: University Place Book Shop.

Sartre, J-P. (1964). *Words.* (Irene Clephane, Trans.). London: Hamish Hamilton.

Sartre, J-P. (1988). *What Is Literature? and Other Essays.* Cambridge: Harvard University Press, 1988.

Suhl, B. (1970). *Jean-Paul Sartre: A literary and political study.* New York: Macmillan.

Ungar, S. (1988). Introduction. In J-P. Sartre, *What Is Literature? and Other Essays*, (pp. 3–20). Cambridge: Harvard University Press.

Vattimo, G. (1988). *The end of modernity: Nihilism and hermeneutics in postmodern culture.* London: Polity.

Section V

BAKHTIN AND BEYOND

The concluding article in this collection is among the most recently written. It serves as a tribute to the powerful and creative theorizing of Mikhail Bakhtin. Like the others who have contributed greatly to my narrative identity, Bakhtin helped me to name, and therefore to own, ideas that previously resided in my pre-understanding, resting beneath the surface of my consciousness, and diffused throughout the texts I have written. Chapter 14 (1995) appreciates Bakhtin's insights about how a polyphonic novelistic form of discourse can honor multiple perspectives—those of writer, characters, and reader—in a manner that engenders trust among them. The result can be an educational inquiry text that temporarily surmounts the attitude of distrust recommended by skeptical postmodernists, thereby promoting emancipatory moments within some readers, and achieving a kind of critical significance.

Chapter 14

Persuasive Writings, Vigilant Readings, and Reconstructed Characters: The Paradox of Trust in Educational Storysharing (1995)

I really am looking for new narratives to replace the old ones. I distrust words and stories and yet probably they are what I value most. Paradox rules.
　　　　　　　　　　　　　　　　　　　　　　—Lynne Tillman (1991)

Can educational stories be trusted? This may appear to be a curious question at a time when the research community seems to have advanced beyond positivistic anxieties regarding the distorting tendencies within personal accounts. Nonetheless, several prominent narrative researchers have suggested caution in trusting stories for reasons that have not occurred to more traditional educational research methodologists. What are they?

The first is that an account may not be phenomenologically truthful. Grumet (1988), for example, described stories as "masks through which we can be seen," and asked about trustworthiness when "every telling is a potential prevarication" (p. 69). Nespor and Barylske (1991) contended that a portrait of oneself will vary with the "specific situation within fields of power, history, and culture" (p. 811).

A second reason cited for not fully trusting story accounts is that they tend to record unmediated experienced phenomena in a superficial manner. For some critics, the superficiality of stories composed in the vernacular bespeaks a lack of penetrating scholarship. Narrative accounts unaccompanied by scholarly analysis are viewed as incapable of advancing knowledge about educational matters.[1] A session at the 1993 annual meeting of the American Educational Research Association explored the question of whether case studies of teaching need to be surrounded by theoretical discourse before they are deemed publishable.[2] Indeed, the prevailing vision of what constitutes legitimate scholarship may partially explain the relative scarcity of published examples of autobiographies, biographies, and other fictional and nonfictional stories about schoolpeople written entirely in the vernacular (Barone, 1992). Stories by and about teachers and students in professional journals are nearly always folded within didactic material aimed at extracting scholarly meaning from the accounts.

For other narrativists, a life story unaccompanied by textual analysis exhibits a second deficiency. Stories, this argument goes, may recreate life experiences, but they cannot critically examine the political, cultural, and ideological systems engendering experience. Thus, the story may contain a record of constrained consciousness (Goodson, 1992). For Goodson, life stories are less than "critical" because (unlike many life histories) they cannot be trusted to challenge stereotypical, taken-for-granted ideas and beliefs or to shed light on the cultural forces conspiring to constrain the awareness of the "self" being described. Some scholars have provided examples of how this perceived failure can be corrected by focusing theoretical lenses on the lived experiences of schoolpeople, lenses crafted within various schools of emancipatory-minded social science, including poststructural literary criticism, neo-Marxism, and feminism. For example, Britzman (1991) presented and analyzed the stories of two student teachers from feminist, deconstructivist, and critical ethnographic perspectives. McLaren (1989) brought Marxist/critical theory to bear on a literary-style journal of his own teaching experiences.

In this essay, I revisit the issue of trust/mistrust of storytelling forms of discourse. I concede that a story never tells the absolute truth. Since the onset of deconstructivism, who can believe that any text does? Life stories are now suspect because of the power relationships discovered hidden in their authorial baggage. However, I contend that stories about schoolpeople can achieve a degree of critical significance. Just as discourse partaking of a critical science format and patois can promote emancipatory moments, so can story genres (biography, autobiography, literary journalism, and the novel) that are derived from literary forms and that honor the norms of everyday speech. I further argue that if educational stories are to reach maturity as a form of educational research, some of the most insightful among them must be left, at least momentarily, unaccompanied by critique or theory. To that end, I identify examples of literary style with emancipatory potential. My goal is to generate dialogue on what I term *emancipatory educational storysharing.*

I begin with an important reminder from the schools of literary criticism known as reader-response and poststructuralism. Critics in these fields have taught us no longer to view the literary text, the story, as a noun, a thing, whether a reified textual object or a piece of ghostly "mental furniture" (Ryle, 1949) in the mind of the writer or reader. They have persuaded us to regard it, instead, as a verb, as an activity, a literary experience characterized by a process of construction (by the writer) and of deconstruction and reconstruction (by the reader). The reality of the text, therefore, resides within the interaction between the writer and the reader, who, Polkinghorne (1988) noted, "function as parts in a whole communication event that occurs when the created narrative text is taken to be understood by different individuals" (p. 99).

Many deconstructivists view authoring and reading, in one sense, as identical activities. Writers, for example, must continuously read what they have written in order to proceed; we know that writing is silent dialogue. Readers become writers, as Agger (1990) has expressed it, when they read "strongly . . . engag[ing] dialogically with texts and thus remak[ing] them and the world to which they are an address" (p. 178). Furthermore, Bakhtin (1981) has introduced a third set of agents into the dialogue. These are the characters constructed by the author and reconstructed by the readers. For Bakhtin, many literary texts are a dialogue exchange between a multiplicity of voices speaking simultaneously (Holquist, 1990).

Each utterance within a dialogic exchange, moreover, should not be viewed as the exertion of the private will of an existential isolate operating within a cultural vacuum. It is an action that is historically contingent, never impervious to social conditions within a specific culture and time. To inquire, therefore, into the nature of particular stories about schooling is not to examine the qualities of textual objects but to consider attributes, including the power relationships, that adhere to the engagements within which stories are written and read. Indeed, I would like to distinguish between the activities of composing stories and of reading them in terms of the primary attitudes adopted by writers and readers, and the stances they take vis-a-vis the persons or characters portrayed in the stories.

Specifically, I propose that inevitably associated with the act of writing is the attitude of persuasiveness. When the act is a literary one, the form of persuasion can be identified as not argumentative or declarative but artistic. Moreover, since an important intention of the writer is indeed the intention to persuade, then the corresponding stance of the storyreader is understandably one of vigilance against abuse of authorial power. Writers and readers of narrative can also occasionally share a mutual aim in their textual activity. This is the aim of securing power for the characters whose stories they choose to craft and remake. Pursuance of this common goal can lead to dialogue in which mistrustful, writer-versus-reader antagonisms are temporarily suspended, as all agents conspire within an emancipatory moment.

Artfully Persuasive Storytellers

Within modern western culture, authors of texts have traditionally assumed a position of privilege, with special access to supposedly objective (and therefore politically neutral) truth, reason, and virtue. Their agenda has been to enlighten, educate, and perhaps even to instill moral values in their readers. The persuasive power of the modernist author resided in the assumption that there existed a single, literal reading of a textual object, the one intended by the author. As Rosenau (1992) put it:

> The modern author in society is a "legislator," defined as a specialist, a manager, a professional, an intellectual, or an educator . . . they "know" and "decide things" by weighing up the positive and negative and determining what is "true." [They] arbitrate in the sense of choosing between opposing points of view in controversy. What they select becomes "correct and binding" (Bauman, 1987). p. 27

Part of the postmodern intellectual attitude is a repudiation of the modernist notion of textual authorship. An author may no longer claim to provide universal truth as a morally or politically neutral translation of reality. The act of authoring is now exposed as arising from within a peculiar perspective bound to issues of personal meaning, history, and power. Having listened to Barthes' (1977) proclamation of the "death" of the modernist author, the black South African, Zoe Wicomb (1991), has celebrated her rebirth as a writer: "As a writer [unlike an author] I do not have an agenda [in the sense of a list of things to accomplish]. But like everyone else I write from a political position" (p. 14).

The realization that the creation of story narrative is indeed political is implicit in the work of Nespor and Barylske (1991). Using a metaphor or reification, these authors described story narratives as representational technologies, tools or "devices tied to specific cultural uses" (p. 807). When, for example, teachers tell stories about themselves, they are not revealing or expressing, but crafting and constructing, those "selves." Nespor and Barylske elaborated by quoting Kondo (1990):

Rather than bounded, essential entities, replete with a unitary substance and consciousness, identities become nodal points repositioned in different contexts. Selves, in this view, can be seen as rhetorical figures and performative assertions enacted in specific situations within fields of power, history, and culture. (cited in Nespor & Barylske, 1991, p. 811)

Similarly, the situated self, the persona constructed in the act of writing a story, can be viewed as a rhetorical figure employed in the interests of the writer. We may recognize this move toward regarding the devices of language as tools for constructing our views of "reality" as Wittgensteinian. Wittgenstein (1953/1968) reminded us that when we choose to employ alternative grammars and vocabularies, we are choosing to alter that reality. Rorty (1989) underscored the importance of using this redescriptive power of language to make new and different things possible and important. We must employ alternative descriptions of phenomena for the purpose of tempting others to accept and act upon those redescriptions of our own or other "selves" (Rorty, 1989, p. 41). Moreover, as Rorty noted, the devices of the storyteller, whether as ethnographer, journalist, autobiographer, dramatist, or novelist, are well suited for creating these powerful redescriptions.

One of these devices is the story form. The powerful allure of a format that invites the reader to join in solving a human problem, followed by an accumulation of meaning as the plot unfolds, and the relaxation of tension in a resolution of the central dilemma, is well known not only to aestheticians, but also to consumers of novels, dramas, short stories, biographies, and autobiographies. Because its powerful formal properties distort reality, story narrative is more suspect than other forms of discourse. As Holquist (1990) put it,

In a literary text, the normal activity of perception, of giving order to chaos, is performed to a heightened degree. . . . Every time we give order to the world: every time we write or read a literary text we give the greatest degree of (possible) order to the world. (p. 85)

Elegantly structured "high literature" prized by formalists often appeared too stunningly beautiful to be marred by acts of substantive criticism. Some poststructuralists, on the other hand, have championed stories that, even as they "sell" their redescriptions, invite discourse and critique rather than squelch it. These stories achieve this quality through rhetorical strategies that are distinct from (and at their best more delicate and indirect than) the tactics associated with other discursive forms. What are some of these strategies?

The human dilemma around which a story plot is erected is introduced within the context of what Iser (1974) called a virtual world (p. 42). The writer entices the reader into living vicariously within this hypothetical world, whether "fictional" or a version of actual events fashioned by the writer. Within the storysharing contract, the reader is asked to refrain from thinking of this storied world as a mirror image of reality, a literal construal of events. Instead, the reader is encouraged to travel outward into the hypothetical realm, although not to remain adrift in some unreal aesthetic remove. The reader is offered a configuration of lived phenomena sufficiently distanced from present realities to stand against, and thus comment upon, the life world of the reader. In this manner "we [readers] may come to notice," as Rorty (1989) suggested, "what we ourselves have been doing" (p. 141), or (I would add) what is being done to us.

This realization can be dangerous, transgressive, and disruptive of our comfortable views of the world (Foucault, 1977). Storytellers can entice some readers into reconsidering comfortable attitudes and values and others into affirming latent perspectives not sanctioned by the dominant culture. The act of writing an artfully persuasive educational story is one with the potential for luring readers into reconstructing the selves of schoolpeople or into rethinking their own selves and situations as educators. For this invitation to be effective, the storyteller must maintain a delicate balance between two countervailing tendencies. If the writer is to comment persuasively on the nearby world, she or he must be credible, offering observations that do not stray far afield from the lived experiences of the reader. The writer must strive for what Bruner (1987) called *verisimilitude* (p. 11), detailing familiar minutiae of daily life as lived within a particular moment of history and societal context. This quality implies a careful scrutinizing of the empirical world by the writer. On the other hand, the reader is coaxed into participating in the imaginative construction of literary reality through carefully positioned blanks (Iser, 1974, p. 113) in the writing. These blanks are pauses that the active reader must fill with personal meaning gathered from outside the text. They foster a kind of indeterminacy, an ambiguity of meaning that distinguishes literary activity from propaganda and other didacticisms.

The aim of storytellers therefore is not to prompt a single, closed, convergent reading but to persuade readers to contribute answers to the dilemmas they pose. For Bakhtin (1981), acts of writing that invite readers into this kind of dialogue possess the attribute of *novelness* (cited in Holquist, 1990, p. 84). Novelness (often found in literature but not exclusively in novels) adheres to that body of utterances that are least reductive of variety for through it a multiplicity of voices—readers, writers, characters—offer varied interpretations of phenomena. The invention of the novel resulted in the demise of two myths: "the myth of language that presumes to be the only language, and the myth of a language that presumes to be completely unified" (Bakhtin, 1981, p. 68).

Of course, not all acts of storytelling possess novelness. Those that do not recognize change or that suppress diversity (for example, socialist realist literature) belong, according to Bakhtin (1981), to the genre of the epic: "The epic world is constructed in the zone of an absolute, distanced image, beyond the sphere of possible contact with the developing, incomplete and therefore re-thinking and re-evaluating present" (p. 17). Like most forms of non-literary discourse, epic writing yields *declarative texts* (Belsey, 1980, p. 91), texts meant to impart knowledge and thus to shut out other voices, to limit interpretive options. Epic writing, in Iser's (1974) lingo, is devoid of gaps to be filled in by the reader. An example of educational storytelling that is epic and declarative is the kind imagined by Berliner (1992). Berliner suggested that stories peopled with teachers and students be composed and used to explicate and illustrate findings previously derived and legitimized through research strategies based on the "hard sciences."

The declarative author-persuader, therefore, seeks direct control over the interpretations placed upon the text in the act of reading; the artful writer-persuader understands the necessity of relinquishing control, of allowing readers the freedom to interpret and evaluate the text from their unique vantage points. In other words, the writer grants to the reader a greater degree of trust. But such generosity is, alas, sometimes beyond the capacity of even (because of their fervid dedication to an agenda) the most emancipatory-minded writers. Indeed, a desire for control may partially account for the penchant of educational narrative researchers for covering exposed stories with blankets of didactic analysis. Consider, for example, this account (in Lancy, 1993) of the decision by McLaren, while writing *Life in Schools*, to augment his narrative with theory:

> McLaren (1989) . . . had doubts about how his journal was being interpreted: "I ran the risk of allowing readers to reinforce their stereotypes of what schooling was like in the 'blackboard jungle'" (p. ix). Hence, he turns his (auto)biography into a case study by incorporating it into an overview of Marxist/critical theory. . . . So . . . instead of the "interpretations being as numerous as readers," McLaren tells us how the journal should be interpreted. (Lancy, 1993, p. 182)

McLaren apparently assumed that the only way to lead his readers away from a state of restrained consciousness was to persuade them declaratively to view his characters from his own preferred perspective.

Other emancipatory-minded writers, those more trusting of their readers, offer novelness. They write, as Wicomb (1991) suggested, from an obvious political perspective but without an agenda, and still succeed in (artfully) persuading readers through narrative unadorned by declarative critique either to question stereotypical notions about the story's characters; or, paraphrasing hooks (1991), to put together the bits and pieces and see anew one's own self as a whole being. To elaborate on this point, I invite these characters of the storyteller into our discussion.

Storied Characters as Reconstructed Selves

About whose "selves" does the storyteller write and the reader read? And why those particular selves? One set of answers can be found in the works of Richard Rorty (1989) and Clifford Geertz (1988). These writers emphasize the generation of empathic identification between society's strangers. Rorty expressed a need for powerful redescriptions of certain selves with whom it is difficult to feel a sense of human solidarity, who are viewed as Others. For example, the technocratic superstructure of schooling institutions ensures that teachers, administrators, and their distanced and bewildering students are included in this list of existential foreigners. Following Rorty's view, sharing vivid depictions of their modus vivendi may serve to reduce this alienation among schoolpeople and with those outside the school. This humanistic goal of storytelling seems congruent with Geertz's (1988) hopes for the future of ethnography:

> The next necessary thing is to enlarge the possibility of intelligible discourse between people quite different from one another in interest, outlook, wealth, and power, and yet contained in a world where, tumbled as they are into endless connection, it is increasingly difficult to get out of each other's way. (Geertz, 1988, p. 147)

For some story readers and writers, however, solidarity and empathy are not enough. Keenly disturbed by a maldistribution of power, emancipatory-minded storytellers and readers focus on members of groups who have been disenfranchised and disempowered.[3] These storytellers aspire, as hooks (1991) suggested, to provide more than "chronicles of pain," for such "colorful spectacles" can easily be appropriated "to keep in place existing structures of domination" (p. 59). They aim to do more than merely "converse across societal lines" (Geertz, 1988, p. 147), especially when those lines serve to demarcate the boundaries between the powerful and the powerless. Instead, they hope subtly to persuade readers to ask questions about the interests served by these lines and about the necessity of their existence.

In Habermasian terms, understanding within the world view of characters yields knowledge in the practical domain (Habermas, 1972). While such knowledge may facilitate social integration, these understandings are reached in the context of the limited state of social development at the time (Bredo and Feinberg, 1982). No consideration is given to the adequacy of these understandings in terms of broader interests of human development. This is not desirable within openly ideological critical science, nor within emancipatory-minded literature. Although these two approaches to socially conscientious inquiry honor different research protocols and rhetorical strategies, their primary interest is identical: namely, the general human interest of emancipation through the transformation of an unjust social system into one that is more democratic.

In order to accomplish this emancipatory goal, the writer cannot portray the self as operating within a moral and political vacuum. Instead, linkages must be established "between the structural dynamics of class, race [gender-based forms of hegemony], and the projects of human agents embedded in these historically constituted structures" (Sullivan, 1984, p. 124). Indeed, emancipatory-minded storytellers operate from the premise that these debilitating structures invade and, to some degree, condition the self. They must therefore be exposed if an alternate conception of the self is to be realized.

But what is the sociopolitical position of these selves vis-a-vis the writer? Elsewhere (Barone, 1994), I have recommended a tradition of storytelling identified by Sartre (1948/1949). Committed literature (or *litterature engagee*) consists of stories told by privileged writers on behalf of members of oppressed classes, those who have been robbed of their voices and cannot (yet) speak for themselves. Dedicated to the fundamental project of power redistribution, socially committed writers choose as their primary focus issues of social justice, and, as their overriding goal, reader action toward enfranchising the disenfranchised. Rorty (as well as Sartre) identified examples of prominent writers outside the field of education—Charles Dickens, Victor Hugo, John Steinbeck, Upton Sinclair, Nadine Gordimer—who as members of privileged groups have published stories of oppressed and marginalized characters. In the educational sphere, one may consider works by Kozol (1991), Sparkes (1994), and Barone (1989).

Sparkes (1994) and others have offered justifications for acts of writing that cross over social boundaries of race, class, gender, and/or sexual orientation. These justifications include: (a) people who hold advantaged positions can more effectively challenge their privileged peers on behalf of the less privileged; (b) self-studies by members of marginalized groups may be coated with self-protective ideology (and therefore phenomenologically untrustworthy); (c) a vulnerable member of a marginalized community may not as yet possess the resources (time, interest, cultural capital) for telling her or his own story; and/or (d) the stories may reflect false consciousness (and therefore be politically untrustworthy). Why, advocates of committed literature ask, should we invest our trust in autobiographies of the downtrodden any more than in tales about their lives told by empathic, but critical, privileged researchers? There is, moreover, Bakhtin's (1981) point that boundaries between selves are illusory, that there are no stable identities, and so we all inevitably speak in many possible voices, for ourselves and for each other. Fine (1992) has similarly cautioned against a romancing of oppressed selves as uncontaminated by dominant perspectives. No one, in other words, is sole proprietor of her or his own story.

In our postmodern age, these justifications require highlighting, for the weight of the *Zeitgeist* (Bakhtin and others notwithstanding) leans against writers who presume to tell the stories of other kinds of people. The thrust of the counterargument is seen in a quote from Owens (1989): "Perhaps it is in [the] project of learning how to represent *ourselves*—how to speak to, rather than for or about, others—that the possibility of a global culture resides" (p. 89). *Narratives of struggle* is the term hooks (1991) has used to describe an alternative tradition of emancipatory-minded stories, stories in which the writer speaks autobiographically as a member of an oppressed group. The selves that these narrators revisit are their own, or those of members within their own oppressed category of race, ethnicity, class, gender, or sexual orientation. The self-redescriptions, however, point in a specific political direction, for they arise out of a "coming to consciousness in the context of a concrete experimental struggle for self-actualization and collective . . . self determination. . . . [These writers] enrich resistance struggles" (hooks, 1991, p. 54) as they, in a gesture that is simultaneously literary and liberatory, imagine their oppressed selves otherwise. Narratives of struggle include (among many) Salvadoran writer Manuel Argueta's (1980/1983) *One Day of Life*, Toni Morrison's (1970) *The Bluest Eye*, and Zora Neale Hurston's (1937) *Their Eyes Were Watching God*. Two examples from education are (auto)biographical accounts: Mike Rose's (1989) *Lives on the Boundary*, and Basil Johnston's (1988) *Indian School Days*.

My argument is for catholicity: I see a need for both socially committed literature and stories of struggle in the future of educational narrative research. Effective emancipatory-minded storytellers within each of these traditions seek to demystify and transform facets of the selves of the disenfranchised. Whether a compassionate, committed, observant stranger, or someone less privileged who comprehends and critiques the nature of the sociopolitical web that constrains her or him, or (as Bakhtin and others would prefer) a person who is an amalgam of privilege and oppression, an emancipatory-minded storyteller wrestles with a paradox: *She or he must trust her or his readers, grant them interpretative space, even as she or he artfully persuades them to reflect critically upon and reconstruct the selves of particular characters.* It is to the attitude assumed by the reader in the dialogue that we now turn.

Vigilant Readings and Emancipatory Moments

The varied descriptions of writers of emancipatory-minded stories also apply to readers. Readers who identify with an oppressed group may achieve a unique outcome through reading about rhetorical figures who are metaphors for themselves. Self re-cognition may result in an imaginative naming of one's condition. Such readings may also promote a previously absent sense of collectivity, an awareness of the presence of others whose life stories overlap with those of the reader (Richardson, 1990).

Readers within privileged groups may, on the other hand, be disturbed to find that their narrow interests are challenged. Persuaded to divert their eyes no longer, they may recognize their implication in an unjust system and feel compelled to "take stock of their responsibilities" (Sartre, 1948/1949, p. 80). Finally, following Bakhtin, who is ever wary of the totalization of any character, the reader may, at different moments, respond as both privileged and oppressed.

Whether privileged, oppressed, or both, skeptical poststructuralists are *revolutionary readers* (Belsey, cited in Wicomb, 1991). Revolutionary readers are reticent to relax their critical faculties, even in the presence of a potentially emancipatory story written by a storyteller with novelness as an aim. Literary persuasion may appear relatively benign when compared with the positioning of the declarative text that implicitly denies the presence of any values undergirding the writing process.

But is the artful persuader really that virtuous? Rorty (1989) quoted George Orwell's chilling observations concerning the rhetorical strategies employed within the literary text:

> "Imaginative" writing is as it were a flank attack upon positions that are impregnable from the front. A writer attempting anything that is not coldly "intellectual" can do very little with words in their primary meanings. He gets his effect, if at all, by using words in a tricky roundabout way. (p. 174)

Orwell admitted that in writing *Animal Farm* he was, in fact, doing the same kind of thing (attempting to persuade through rhetorical devices) as his opponents, the apologists for Stalin, were doing (Rorty, 1989, p. 174). Revolutionary readers recall the insistence of postmodern critics from Barthes to Derrida that even texts of well-intentioned authors possess a surplus of meaning as supplied by a dominant culture. Despite the style of persuasion-by-participation adopted by the literary text, the revolutionary reader honors the responsibility to uncover and inspect as much of that surplus as possible.

But sometimes, within certain rare conferences between reader, writer, and characters, there appears the splendid paradox of poststructuralist textual antagonists sharing a moment of trust. As Wicomb (1991) says:

> Had my education offered me the possibility of revolutionary reading, I would have done what I do with any commodity produced in the culture that I am told is good for me: sift out what I consider valuable from that which I find objectionable. (p. 13)

Wicomb suggests (through a reifying metaphor) that in our long overdue march toward deconstructivism, we must not forget that there are some stories worthy of being reassembled and valued.

Indeed, haven't we all listened to storytellers who invite us into astoundingly liberating acts of textual reconstruction, acts that remind us of the fundamental usefulness of storysharing? This is what happens during an occasion of narrative communion when I, the vigilant reader, find that my tired, habitual way of perceiving the selves of particular sorts of strangers (including, perhaps, the stranger that is me) is challenged. I accept the invitation of the storyteller to resituate those selves within the historical and cultural contingencies that shape them so that I may imaginatively identify with these heretofore strangers. I take the offer of perceiving in a strange new way the cruel social and institutional forces that have served to distort these selves and accept the invitation to imagine these rhetorical figures, and their analogues outside the text, remade within more empowering conditions. I, the reader, enter into a *conspiracy* with the storyteller (Barone, 1990), a politically based conversation about the relationship between world-at-hand and world-to-be-made, a sharing of ideals and ideas towards a "possible future" (hooks, 1991, p. 55) in which the selves of the powerless are reconstituted into the selves of the empowered. Such a conspiracy cannot succeed without a suspension of distrust between the co-conspirators.

These conspiratorial moments are fragile, evanescent instants that occur within a unique constellation of historical and personal contingencies. They are rare, even if their effects can sometimes be long-lasting. The sifting, to borrow Wicomb's term, takes patience; the valuable, trustworthy texts are like precious gems among objectionable silt. But emancipatory-minded readers may recall occasions in which his or her negotiations with writer and characters ultimately resulted in something akin to an epiphany (Denzin, 1989), a major transactional moment that disrupts the ordinary flow of life and makes problematic the usual definitions given to facets of one's world. An epiphany "leaves marks on people's lives . . . alters and shapes the meanings persons give to themselves and their life projects. . . . Having had this experience, the person is never quite the same again" (Denzin, 1989, p. 15).

Epiphanies (which also occur, of course, outside reading literature) are both rare and intensely personal, directly accessible only to the reader (or experiencer). Therefore, I can share only a few examples from my own life as an emancipatory-minded reader. I will briefly describe epiphanic moments I experienced in reading Richard Rodriguez's (1982) *Hunger of Memory*, Alex Kotlowitz's (1991) *There Are No Children Here*, and Pat Conroy's (1972) *The Water Is Wide*.

Hunger of Memory is a narrative of struggle, or, in Rodriguez's words, an *intellectual autobiography*. I have read and reread this life story from my privileged perch as a white, male, middle-class university professor. Due to my ignorance of the existential issues that might confront a poor, academically adept Mexican American, my initial reconstruction of the self of the protagonist was an exercise filled with awe. Why, for example, had I never considered that a talented Hispanic's success in the Anglo world might be accompanied, as was Rodriguez's, by several degrees of alienation from his native language, from his family, and ultimately from his own feelings and emotions? Moreover, the author's lucid descriptions moved beyond the generation of empathic understanding as they sensitized me to certain issues surrounding bilingual education (and education generally). It is true that upon rereading the text, I became disenchanted with it, more skeptical of the author's ultimate claims about the wisdom of a form of education that led to a denial of his primary form of being, to a separation from his parents and their culture, in favor of an intellectualism that gave him "ways of speaking and caring about that [separation]" (Rodriguez, 1982, p. 72). But conspiracies, like the effects of epiphanies, rarely last forever.

There Are No Children Here is not an autobiography, but literary journalism: a poignant, harrowing, convincing account of two African-American children growing up in an inner-city housing project. Its theme is innocence lost as the selves of these two brothers are pulled apart by powerful cultural forces. My moment with this story was generally one of horror. I felt I was participating in what Fine (1993) has called a *story of despair* (p. 36). This story is not a merely sensational, strictly emic, *chronicle of pain* (hooks, 1991, p. 59). One hears not only the still-weak voices of the two young protagonists but also the voice of the author. Kotlowitz chooses not merely to recreate their horrific experiences for the reader but to contextualize them, to examine critically (in story language and format) some features of the political and cultural systems that engender such experiences. Radically subverting and challenging the dominant discourses, the writer ultimately persuaded me to revisit my stock of responsibilities, to become more engaged in educational activism aimed at attacking forces within social institutions (such as the modern American school) that inflict cruelties on their inhabitants.

I therefore reject any suggestion that, through my reading, a secure, white, middle-class male was merely indulging in a bourgeois act of cross-cultural voyeurism. Granted, reading these stories by Rodriguez and Kotlowitz was an observance from a distance. Still, my reading expedition represented not a kind of tourism of the soul, but a serious quest for comprehending, through particular cases, the forces of domination deplored by all citizens who yearn for democracy that is more than superficially political.

The last emancipatory-minded reading I will describe involved a conversation within an autobiographical novel written by a schoolteacher. I read Pat Conroy's (1972) novel *The Water Is Wide* two decades ago while still a high school teacher. Conroy's tale depicts one year in his life as a white schoolteacher of black children in an isolated school in South Carolina. Conroy confronts the constrained consciousness of administrators and others, victims themselves of a repressive, racist system, who confound his efforts at true education. Labeled a "troublemaker," Conroy was fired after eighteen months. Although my situation was less extreme than Conroy's, I recall a profound identification with his plight. I realized that the distorted features of his social and institutional milieu were not locally contained; they roamed the expanses of American culture and schooling. I began to see them in my own workplace. I recall my initial entertainment of the now-obvious notion that teachers are themselves victims of oppression, and I began to wonder what could be done to alter that fact. Now calling on bell hooks (1991) to speak for me, I do not equate the challenges faced by an African-American woman with a white, male high school teacher. I do so because I cannot better express my sense of what this novel (along with other writings) gave to me:

> [N]ovels brought me close to myself, helped me to overcome the estrangement that domination breeds between psyche and self. Reading, I could vicariously experience, dare to know and feel, without threat of repression, retaliation, silencing. My mind became a place of refuge, a sanctuary, a room I could enter with no fear of invasion. My mind became a site of resistance. (p. 54)

Shortly afterward, as a result of experiences both vicarious and direct, I left high school teaching to explore the possibilities of resistance from a distance, within the habitue of a teacher educator. My explorations continue. But would they have commenced as early had I not confronted a vivid alternative to my fuzzy picture of the vaguely unacceptable conditions in my own professional life? A writer of a fictionalized version of his life story offered me a novel reading of my own. I was artfully persuaded to trust a writer who had trusted me, persuaded to conspire with him in a mutual struggle.

Closure

These three acts of educational storysharing, varied in elements such as genre, style, or relationship of writer to characters, are each an act of inquiry with integrity, a distinct moment in an ongoing educational dialogue. My point (in this non-storied form of discourse) is not to privilege the story over other discursive modes heard in that dialogue. Storytellers who aspire to novelness welcome, in due course, critique in all discursive forms, including historical, philosophical, or sociological theory, as well as counterstories that redescribe the conditions of the selves at hand. Indeed, the end of a story is best seen as an invitation to begin a new phase in the conversation. But I have attempted to demonstrate that some stories deserve their own space, with inviolable boundaries surrounding the message that they attempt to convey in their chosen format and language. We do not always need, within the same textual breath, to deconstruct in another style and format the epiphanies they foster. Sometimes the conversation between writer, reader, and characters should be allowed to wane before additional voices inject themselves into the dialogue.

To value such emancipatory-minded stories, editors of educational books and journals will need to be willing to publish them, even though they are not enclosed within a textual envelope of traditional scholarly writing. It means that members of the educational research community (expanded to include teachers, school administrators, and students?) must learn to overcome a legacy of mistrust of all storysharing. (Is it surprising, that two of the three writers I referenced above—Kotlowitz and Conroy—write from outside that community?) Of course, judgments will still need to be made about the potential trustworthiness of each composition. Reader-references must ask whether other readers of the story are likely, in conference with writer and characters, to experience an emancipatory moment. This is hardly an easy task, given the complexities of writing and reading I have outlined here. But in my experience, the rewards of emancipatory educational storysharing—singular, liberating moments of heightened awareness in which new definition is given to the selves of others and to one's own being—are worth the effort.

Notes

1 Narrativists in the field of education sometimes conflate the terms narrative and story (e.g. Nespor and Barylske, 1991). In this essay, I do not. Narrative has been defined in various ways, but its root is in the Latin *narrare*, "to relate." Narrators, therefore, can be said to relate accounts of incidents and events. Many kinds of narrative accounts have been identified, including oral anecdotes and folklore, diaries, or historical treatises (Connelly and Clandinin, 1990). In this essay, narrative is defined in this broad sense, while story is one species huddled under that umbrella.

Of course, story can be a promiscuous term. Some radical rhetoricians of science even conflate the terms science and story, pointing to storylike dimensions of scientific texts (Lawson and Appignanesi, 1989; Nelson, 1987). While not denying the spectrum of rhetorical /literary possibilities, I choose the more traditional, Aristotelian definition of story. I use the term story to indicate a discourse with two particular attributes. The first is an eidetic structure, a particular sort of dynamic form. This form has been, over the years, segmented by literary critics into a varying number of phases. These phases, however, are generally viewed as integral parts that flow together within a single coherent and unified structure. An early phase involves the introduction and situation of characters within a human dilemma. The story then moves to a building phase in which complications arise and meaning continuously emerges until, in a final phase, a tentative, sometimes ambiguous, resolution to the dilemma is suggested. I am conscious of the middle-class, Eurocentric tendency here as I exclude narrative forms from other cultures that are not temporally organized (Nespor and Barylske, 1991; Rosaldo, 1989).

The second hallmark of a story, as I employ the term, is its participation in vernacular forms of speech. By this I mean that the storyteller tends to display everyday, informal language rather than speech that is narrowly technical or identified with a particular institution. Stories about teaching, therefore, are told, not in the argot of the social science professional, but in the language emanating out of the "dailiness" of classroom experience. This is not to posit a singular, totalized vernacular; various speech communities within a culture employ their own transinstitutional idioms. A female, Native American teacher in Window Rock, Arizona, may not employ the same style of language as a male Jamaican teacher. Moreover, stories obviously represent only one of many sites of such everyday speech.

2 The session, entitled "Educational Discourse and Constructions of Profession," was organized by Margaret Marshall and Anthony G. Rud, Jr.

3 It may be argued that in an oppressive society this includes all of us, including those for whom we usually reserve the label "oppressor." Writers as diverse as Paulo Freire and James Baldwin have insisted that the oppressor is also the oppressed. The very act of oppression, this argument goes, demeans the oppressor,

makes him less than fully human, prevents him from joining those who are able to gain mastery over their world without resorting to the narcotic of controlling others. Stories that investigate and reveal the webs of meaning in the lives of superficially powerful people without demonizing them are also emancipatory-minded stories.

References

Agger, B. (1990). *The decline of discourse: Reading, writing, and resistance in post modern capitalism.* New York: Falmer.

Argueta, M. (1980/1983). *One day of life* (B. Brow, Trans). New York: Vantage.

Bakhtin, M.M. (1981). *The dialogic imagination: Four essays.* Austin: University of Texas Press.

Barone, T. (1989). Ways of being at risk: the case of Billy Charles Barnett. *Phi Delta Kappan, 71,* 147–151.

Barone, T. (1990). Using the narrative text as an occasion for conspiracy. In E. Eisner & A. Peshkin (Eds.), *Qualitative inquiry in education: The continuing debate* (pp. 305–326). New York: Teachers College Press.

Barone, T. (1992). A narrative of enhanced professionalism: Educational researchers and popular storybooks about schoolpeople. *Educational Researcher, 21,* 15–24.

Barone, T. (1994). On Kozol and Sartre and qualitative research as socially committed literature. *The Review of Education/Pedagogy/ Cultural Studies, 17* (1), 93–102.

Barthes, R. (1977).The death of the author. In R. Barthes (Ed.), *Images, music, text* (pp. 142–148). New York: Hill & Wang.

Bauman, Z. (1987). *Legislators and interpreters: Modernity, post-modernity and intellectuals.* Ithaca, NY: Cornell University Press.

Belsey, C. (1980). *Critical practice.* London: Methuen.

Berliner, D. (1992). Telling the stories of educational psychology. *Educational Psychologist, 27,* 143–161.

Bredo, E., & Feinberg, W. (1982). *Knowledge and values in social and educational research.* Philadelphia: Temple University Press.

Britzman, D. (1991). *Practice makes practice: A critical study of learning to teach.* Albany: State University of New York Press.

Bruner, J. (1987). *Actual minds, possible worlds.* Cambridge: Harvard University Press.

Connelly, F.M., & Clandinin, D.J. (1990). Stories of experience and narrative inquiry. *Educational Researcher, 19,* 2–14.

Conroy, P. (1972). *The water is wide.* Boston: Houghton Mifflin.

Denzin, N. (1989). *Interpretive interactionism.* Newbury Park, CA: Sage.

Fine, M. (1992). *Disruptive voices: The possibilities of feminist research.* Ann Arbor: University of Michigan Press.

Fine, M. (1993). A diary on privatization and on public possibilities. *Educational Theory, 43,* 33–39.

Foucault, M. (1977). *Discipline and punish: The birth of the prison.* New York: Vintage.

Geertz, C. (1988). *Works and lives: The anthropologist as author.* Stanford, CA: Stanford University Press.

Goodson, I. (1992). Studying teacher's lives: An emergent field of inquiry. In I. Goodson (Ed.), *Studying teacher's lives* (pp. 1–17). London: Routledge.

Grumet, M. (1988). *Bitter milk: Women and teaching.* Amherst: University of Massachusetts Press.

Habermas, J. (1972). *Knowledge and human interest.* Boston: Beacon Press.

Holquist, M. (1990). *Dialogism: Bakhtin and his world.* London: Routledge.

hooks, b. (1991). Narratives of struggle. In P. Mariani (Ed.), *Critical fictions: The politics of imaginative writing* (pp. 53–61). Seattle: Bay.

Hurston, Z. N. (1937/1990). *Their eyes were watching God.* New York: Harper & Row.

Iser, W. (1974). *The implied reader.* Baltimore: Johns Hopkins University Press.

Johnston, B. (1988). *Indian school days.* Norman: University of Oklahoma Press.

Kondo, D. (1990). *Crafting selves: Power, gender, and discourses.* Chicago: University of Chicago Press.

Kotlowitz, A. (1991). *There are no children here: The story of two boys growing up in the other America.* New York: Doubleday.

Kozol, J. (1991). *Savage inequalities: Children in America's schools.* New York: Harper Collins.

Lancy, D.F. (1993). *Qualitative research in education: An introduction to the major traditions.* New York: Longman.

Lather, P. (1986). Issues of validity in openly ideological research: Between a rock and a soft place. *Interchange: A Quarterly Review of Education, 17,* 62–84.

Lawson, H., & Appignanesi, L. (Eds.). (1989). *Dismantling truth: reality in the postmodern world.* London: Weidenfeld & Nicholson.

McLaren, P. (1989). *Life in schools: An introduction to critical pedagogy in the foundations of education.* White Plains, NY: Longman.

Morrison, T. (1970).*The bluest eye: a novel.* New York: Holt, Rinehart & Winston.

Nelson, J. (Ed.). (1987). *The rhetoric of the human sciences.* Madison: University of Wisconsin Press.

Nespor, J., & Barylske, J. (1991). Narrative discourse and teacher knowledge. *American Educational Research Journal, 28,* 805–823.

Owens, C. (1989). The global issue: A symposium. *Art in America, 77,* 86–89, 151–157.

Polkinghorne, D.E. (1988). *Narrative knowing and the human sciences.* Albany: State University of New York Press.

Richardson, L. (1990). *Writing strategies: Reaching diverse audiences.* London: Sage.

Rodriguez, R. (1982). *Hunger of memory: the education of Richard Rodriguez.* Boston: David R. Godine.

Rorty, R. (1989). *Contingency, irony, and solidarity.* Cambridge: Cambridge University Press.

Rosaldo, R. (1989). *Culture and truth.* Boston: Beacon.

Rose, M. (1989). *Lives on the boundary*. New York: Penguin.

Rosenau, P. (1992). *Post-modernism and the social sciences: insights, inroads, and intrusions*. Princeton, NJ: Princeton University Press.

Ryle, G. (1949). *The concept of mind*. New York: Barnes & Noble.

Sartre, J.P. (1948/1949). *What is literature? And other essays* (B. Frechtman, Trans.). Cambridge: Cambridge University Press.

Sparkes, A. (1994). Life histories and the issue of voice: Reflections on an emerging relationship. *International Journal of Qualitative Studies in Education, 7*, 165–183.

Sullivan, J.P. (1984). *A critical psychology*. New York: Plenum.

Tillman, L. (1991). Critical fiction/ critical self. In P. Mariani (Ed.), *Critical fictions: The politics of imaginative writing* (pp. 97–103). Seattle: Bay Press.

Wicomb, Z. (1991). An author's agenda. In P. Mariani (Ed.), *Critical fictions: The politics of imaginative writing* (pp. 13–16). Seattle: Bay Press.

Wittgenstein, L. (1953/1968). *Philosophical investigations* (3rd ed.) (G.E.M. Anscombe, Trans.). New York: Macmillan.

Wright, R. (1945). *Black boy, a record of childhood and youth*. New York: Harper & Row.